The Idea of English in Japan

CRITICAL LANGUAGE AND LITERACY STUDIES
Series Editors: **Professor Vaidehi Ramanathan**, *University of California, USA*, **Professor Bonny Norton**, *University of British Columbia, Canada* and **Professor Alastair Pennycook**, *University of Technology, Sydney, Australia*

Critical Language and Literacy Studies is an international series that encourages monographs directly addressing issues of power (its flows, inequities, distributions and trajectories) in a variety of language- and literacy-related realms. The aim with this series is twofold (1) to cultivate scholarship that openly engages with social, political and historical dimensions in language and literacy studies, and (2) to widen disciplinary horizons by encouraging new work on topics that have received little focus (see below for partial list of subject areas) and that use innovative theoretical frameworks.

Full details of all the books in this series and of all our other publications can be found on http://www.multilingual-matters.com, or by writing to Multilingual Matters, St Nicholas House, 31–34 High Street, Bristol BS1 2AW, UK.

CRITICAL LANGUAGE AND LITERACY STUDIES
Series Editors: Vaidehi Ramanathan, Bonny Norton and Alastair Pennycook

The Idea of English in Japan
Ideology and the Evolution of a Global Language

Philip Seargeant

MULTILINGUAL MATTERS
Bristol • Buffalo • Toronto

Library of Congress Cataloging in Publication Data
Seargeant, Philip.
The Idea of English in Japan : Ideology and the Evolution of
a Global Language / Philip Seargeant.
Critical Language and Literacy Studies: 3.
Includes bibliographical references and index.
1. English language--Study and teaching--Japanese speakers.
2. English philology--Study and teaching--Japan. 3. Second
language acquisition. 4. English language--Japan. 5. English
language--Globalization.
I. Title.
PE1068.J3S437 2009
428.007'052-dc22 2009026139

British Library Cataloguing in Publication Data
A catalogue entry for this book is available from the British Library.

ISBN-13: 978-1-84769-202-3 (hbk)
ISBN-13: 978-1-84769-201-6 (pbk)

Multilingual Matters
UK: St Nicholas House, 31–34 High Street, Bristol BS1 2AW, UK.
USA: UTP, 2250 Military Road, Tonawanda, NY 14150, USA.
Canada: UTP, 5201 Dufferin Street, North York, Ontario M3H 5T8, Canada.

Copyright © 2009 Philip Seargeant.

All rights reserved. No part of this work may be reproduced in any form or
by any means without permission in writing from the publisher.

The policy of Multilingual Matters/Channel View Publications is to use papers that
are natural, renewable and recyclable products, made from wood grown in
sustainable forests. In the manufacturing process of our books, and to further support
our policy, preference is given to printers that have FSC and PEFC Chain of Custody
certification. The FSC and/or PEFC logos will appear on those books where full
certification has been granted to the printer concerned.

Typeset by Integra Software Services Pvt. Ltd, Pondicherry, India.
Printed and bound in Great Britain by the Cromwell Press Group

Contents

List of Figures viii
Acknowledgements ix
Preface xi

1 Introduction 1
   Language as a Concept 1
   The Context of Japan 2
   Structure and Approach 3

2 The Concept of English as a Global Language 6
   Flaws in the Foundational Argument 6
   English and the Concept of a Universal Language 7
   English Today 8
   The Lingua Franca Approach 11
   English as Axiom 14
   English Versus Japanese 15
   'See, listen, and eat English' 16
   Conclusion 20

3 Language Ideology and Global English 22
   Politics and the Emergence of the World Englishes Paradigm . . . 22
   Language Ideologies 25
   The Concept of Ideology 27
   Indexicality and Symbolic Meaning 29
   The Historical Ontology of Language 32
   Culture and the Context for Analysis 36
   Methodology and the Objects of Analysis 38

4 English in Japan: The Current Shape of the Debate 43
   The State and Status of English Language Teaching in Japan . . . 43
   Identifying the Issues 45
   Creating an Historical Context 47
   The Communicative Approach 50

	Internationalism and the Ethnocentric Debate	53
	Practice and Policy	56
	Conclusion	61
5	**Globalization: 'Enriching Japanese Culture Through Contact with Other Cultures'**	**63**
	Conceptual Case Studies	63
	The Future as a Foreign Country	67
	Dejima Mentality	69
	The Theme Park of the World	70
	Local Variations of Globalization	73
	The Absorption of English: Loanwords	75
	The Absorption of English: Ornamentalism	77
	The Promulgation Function	78
	Literary and Artistic Reconfigurations	81
	Conclusion	85
6	**Authenticity: 'More English than England Itself'**	**87**
	Alternative Visions of 'Realistic' Language Practice	87
	What Is Authentic?	89
	The Authentic Text and Authenticity of Interaction	91
	ELT in Japan: The Commercial Sector	94
	The McUniversity and Theme Park Education	99
	The Simulation of Authenticity in English Language Practice	100
	Conclusion	104
7	**Aspiration: 'Enhancing Lifestyles and Living Out Dreams'**	**106**
	A Desire for English	106
	Aspiration and Education	107
	Motivation and Language Learning	109
	'Audacious Life Goals'	110
	Language, Travel and Social Mobility	114
	Aspirational Orientations	120
	Attitudes to English	123
	Conclusion	130
8	**The Unknown Language**	**132**
	An Imaginary Japan	132
	English Encounters	134
	Perceptual Disjuncture and Ideological 'Erasure'	138
	Semiotic Hierarchies	141
	The Disregarded Linguistic Residue	144

Dual-process Interpretation of English 146
Conclusion 152

9 **Rival Ideologies in Applied Linguistics** **154**
An Ontology of English in Japan 154
Rival Authenticities 156
Evaluation as Interpretation 160
The Limitations of a Lingua Franca Usage Model 163
Conclusion 165

Notes 169
References 174

List of Figures

2.1	McPal 'lesson plan'	18
5.1	Global warming campaign: *Sutoppu za ondanka taisô*	76
5.2	L'Académie française and The National Institute for Japanese Language	81
5.3	Muneteru Ujino's 'One Room Mansion'	84
6.1	Nova's diagram of contrastive 'wave-lengths' for Japanese and English	98
7.1	The 'aspiration' motif in university publicity	108
7.2	Gaba language school advert	111
7.3	Study abroad magazine *Wish*	115
7.4	The personal narrative of a successful career woman	118
7.5	Table of interview participants	125
8.1	Preston's triangle of approaches to language data (adapted)	138
8.2	The hierarchy of semiosis and the symbolism boundary	144
8.3	T-shirt design	144

Acknowledgements

I would like to gratefully acknowledge the assistance and support of the following people in the preparation of this book: Casimir Adjoe, Nozomi Azechi, Tomoko Bettoyashiki, David Block, Jan Blommaert, Beth Erling, John Hardcastle, Noriko Inagaki, Anna Jones, Yukiko Kawaguchi, Gunther Kress, Claudia Lapping, Bob Tsukada-Bright, Cathie Wallace and Atsuko Watanabe-Suzuki.

Earlier versions of certain sections of the book have appeared in the following articles: 'Globalisation and reconfigured English in Japan' (2005) *World Englishes*, 24:3, pp. 309–319 (with kind permission of Blackwell Publishing); ' "More English than England itself": the simulation of authenticity in foreign language practice in Japan' (2005) *International Journal of Applied Linguistics*, 15:3, pp. 326–345 (with kind permission of Blackwell Publishing); 'Ideologies of English in Japan: the perspective of policy and pedagogy' (2008) *Language Policy*, 7:2, pp. 121–142 (with kind permission of Springer Science and Business Media).

I am grateful to John Benjamins Publishing Company, Amsterdam/Philadelphia for their kind permission to use Figure 0.1 from Preston, D., *Handbook of Perceptual Dialectology*, Volume 1, 1999, p. xxiv. I would also like to thank the following for their kind permission to use selected images: l'Académie française, ALC Press Inc., Gaba Corporation, Glasgow Caledonian University, Nagoya University of Commerce and Business Administration, the National Institute for Japanese Language, Team-6% Committee & Ministry of the Environment and Muneteru Ujino. Every effort has been made to contact copyright holders, and if there are any errors, they would be rectified in a future edition.

Preface

That 'globalization' has become a catchall word in a variety of academic and nonacademic domains now is a truism. Government policy-makers sometimes attribute their country's economic woes to its onslaught, environmentalists lament the destructive impact of its onward march and advocates of indigenous communities blame the disappearance of smaller cultures and minority languages on it. The multiple and disparate ways in which this term is used has turned this concept into a global symbol of sorts, with its meanings becoming inflated and the risk of its becoming a cliché. However, it is when we attempt to understand it in terms of local realities – the forms and nuances it assume in very particular articulations, in specific places on our planet – that the worn nature of this term is contested. There is in applied linguistics a growing awareness of global flows (Alim et al., 2009; Pennycook, 2007), the role of language, specifically English, in cross-national movements (Tan & Rubdy, 2007) and the ways in which language ideologies permeate and position people and communities, that open up ways to address the untidiness and spillage associated with the term globalization.

It is precisely this set of issues that informs the present volume. Seargeant's insightful analysis of how English is positioned in Japan, both as a linguistic system and as a set of free-floating ideologies, shows us how different forms of knowledge about language have an effect upon the way in which language is regulated within society. This focus on language ideology is a significant one for studies of global English. Some critical approaches to the spread of English see ideology as a reflection of a neoliberal, English-speaking empire (Phillipson, 2008), the means by which the inequitable relations between English and other languages are maintained. Seargeant, by contrast, draws on broader studies of language ideology (see Blommaert, 1999; Kroskrity, 2000), which, deriving from an anthropological tradition, are interested centrally in the ways in which language is understood locally. This work is of great, and as yet rather untapped, significance for applied linguistics generally and studies of the global spread of English more specifically since it looks at ideology not as a top-down imposition reflecting only an economic order but rather as a local manifestation of how language is understood.

Amongst other things, this focus allows on the one hand for a much more complex understanding of language ideology: The ways languages are understood is a product of local cultures, histories, aesthetics, educational orientations and so on. And on the other hand, it helps us to question the very solidity that is ascribed to language: If it means different things to different people, then what constitutes English is less clearly defined by recourse to grammar, lexicon or naming practices, and instead is a product of particular conditions of locality. As Seargeant points out, defensive positions and clamours to hold on to traditions – partially revealed in Bunmei Ibuki's (Japan's Minister of Education) comment on the need to ensure that students write and speak decent Japanese – calls attention to English's binaristic positioning in that landscape. 'The English language is assigned a particular emblematic meaning...' (p. 25), and Seargeant evocatively captures this by showing, among other things, how McPal (and the initiative that tries to use McDonald's as a site for English language learning) sets in motion an ideology that brings together food, Americanization and ELT pedagogy and justifies it in terms of 'citizens expecting a better life in the 21st century' (p. 28).

The dynamics of such local ideologies are needless to say, imbued with power (Blommaert, 2005; Kubota, 1998, 1999). The hierarchies and stratifications they reproduce point to their material articulations while their *mentaliste* aspects (world views and beliefs) make us aware of the prediscursive space before enactments happen. The entanglements and complexities that make up the ineffability of ideologies (impossible as they are to pin down either through language or artifact) call for modes of inquiry that go beyond traditional methods associated with sociolinguistics to others that capture 'concepts' of ideologies. This is an important deviation because it proceeds from the assumption that the best way to address power dimensions in ideologies is through variously scattered signs and icons. Seargeant's focus on such 'symbols' – whether it is through a commentator in the media describing Japanese as being 'deep, profound, at times esoteric language [which is] very different from the shoot-from-the-hips English' or the analysis of particular written texts including educational policies regarding EFL, or how the tourist industry partially dictates particular kinds of self-presentation – underscore how particular vignettes in cultures provide very valuable insights into the messiness, collisions and deliberations in and around ideologies. The globalizing surges that bring in English loanwords, create contexts for Japanese rap lyrics (Pennycook, 2003) and open up possibilities for changing language policies in educational settings permit us glimpses into the completely intertwined nature of both Japanese and English in modern Japan. Indeed, English, in some contexts becomes a powerful way to present oneself and anticipate a future identity (Norton, 2000; Norton & Kanno, 2003).

These snapshots of local ideologies move us toward conceptualizing 'the local' in Applied Linguistics. While the local-global dichotomy may be commonplace now in some contexts of the field, the local is a vital space in the discipline since it is a site of meaning construction (around Japanese and English in the present case) or power struggles (moments of defensiveness while also surging forward), and social action and agentiveness (in the face of societal constraints). So rather than think in terms of local and global as opposites, it may be more productive to view them as mutually constitutive. Such an orientation is one that the three of us support in this series, and which also emerges in forthcoming work on English in East African contexts (Higgins, 2009). It lends support to Appadurai's claim (1996) that local knowledge is not only local in itself, but even more important, for itself (thus affording an interesting contrast to the Geertzian notion of the local being a somewhat autonomous site). Locality is always supralocal; it emerges only in relation to other localities (just as the global force of English emerges only in relation to local languages). This point is an important one because it is at once translocal and critical – indeed a particular kind of critical translocalism – and is ideal for addressing ideologies and globalization. It focuses on connections between several local spaces (Ramanathan, 2005), exploring local-to-local networks, and works in some ways to counter the center–periphery dichotomy. As Sergeant's work effectively points out, it removes the West from the center of intercultural relations and moves English away from its native speaking population to reveal uneven in-betweens, movements that are at once intercontextual and interdependent.

In terms of disciplinary locales, the space that Sergeant's book carves for itself is between English and a certain cultural geography, with a vision toward economic geography in its related political, cultural and applied turns. Geography – spaces, actual physical domains in the natural world – is crucial here and it is its role in future economic prospects of the country through English that is relevant. The wider ideational scope of this project explores questions around this crux of issues, and in so doing locates itself at the crossroads of contemporary issues in cultural and economic studies of ELT. These theoretical currents – cultural studies, critical geography and political economy – applied to ELT derive both the poststructural shifts in social theory as well as the complex political, economic and cultural conditions at stake as a result of processes of globalization. In all of this, Sergeant is clear that the complexities around English as a global language far exceed current disciplinary debates about it, especially those pertaining to intelligibility. As he points out, 'if intelligibility were the primary concern for the success of a global language, then decisions about a model for teaching could be resolved on the basis of rudimentary linguistic knowledge.... But a global language is not simply a matter of mutual intelligibility. The role that ideology plays in language conceptualization and language use results in a far more complex picture of what a global language is', opening up the possibility of viewing language itself as a political construction (Pennycook & Makoni, 2007).

The various disciplinary narratives around English that such a position both draws on but also moves beyond need careful articulation and Seargeant shows how complexly his work culls from various strains in the field – world Englishes, English as an international language or English as a lingua franca – but goes beyond them as well (Ramanathan, 2008). He also shows us how 'ethnography' is not enough since what we regard as 'ethnographic' always proceeds from implicit or explicit modes of critical and theoretical interpretation. Theory affords us mappings of worlds so that we can understand, among other things, relationships between various ethnographic claims, and Seargeant shows us, by an explicit articulation of some theories, how diverse representations and interpretations position English in simultaneous conflicting and competitive struggles for authority. People's lives and communities are enmeshed in such tensions and this book compels us not only to think about the relationship between an icon and its referent differently, or between languages and their associative meanings in unusual ways, but about how English is positioned evermore in local-to-local connections that indicate *supralocality* – connections between several different local sites, sometimes in the same geographic territory, but not necessarily – and less and less on center–periphery links that perpetuate dependence. Seargeant accomplishes this with finesse.

Vaidehi Ramanathan, Alastair Pennycook
and Bonny Norton

References

Alim, S., Ibrahim, A. and Pennycook, A. (eds) (2009) *Global Linguistic Flows: Hip Hop Cultures, Youth Identities, and the Politics of Language*. New York: Routledge.

Appadurai, A. (1996) *Modernity at Large: Cultural Dimensions of Globalization*. Minneapolis: University of Minnesota Press.

Blommaert, J. (ed.) (1999) *Language Iedological Debates*. Berlin: Mouton.

Blommaert, J. (2005) *Discourse: A Critical Introduction*. Cambridge: Cambridge University Press.

Canagarajah, S. (2005) *Reclaiming the Local in Language Policy and Practice*. Mahwah, NJ: Lawrence Erlbaum Associates.

Higgins, C. (2009) *English as a Local Language: Post-Colonial Identities and Multilingual Practices*. Bristol: Multilingual Matters.

Kanno, Y. (2003) *Negotiating Bilingual and Bicultural Identities*. Mahwah, NJ: Lawrence Erlbaum.

Kroskrity, P. (ed.) (2000) *Regimes of Language: Ideologies, Politics and Identities*. Santa Fe, NM: School of American Research Press.

Kubota, R. (1998) Ideologies of English in Japan. *World Englishes* 17 (3), 295–306.

Kubota, R. (1999) Japanese culture constructed by discourses: Implications for applied linguistics research and ELT. *TESOL Quarterly* 33 (1), 9–35.

Norton, B. (2000) *Identity and Language Learning: Gender, Ethnicity and Educational Settings*. New York: Longman.

Norton, B. and Kanno, Y. (eds) (2003) Imagined communities and educational possibilities. Special issue of *The Journal of Language, Identity and Education* 2, 4.

Pennycook, A. (2003) Global Englishes, Rip Slyme and performativity. *Journal of Sociolinguistics* 7 (4), 513–533.

Pennycook, A. (2007) *Global Englishes and Transcultural Flows*. New York: Routledge.

Pennycook, A. and Makoni, S. (eds) (2007) *Disinventing and Reconstituting Languages*. Clevedon: Multilingual Matters.

Phillipson, R. (2008) The linguistic imperialism of neoliberal empire. *Critical Inquiry in Language Studies* 5 (1) 1–43.

Ramanathan, V. (2005) *The English-Vernacular Divide: Postcolonial Language Politics and Practice*. Clevedon: Multilingual Matters.

Ramanathan, V. (2008) Poverty, TESOL's narratives, and "other" languages. *Kritika Kultura* 11, 26–35.

Tan, P. and Rubdy, R. (2007) *Language as Commodity: Global Structures, Local Marketplaces*. New York: Continuum.

Chapter 1
Introduction

Language as a Concept

The postulate of this book is that language exists not only as a medium of expression but also as a concept; that we talk not only via language but also about language; and that, in fact, our use of language is always influenced by the ideas we form of language. Such ideas are therefore of interest from a linguistic point of view (in that metalinguistic reflection is an aspect of all language practice), but they also exist as an index of beliefs about the place and significance that language has within the lived human experience. That is to say, ideas about language always reflect the ideas we have about ourselves as social beings. They are, in a sense, a metaphor for our manner of participation in social process. And thus, in the early 21st century, the idea of English as a global language is an idea also of a globalized world and the idea of the challenges this ushers in for contemporary society.

Taking this contention as its point of departure, the book provides a theoretical examination of English within a globalized context, considering specifically the manner in which the language is conceptualized, and how the resultant language ideologies – drawn in part from universal discourses; in part from context-specific trends in social history – inform the relationship that people take toward the language.

The design of the book is broadly twofold. Its nucleus consists of an investigation of the way in which English is conceptualized in contemporary Japanese society. Analysis is made of the nature of such conceptualization as it occurs in two forms: talk about the language (that is, discourses *of* the language and discourses that *cite* the language); and the positioning and presentation of the language within the sociocultural environment. Given that Japan is not an expressly multilingual society, or at least, does not self-attest to being such (Maher & Yashiro, 1995), the focus is not solely on the way that English usage is manifest in everyday verbal utterance (a sociolinguistics of 'Japanese English'), but on the way in which it is displayed as part of a far wider field of semiotic practice (what might conventionally be understood as 'nonlinguistic' usage), and how a discourse of the language is constructed by the voices *and* actions of the society. The study thus considers two issues: the specific nature of the language's symbolic meaning in Japan; and how this meaning is expressed and negotiated in society. Thus, a detailed mapping of the ideological frameworks around and involving English within Japan is carried out.

The other branch of the book is a discussion of how the specific symbolic meanings on show here might have implications for the concept of 'English as a global language', and how the concerns that motivate research into and regulation of the English language within the world today can incorporate these theoretical implications into their wider project. To this end, the book considers the question of what constitutes a 'global' language, and how, if at all, a balance can be struck between the universal and the historically contingent when it comes to formulating a theory of language use within the world. This question, it is suggested, is of fundamental importance if applied linguistics is to contribute to sustainable, productive and ethically aware regulation of the language, and it thus provides the skeletal structure for the book as a whole.

The twofold focus of the book is a product of the general theoretical approach that I am pursuing. The contention is that research into and theory generation for English as a global language must combine general linguistic precepts with an ethnographic appraisal of the way in which the language is conceptualized within a given community. The hypothesis is that meanings associated with the language (meanings produced by the act of conceptualization) are culturally constructed within the society in which the language is operational, and are thus specific to that particular society rather than to the language itself. By describing and analyzing the diverse language practices associated with English in one particular (national) context, therefore, the book is able to interrogate current applied linguistic theories about English's status as a global language, and consider their relevance to the actuality of the lived linguistic experience. Working inductively from data provided by the situated case study, it is hoped that the book can, thus, offer an alternative survey of the existence of a 'global language'.

The Context of Japan

Any number of societies in which English is accorded a specific significance due to its global status will offer intriguing case studies for this type of investigation, and dedicated investigations of diverse contexts of use will always augment our understanding of the linguistic. That being said, the context of Japan and of Japanese society is a particularly compelling case for such a study, and there are a number of reasons for this. Chief among these is the intense fascination that is shown toward English in the country (McVeigh, 2002; Strevens, 1992); a fascination which is exhibited both in acts of cultural display (in advertising and popular culture, for example) and in forms of social practice (the recreational pursuit of English language education, for instance). Yet despite the strong visual and conceptual presence that English has within Japanese society, the language currently has no official status, nor, in relative terms, do the majority of citizens require any particular fluency in it for their everyday lives (Yano, 2008). Indeed, one of the most frequently voiced opinions about English in Japan is that the high profile of, and immense interest in, the language is not matched by an equally high level of communicative proficiency among the population. This situation has attracted a great deal of attention from the TESOL community (e.g. Gorsuch, 2001; Koike, 1978; LoCastro, 1996), and has been an influential factor in policy reform over the last two decades (MEXT, 2002; Monbusho, 1989). Yet, as Kubota (1998, 1999) has noted, little analysis has taken place of the wider cultural role that English plays as a structuring concept within Japanese society.

It is for these reasons that Japan offers an appealing case study for the global language paradigm, as conceptualizations of the language within the country are not concentrated solely around instrumental ambitions for a code for international communication, but instead are dispersed in diverse ways across the social landscape, presenting various conundrums for traditional applied linguistics theory. Here again, therefore, the book's focus is guided by twin ambitions: the first, a substantive study of English linguistic practice within the Japanese context itself; the second, the contrastive insights that such a study can offer for canonical conceptions of a global language. For just as anthropologists traditionally turn their gaze to communities that are not constrained to be standardized in the way that most postindustrial societies are, and in so doing are able to learn something of the diversity of human practice, so the linguist has much to learn from environs in which language practices appear uncharacteristic and where the very ontology of the object of study seems unfamiliar. Japan, I would suggest, provides just such a context.

Structure and Approach

The book is loosely divided into three parts to accommodate this dialectic between universal and historically contingent approaches to the concept of global English. The core of the book provides an interrogation of the beliefs that constitute the symbolic meaning attributed to English within Japan. Research into this question proceeds by means of an analysis of discourses about English and its status as a global force as they are articulated within Japanese society. It thus takes the form of detailed studies of critical cases of English language-linked social practice in the country. Within this context, the discourse of the language is deemed to be not merely textual articulation of ideas about the language, but also the deployment and arrangement of more general semiotic resources. These include material artifacts such as pictorial advertisements, the architecture and ornament of schools and tourist attractions and social practices such as the employment policies of educational institutions. All of these convey a specific attitude toward the language and thus contribute to its symbolic meaning, and as such are important sites for analysis. The research focuses primarily upon the two fields within society in which language-linked practice is most evident: namely, the field of education (at the level of both policy and practice) and the field of the media and popular culture.

The purpose throughout is to consider the meanings invested in the language, both in linguistic terms (the assumptions made about the nature of language as an essential aspect of human behavior), as well as in wider social terms (the relationships the language establishes with issues such as cultural identity), and the role it plays as a determining cultural force within society. The details of this context-specific case study can then be placed alongside conceptualizations of the language that are articulated in applied linguistics research and theory. To this end, the extended case study at the centre of the book is framed by a discussion of more general theoretical issues related to English as a global language.

The division and structure of this approach is as follows. Chapter 2 firstly rehearses the major issues summoned up by the promotion of the concept of English as a global language. It begins with a review of the current state of the debate over global English, before moving to two scenarios from contemporary Japan which present issues which mainstream approaches in applied linguistics appear ill-equipped to address. In response to the problematic highlighted in these two examples, Chapter 3 then introduces a 'language ideologies' framework as a means of anatomizing the multiplex nature of English's existence in the world today. It then proceeds to a consideration of how such an approach – which has been developed from work in linguistic anthropology – can be productively applied to the world Englishes paradigm.

Chapter 4 makes the shift from the generic to the specific, and introduces the site of the case study for the book by examining the ideologies of language which underpin mainstream applied linguistics research and foreign language education policy in Japan. The contention here is that a great amount of research and policy recommendation is structured around a relatively narrow spine of presuppositions about the role of a global language, and that because of this a certain determinism exists within debate about the language which disregards the actuality of demotic practice. Chapters 5–8 thus expand the field of view to provide a detailed empirical study of the wider Japanese situation beyond this 'official' discourse. Structured around three major 'motifs' in the ideology, these chapters examine the ways in which English is allied in popular cultural practice with certain salient concepts in the contemporary social landscape. Chapter 5 examines the role played by English in the relationship that Japan conducts with the rest of the world – that is to say, in the way that Japanese society deals with the challenges (both perceived and real) of 'globalization'; Chapter 6 examines the way in which the concept of 'authenticity' operates as a key motif in the construction of the symbolic meaning of English and how the language plays a crucial role in evolving discourses of cultural identity; and Chapter 7 explores the relationship between 'aspiration' and the learning of English as a global language, identifying particularly a 'desire for English' as a key trope in the ideology of the language. Chapter 8 concludes this empirical study by considering the relationship between mainstream ideas of English language use within Japan – those focusing upon its use as a communicative code for the relay of ideational meaning – and the many other ways in which it is dispersed across the wider cultural landscape. In doing this, it examines how the barrier that is erected between sanctioned and unsanctioned English becomes a key site for ideological struggle over the language.

Following the situated case study, Chapter 9 returns to the issues articulated at the beginning of the book, and to the debates in contemporary applied linguistics over the global English question. The intention in this final chapter is to incorporate significant structural factors from the language ideologies that constitute the symbolic meaning of English in Japan into these contemporary debates about the function of a global language. Thus, it is hoped that two things can be achieved. Firstly, insights can be provided into how both language theory and linguistic ethnography can be drawn upon to produce a context-sensitive approach to the regulation of English within the context of globalization; and secondly, the study can expand our understanding of how the concept and practical reality of English as a global language operates in the world today.

Chapter 2
The Concept of English as a Global Language

Flaws in the Foundational Argument

There is a simple argument that runs as follows: Premise One – the English language is spread widely across the globe, with at present an estimated 1.5–2 billion speakers. Premise Two – a single language which will allow the peoples of the world to communicate freely with each other is a desirable thing. Conclusion – therefore English, already so widely spread, is the ideal candidate to fill such a role.

A version of this argument – either explicitly unpacked as above, or nested as an assumption within proposals about English as an international language – is to be found reiterated in a variety of settings and contexts. Here, for example, it provides the introductory rationale in an announcement made by the British prime minister, Gordon Brown (Prime Minister's Office, 2008), about a government-backed TESOL initiative:

> The English language, like football and other sports, began here [in the UK] and has spread to every corner of the globe. Today more than a billion people speak English. It is becoming the world's language... the pathway of global communication and global access to knowledge. And it has become the vehicle for hundreds of millions of people of all countries to connect with each other, in countless ways. Indeed, English is much more than a language: it is a bridge across borders and cultures, a source of unity in a rapidly changing world.

Similarly, a policy recommendation from Japan's Ministry of Education (MEXT, 2003) states that:

> Globalisation extends to various activities of individuals as well as to the business world. Each individual has increasing opportunities to come in contact with the global market and services, and participate in international activities.... In such a situation, English has played a central role as the common international language in linking people who have different mother tongues. For children living in the 21st

century, it is essential for them to acquire communication abilities in English as a common international language.

Providing that one accepts the two premises upon which this oft-voiced argument is built (and the second one especially is the cause of some controversy), the conclusion appears to be sound. The logic involved is secure enough and seems to present a persuasive line of reasoning. There are, however, two possible flaws in this reasoning, and paradoxically they are both due to the way that language itself is being used in the framing of this argument. These two flaws are both related to how we are to define the key concepts upon which the argument rests – that is, how the words 'English' and 'language' are being used. In understanding the problems of (and possible solutions to) the issue of English as a global language, we need to begin with a detailed understanding of what is meant by both 'English' and 'language', for otherwise our elaborate plans may turn out to be built upon decidedly porous foundations.

English and the Concept of a Universal Language

English qualifies for description as a world language because it is so widely spread across the globe (Crystal, 1997). In the many different contexts in which it exists, however, it has markedly different incarnations. Indeed, it would be difficult to identify with any certainty the essential properties which unite these disparate varieties, other than maybe the appellation 'English' itself. And even then there are pidgins and creoles which do not share this name (Tok Pisin, for example, or Krio), as well as certain historical and regional varieties (the Inglis of 13th century Scotland is one, as are recent coinages such as Singlish in modern day Singapore). In addition, grammar varies from one variety to another so that identical forms can have divergent meanings, while the lexicon too presents ample opportunity for misunderstanding, allowing for scores of books dedicated to the recording of awkward discrepancies (Mencken's *The American Language* (1947) is a classic example). As such, perhaps Wittgenstein's concept of 'family resemblances' (1953) would be the best way to group the many different codes that are often included under the term English: there are amongst them several points of overlap, be they in grammar, lexicon or history, but the diversity is the result of constant change in all directions.[1] Because of this huge diversity it is extremely difficult – not to say hazardous – to generalize too assertively about English in the world today, and thus a true understanding of the form, function and status of the language in any one context must need begin with an examination of that particular context.

At the same time, however, this global spread of English has revitalized the concept of a universal language: one tongue to unite the disparate peoples of the world. Often today, if one talks of the teaching of English, it is with this concept hovering somewhere in the background, and explicit promotion of the language, especially in parts of the world where its influence is historically slight, draws directly upon this idea as one of the most positive factors in the language's favor. The perception is that to have English is to have access to the wealth of the world that is otherwise obscured behind linguistic barriers. As one recent policy document from Japan asserts, 'knowledge of English as the international lingua franca equips one with a key skill for knowing and accessing the world' (CJGTC, 2000a: 10).

In actual fact, there are two distinct issues here, despite the inevitable melding that occurs between them. There is the spread of English historically, culturally and diversely; then there is the benefit that English can, in theory, bring for enhanced linguistic mobility – an idea which leads, by small increments, to the concept of the universal tongue. And while this conceptual confusion may be inevitable – especially within the context of globalization, which preaches the acute importance of communication across cultures – it is also problematic. For immediately we can see that while English in the world is far from unitary in any aspect of its existence, a universal language has, as its one essential characteristic, the function of uniting in dialogue the speakers of disparate languages, and of providing an antidote to the *confusio linguarum* which has bedevilled human civilization since its inception. To unite by means of something that is itself only unitary in the imagination seems logically impossible. And yet discourses of English across the globe have become entangled with this persuasive discourse of English as a universal tongue, and the result is a complex of both practical and ethical issues. Much of applied linguistics today is engaged in navigating through the opaqueness of this conceptual fog, and trying to anchor the ambition to the constraints of actuality.

English Today

A key intellectual dispute which marks an early attempt to resolve these issues is the exchange of papers in the early 1990s between Randolph Quirk (1990) and Braj Kachru (1991) in the journal *English Today*. The substance and structure of this dispute, related as it was to the status (and particularly the teaching) of English around the world and how global varieties should be classified, has had great impact on the development of the discipline, and its narration has become an emblematic motif in

The Concept of English as a Global Language

commentaries and textbooks on the global English question ever since (see, for example, Graddol *et al.*, 1996; Jenkins, 2003; Seidlhofer, 2003). Although the basic issues had been an undercurrent in associated debate before this time (the editorial statement of the renamed *World Englishes* journal in 1985 gives a pertinent summary of the emergence of these concerns (Kachru & Smith, 1985)), the Quirk–Kachru dispute crystallized them, and thus did much to define the ground for applied linguistics research in the global context and for the contested concept of English as an international language.

While I do not wish to revisit this debate in any great detail here, what I would like to do is reflect upon the object of study presented within it, as well as the underlying assumptions, especially as they relate to the concept of a global language. English within the global context is, of course, an issue of great interest for the present historical period due to the fact that it affects, either directly or indirectly, large swathes of the world's population. Without wishing to hyperbolize, if language (as an abstract faculty) is at the heart of the human experience, then the *use* of language – and the way that this use is regulated – has profound consequences for the lived reality of any and every member of the species. And it is this context that motivates the opinions of Quirk and Kachru, and the many other scholars actively addressing the issue. For while language itself (that abstract notion) is mostly an unproblematized given in social existence, the discussion of any *specific* language – or indeed any variety, dialect or register – almost immediately provokes talk of vexed issues such as rights, cultural identity and social capital. To put it another way, there is today no controversy over whether people should have access to language *per se* (gone are the days when the Holy Roman Emperor could quarantine infants away from human society as a linguistic experiment (Eco, 1994)), yet the actual nature of that language – its real-world shape and use – is a supremely political question for all levels of society. And in this current era of globalization, the English language (as both concept and specific code) has become implicated in a great number of these political debates, with ramifications which ripple out across the species.

The issues that the Quirk–Kachru debate presented concern the way in which the language (and by extension the linguistic practices of those who use it) should best be regulated. In short, the key argument divides along the lines of whether English should be perceived as a unitary entity tied to the model of an Anglo–American standard, or whether local varieties (Indian English, Nigerian English, maybe Japanese English, etc.) should be afforded a legitimacy of their own. Quirk (1990: 8) summarizes the issues by recounting that:

A colleague of mine who this year spent some time working in Kenya told me in a letter: 'There is heated debate here as to whether there is such a thing as "East African English" or whether the local variety is just the result of the increasing failure of the education system'.

To a great extent, this question sets the parameters for most subsequent debate: the opposition between diversity and a single world standard which can function as a model for any educational practice and against which divergence should be judged as lack of competence. And despite the fact that this debate is now over a decade and a half old, the substantive issues still animate both theorists and practitioners (Seidlhofer, 2005).

The positions that both Quirk and Kachru take are, in fact, attacks against the way the language is, from their perspective, being regulated at present – and are thus manifestos for how they believe it should be regulated. The basic battle here is between pluricentrism (Kachru's advocacy of a diffusion of world Englishes) and monocentrism (Quirk's 'single monochrome standard' (1985: 6)).[2] Quirk's position is to consider non-native varieties as imperfectly learnt versions of a 'correct' English, and thus not suitable for use as teaching models. Kachru responds by insisting that local varieties are not simply 'interlanguages' (Selinker, 1972) – that is to say, partially realized internalizations of the type of full proficiency that can be found only in native speakers – but are sophisticated and rule-bound systems in their own right, often with institutionalized authority within the society in which they exist. Furthermore, he points out, native speakers need not enter the equation at all, as English is often used as a lingua franca between speakers who do not share a mother tongue, while it also operates for intranational purposes in many countries (the case of India being, for him, a paradigmatic example). Quirk's position, he thus contends, is out of touch with 'sociolinguistic realities', and is an attempt to impose an ideological idealism on social situations which are neither amenable to, nor compatible with, such a programme.

One paradox of this situation is that the two men are, in fact, both advocating a similar democratic position. They simply choose to do so in very different fashion, based upon their own reading of contemporary social politics. Quirk is of the belief that social mobility – which he sees as a key rationale for the learning of English around the world – is most likely to result from being fluent in a standard which is the acknowledged bearer of social capital across the globe. It is only through this that learners will, in reality, be able to 'increase their freedom and their career prospects' (1990: 7). To his mind, an insistence on variety is likely to have the very opposite effect, and constrain the learner to his or her original social position. Kachru's counterargument is that there are issues of political, social and even psychological identity that are directly related to the form of language that one speaks, and that an insistence on elevating native speaker norms as the only acceptable target ignores this. Thus, far from being emancipatory, the single world standard of Quirk's prescription is, in Kachru's view, fundamentally divisive.

Of key importance for our discussion here is that Quirk is explicitly advocating the agenda of a universal language. He writes of his belief that 'the world needs an international language and... English is the best candidate at present on offer' (1990: 10) – a rationalized approach that conforms to the outline of the argument that I cited at the beginning of this chapter. Founded on the need for a single, central variety, this approach has since been promoted by others, most noticeably Crystal (1997: 137), who suggests that a 'World Standard Spoken English (WSSE)' will emerge. While Crystal is less dogmatic about insisting that this WSSE should conform to a native speaker model, he believes it is likely that a standard US variety will be most influential in its development. Kachru's approach, on the other hand, is more cautionary, and he does not give a direct solution to the question of the universal tongue, but instead points to the importance of the 'sociolinguistic realities' which complicate Quirk's position. The concluding paragraph of his paper gives a good summary of the issues as he perceives them:

> What is actually 'deficit linguistics' in one context may be a matter of 'difference' which is based on vital sociolinguistic realities of identity, creativity and linguistic and cultural contact in another context. The questions are: can sociolinguistic realities be negated? And, can international codification be applied to a language which has over 700 million users across the globe? If the answer to the second question is 'yes', it is vital to have a pragmatically viable proposal for such codification. We have yet to see such a proposal. (1991: 11–12)

To an extent, then, there is a conceptual schism between the two perspectives, as the one is moving directly from the prominence of English in the world to the advocacy of a universal language, while the other is calling for a more nuanced understanding of the way in which English (if we can use the single term) actually exists around the globe.

The Lingua Franca Approach

Kachru's explication of the complexities of the situation has, however, been taken by some as a need to formulate a more pluricentric approach to the concept of a universal language. One current effort to do this is the project of English as a Lingua Franca (ELF), which is an attempt to circumvent the double bind that a universal language would seemingly need to be unitary (it is one common language for the entire world), but that a pluricentric view (a commonwealth of local varieties) is the more democratic option, reducing (if not destroying) the hegemony of the Anglo–American model. The way in which ELF seeks to tackle this problem is explained by Jenkins (2006: 161) as follows:

> The existence of ELF is not intended to imply that learners should aim for an English that is identical in all respects. ELF researchers do not believe any such monolithic variety of English does or ever will exist. Rather, they believe that anyone participating in international communication needs to be familiar with, and have in their linguistic repertoire for use, as and when appropriate, certain forms (phonological, lexicogrammatical, etc.) that are widely used and widely intelligible across groups of English speakers from different first language backgrounds.

This approach maintains the ambition of a universal language, but does so in a fragmentary form. It draws upon the repertoire paradigm of language use – the view that speakers have a range of registers or context-specific varietal strategies to draw upon as and when circumstances require. The idea, then, is not simply that lingua franca use exists as a function, but that a complex of core features (though not amounting to what would constitute a variety) also exist, which can be drawn upon to enable communication of primarily ideational meaning. This differs from Crystal's WSSE in that, although he too suggests that a repertoire or bidialectical approach is a democratic solution, he sees local varieties coexisting with something more 'monolithic', to use Jenkins's term.

In a sense it would appear that the 'core features' approach is akin to pursuing a 'common denominator' variety – the identification of some sort of 'universal English grammar' which will result in a reconfiguration of the language so that those inconsistencies which coincide with redundancies for the transmission of ideational meaning are filed off. (The commonly cited example is vestigial inflections such as the 's' on the third person singular of regular verbs (e.g. Seidlhofer, 2004).) The project then seeks to combine this with attitudinal changes that promote pluricentrism over monocentrism, and inclusiveness over exclusiveness (Jenkins, 2007). Research in this area is relatively young, and thus conclusive evidence of its viability is still being pursued. However, this approach does still pursue the idea of the universal language – though in an admittedly very different form from the solutions proposed throughout the 20th century.

If we return to the formula of our original argument therefore, we can see that both these approaches follow the basic logic, but interpret the word 'English' in a different way. And indeed, to make the formula work, they propose specific ways in which the term 'English' – and the social practices to which it refers – should be regulated. For Quirk, English can assume the mantel of an efficient universal language if English is taken to mean a standardized variety based upon native speaker intuition; for Jenkins the formula is made possible if English is taken to mean the dynamic and variegated form that occurs in authentic lingua franca situations across the globe and which is emphatically not to be constrained by native speaker prejudices. As such, both proposals appear to provide evidence for Kristeva's (1989: 325) contention that throughout the history of linguistics, 'representations and theories of languages ... approach through the name 'language' an object that is noticeably different each time'. If we simply replace 'language' with 'English' in this aphorism, we have here a methodological caveat for all research into English as a global language.

Another example of this conundrum can be found in Sandra McKay's book aimed at instructors wishing to teach English as an international language. She writes that 'one of the reasons for considering English an international language is the sheer number of people in the world who will have some familiarity with English. This shift reflects the use of English as a language of wider communication in a global sense for a great variety of purposes' (2002: 13). As has been suggested, this appears, according to the logic that structures mainstream discourse on the subject, to be a sound conclusion to draw: English already has a foothold in diverse regions of the globe; it therefore seems reasonable to promote it as a universal code for communication. Yet McKay notes in the same chapter that the question of 'whether or not to include pidgin and creole speakers in estimates of English users is a subject of debate' (p. 11). Such a question is only controversial, however, if it is necessary to limit the reference of the word 'English', and by extension to regulate the language so that it remains a coherent and unified entity. The 'family resemblances' approach to English violates this premise, and in so doing problematizes the simple equation that says that because 'English' is already so widespread in the world, it is the ideal candidate (from a pragmatic, if not a political point of view) for a world language.

There are linguistic concerns, of course, about the assumptions upon which these various approaches are founded, and part of the analysis of what can qualify as a global language will depend upon the constraints that the faculty of language itself brings to the ambition (Seargeant, 2009). A fully sophisticated notion of what it is that we mean by English could well lead to the conclusion that the logic upon which the promotion of English as a universal language is founded is insolubly flawed. And indeed, much research in this area has involved identifying difficulties with exactly such an idealistic project. Issues such as pragmatic and rhetorical competence (Connor, 1996; Kasper, 1997), for example, point to the way that communication is very evidently reliant on shared assumptions about cultural context, and thus a truly universal language might require a further revolution in the structuring of a global society (a more all-encompassing and uniform globalization).

What it is important to appreciate, however, is that all such approaches both to research and to regulation of the language are based upon certain theoretical assumptions about the nature of language in general and of English in particular. In articulating their arguments, these various approaches contribute to specific conceptualizations of the language which, when converted into practice (through educational policy, for example), can affect – in a fundamental way – attitudes toward linguistic behavior, as well as to wider social issues. As we can see from the above synoptic account of mainstream issues in the field, what is privileged is often a functionally limited aspect of linguistic behavior (the communication of ideational meaning),[3] and when these approaches talk of English in general they are actually referring to a specific dialect – either an existing or an emergent one[4] – and thus they pass quietly over the full breadth of language-as-praxis that constitutes the linguistic dimension of human existence.

English as Axiom

In summary, we have here different conceptualizations of English which act as the basis for different trends within applied linguistics practice. In a statement, problematizing the concept of language with which the discipline of linguistics works, Milner writes that '[i]t is possible to understand the sense in which linguistics does not have language as its object: language is its axiom' (English translation from Harpham, 2002: 58). We can, perhaps, apply this same contention to the global English issue as it is taken up both within applied linguistics and in wider social contexts. A pre-established concept of 'English' is always an axiomatic starting point for any form of English language-related reflective practice. Although research takes English as its object of study, it must first designate what is meant by English, and thus the object of study is not objectively found, but partially predetermined according to the assumptions and interests of the research tradition. In this way, the object is, in Harpham's characterization, 'arbitrary' (2002: 57).[5] The axiom of English does not, therefore, have a fixed or universal value, and it is this difference in starting point which develops into different disciplinary traditions.

In the two approaches outlined above, the ambition of international communication is an ingredient of the axiom, and the notion of English with which they work is molded to an extent to this presumptive function. Both of these particular approaches are abstract and theoretical, and intended to be generalizable across different contexts in which English is used. In this way they stake their claim to being the authoritative interpretation of the nature of the global language. There exist, however, alternative conceptualizations of the language which are generated by a similarly 'arbitrary' designation of function and properties, but within specific cultural contexts which are often beyond the theoretical parameters of applied linguistics. As with the two approaches above, these alternate concepts are centered around the notion of English's international status. Yet in other ways these conceptualizations appear to be in conflict with certain of the tenets upon which the dominant applied linguistics approaches are founded. Before moving on to consider the implications for applied linguistics of these alternate conceptualizations, and to address the question of what function they may perform in their own right within the culture in which they exist, let me provide two introductory examples of the practices to which I refer.

English Versus Japanese

The first example concerns comments made by the Japanese Minister for Education, Bunmei Ibuki, in October 2006[6] – a few weeks after his appointment to the post – about proposed changes to the Fundamental Law of Education. Central to the revision of this bill was a stress on respect for tradition and the fostering of patriotic sentiment in the nation. The wider context for this realignment of policy involves a complex of national and international concerns, including especially the delicate nature of relations with Japan's Asian neighbors which have suffered in recent years due to the controversy over former prime minister Junichiro Koizumi's visits to Yasukuni shrine, the memorial to several Japanese war criminals, and the pledge by his successor, Shinzo Abe, to review Japan's pacifist constitution.

The way in which Ibuki phrased his call for a greater stress on tradition within education policy – and the way in which this was then relayed by the media – was to juxtapose Japanese values (in part symbolized by the Japanese language) against the need to teach English at the elementary level. In an interview with the *Japan Times*, Ibuki is quoted as saying: 'I wonder if [schools] teach children [the] social rules they should know as Japanese.... Students' academic abilities have been declining, and there are [many] children who do not write and speak decent Japanese. [Schools] should not teach a foreign language before improving the situation' (*Japan Times*, 3 Oct. 2006, parentheses in original). At a postcabinet news conference the following day he reiterated the point by use of an enigmatic analogy: 'It is fine [for elementary school pupils] to eat sweets and cakes, but only if they still have an appetite after consuming basic foodstuffs for the sustenance of the body such as protein and starch' (MEXT, 2006).

What is of interest here is the collocation of concepts, and the way in which the English language is assigned a particular emblematic meaning which contrasts very specifically with Japanese values. The *Japan Times*, for example, interprets the minister's comments in the following way: 'Ibuki believes one of the reasons for his appointment is that ... [he] shares Abe's policy goal of placing greater emphasis on reviving traditional values and social norms. [He] is thus reluctant to introduce English education as a formal subject at public elementary schools' (*Japan Times*, 3 Oct. 2006). The logic here is one of mutual exclusivity, of a choice in which, if the study of Japanese promotes traditional values, then English (that is, the language which denotes an international outlook) can only impede such values.

Implicit in both the comments by the minister and the commentary by the newspaper is the idea that assigning a symbolic value to a language is an unproblematic, if not natural, act, and that rational argument about language policy can be structured around such associative meanings. What we can further read from this example is that the symbolic value of the language is thus predisposing people to approach the language itself in a particular way. In this example, the language is being regulated *prior* to any discussion of the type of English that might form part of the curriculum. This regulation prefigures the debate between monocentric and pluricentric standards, yet still draws upon the concept of the global language, and uses this as a key motif within language policy. English is here conceptualized, in part, in a strategy of antagonism with the conceptualization of the Japanese language, in ways which are explicitly political, and also emphatically consequential.

'See, listen, and eat English'

A further example, of rather more infamous character, can offer an illustration not only of how attitudes toward the language may predispose people to a particular relationship with it in gate-keeping scenarios such as policy, but of how they can affect actual practice. It concerns a learning initiative instigated a few years ago by the Japanese educational publisher Shogakukan in partnership with the McDonald's restaurant chain. In addition to its publishing concerns, Shogakukan runs language classes for children, and in 2002, they launched an English school for toddlers, using the McDonald's restaurant as the classroom, and utilizing the dining experience as a type of task-based learning resource (see Figure 2.1). The rationale for the venture, as explained in their publicity material, is this

> All children love McDonald's. There they can enjoy delicious food. *Hamburger, French Fries, Juice, Nuggets, Soup*. These words are always learnt in English class. Children can quickly learn the things they love. The passion to speak about their favourite things helps children learn new words. Because they love it they can remember the word for it. Because they love it they can remember the English word for it. Ages two to three is the perfect stage for "input". Children see English, listen to English, touch English – and eat English?! They experience English. Sooner or later, they will start using those words which were "input" during this term. And their interest in English will grow greater and greater.[7]

The press release for McPal, as it is called, elucidates further on the pragmatics of the learning experience:

> The children, about 15 to a class, will go to the counter and use the English they have learnt to place their orders. Their mothers and teachers will then do the same. After 45 minutes of teaching and singing, the class will be served with the food they ordered earlier. Tuition fees are set at a competitive 1000 yen for mother and child [approximately £5], but don't include dining expenses. The pupils are expected to improve their English significantly over the 12-week course, and will be encouraged to place orders of increasing complexity, including different sizes of drink and various dipping sauces.

This is, to put it mildly, an enigmatic approach to pedagogy. Learning a narrow range of brand-specific vocabulary; conducting 'authentic' exchanges with monolingual Japanese staff who are required, as part of their job, to include certain Americanisms in their pre-scripted dialogue: none of this is likely to show up as good practice in a contemporary TESOL methods manual. The conundrum, therefore, is how such an abnormal version of ELT is not only tolerated (to the extent that it can

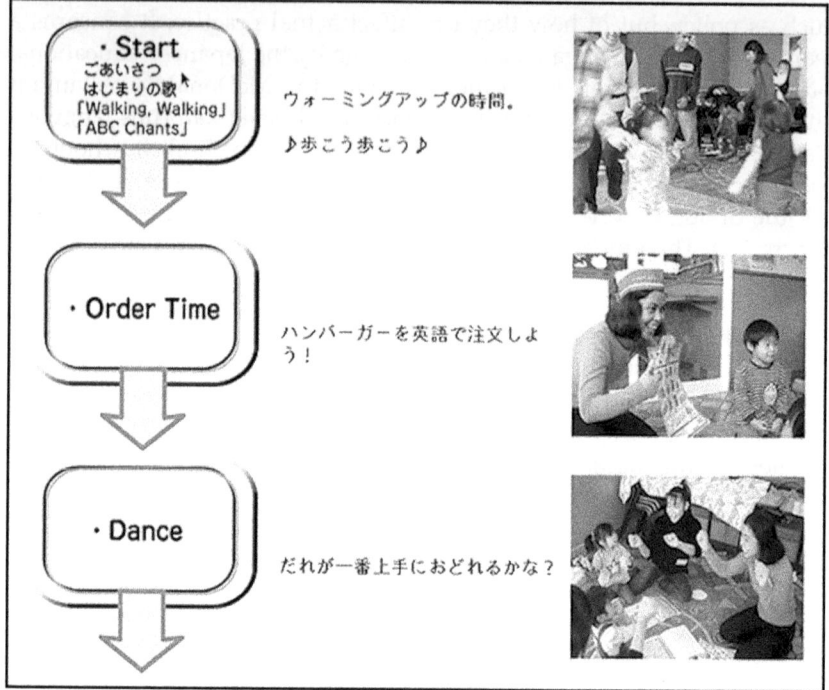

Figure 2.1 McPal 'lesson plan'

succeed as a going commercial concern), but is also sponsored by a reputable educational publisher in a society that views English ability as one of the determining factors for whether its citizens can expect a better life in the 21st century (CJGTC, 2000a), and which pours such financial and intellectual resources into improving language education.

One answer, given the nature of the noneducational company involved, is to view the enterprise in terms of the penetration of corporate marketing strategies into all aspects of society. This type of aggressive marketing policy, where a brand allies itself with a socially responsible institution or initiative, is a phenomenon increasingly common in consumerist society, and has been highlighted by Molnar (1996) in his investigation of the sponsorship of high school programmes in the United States by major corporations (see also Klein, 2000). For this to work successfully a link has to be established between the brand name and the service on offer, and in this case the formula is a simple and traditional one: English = USA = McDonald's. The corporate image has a metonymic relationship with the culture that spawned it, and this culture is, in turn, inextricably linked in the popular imagination with the English language. In essence, the consumption of American fast food is symbolically equivalent to the consumption of the English language within this formula ('Children see English, listen to English, touch English – and eat English') – and in both cases the product itself (the hamburger/the linguistic ability) is of less importance than the aspirational and culturally exotic image that it connotes.

The McPal initiative can certainly be explained in part by this dynamic. Based on his study of America in the mid-90s, Molnar notes how the old adage that 'if education fails, the economy fails' has been replaced by a more sinister mindset: 'The original economic justification for corporate leadership in educational reform has been turned on its head. The emphasis has shifted from the contribution good schools make to everyone's economic well-being to how public schools can be used to increase the profits of a particular business' (1996: 18). The present day agenda of many businesses which take an interest in education is thus not only to exploit the resources of the school population as an untapped market, but in so doing to instil a consumerist ideology into children in an entirely practical manner. As an example, Molnar tells a story of Ronald McDonald teaching children about a fire drill in a school in Milwaukee, and handing out 'a coupon good for a cheeseburger at participating McDonald's stores in return for filling out a safety quiz' (p. 26). A show of social responsibility thus becomes an unlikely promotional opportunity.

The McPal scenario goes further, though, by not only socializing children into ways of acting, but associating a specific consumerist identity with the whole practice of foreign language acquisition. Unlike the fire drill and the cheeseburger, there is no dissociation between product and practice in the McPal scenario – the two are an integral part of the same action. McDonald's, after all, even has its own specific discourse (the often parodied proprietorial use of the 'Mc' prefix), while it, too, operates as a first order symbol of globalization. On a conceptual level then, the marriage of the two is close to intuitive, and is certainly not arbitrary in the way many of Molnar's examples are. Yet it relies for its coherence on very specific cultural connotations which serve to override functional linguistic concerns.

What is apparent, therefore, is that it is the associations that are allied to the English language within Japan that allow for a place like this to exist. Already we are less concerned with linguistic or applied linguistic analyses of the language, and are instead turning to a sociological critique of the context within which the language is being promoted for our explanation of the way it is taught. The English language in this context cannot be seen as a neutral communicative system which parents desire their children to master. If that were the case the flawed pedagogical nature of such a venture would render the enterprise absurd. Instead, the language has to be viewed as having a particular sociocultural meaning which creates the context in which such ventures can exist. Here again, therefore, a very specific conceptualization of the language exists, in this case not articulated in metalinguistic terms (i.e. propositional statements about the language), but enacted in practice – in both the institution of the McPal school, and the behaviors of the parents who sign their children up for classes.

Conclusion

The McPal case is, of course, an atypical example, and the majority of mainstream education in Japan is not predicated on such extreme notions (though see Chapter 6). The contention of this book, however, is that *any* engagement with English in Japan will take place within a similar context of cultural associations and will be duly influenced by these associations. These associations, which coalesce into distinct conceptualizations of the language, are, in the ways they structure social behavior, consequential. As such, an analysis of such associations and the way they reflect and interact with social and political trends within the culture is of great importance for any debate about the place and state of English in Japan. Indeed, we can hypothesize that the conceptualizations of English that exist are not arbitrary in terms of their historical and political genealogy, and are thus likely to be significant in terms of the cultural work they perform. It would be mistaken, therefore, to dismiss them as simply wrong-headed and out of line with contemporary thinking in TESOL and applied linguistics studies.

We are faced, then, with two specific questions. To what end are the conceptualizations of English within Japanese society the way that they are? and, what consequence do the structural dynamics which result in these context-specific conceptualizations have for the generation of the theoretical approaches that were discussed at the beginning of the chapter? The first question is an empirical one, and requires the examination of English language practices as they occur within the specific context of Japanese society. The second question is of a more theoretical nature, and involves detailed consideration of the role played by 'ideology' in language-related social practice. Before moving to the specific case study, therefore, it is worth first reviewing the ways in which global English studies have broached the issue of ideology, while looking also at how an explicit 'language ideologies' approach might provide us with a productive analytical framework for the examination of the idea of English in Japan. This, therefore, will be the subject of the next chapter.

Chapter 3
Language Ideology and Global English

Politics and the Emergence of the World Englishes Paradigm

It is since the outset of the 1990s that politics has become an overt concern for research into world English. Prior to this, it was more specifically linguistic concerns that initially dominated the discipline. These concerns were then recalibrated with the injection of sociolinguistic sensibilities into the research agenda, until the 'critical turn' in applied linguistics arrived to foreground the ubiquity of the political. At present, the discipline appears to be seeking a balance between these two poles, attempting to retain a linguistic focus on the affordances and constraints of the language faculty, while also plotting the effects within the social environment of language and language-related social practices. And it is here that a 'language ideologies' approach can offer great potential, as it takes as its site of inquiry the mediating forces between language form and language function, and places linguistic behavior firmly within an animating cultural context. This chapter will therefore examine theoretical precepts from this approach that might productively be applied to the global English question, and it will consider specifically how these can offer support in the development of a methodology for the analysis of the conceptualization of the English language in Japan. Firstly, though, I will briefly recite the stages of emergence of the world Englishes paradigm, and consider how the concept of ideology has hitherto featured within the genealogy of the discipline.

In his review of the development and diversification of approaches to the study of English within globalized contexts, Bolton (2005) traces a narrative which begins in the 1960s with Randolph Quirk (e.g. 1968) and University College London's Survey of English Usage. This had as its brief the description of diverse varieties of the language, specifically in terms of syntactic structure and historical change. It took a predominantly linguistic approach, with the object of study being linguistic form rather than sociolinguistic function, and the concept of variety being formulated as (syntactic) divergence from a central standard. Ideological evaluation of language practices was thus encoded within the methodology (in the hierarchical ordering of central standard versus peripheral variety), but there was no explicit engagement with the political nature of either language practice or linguistic research.

Concomitant to this was the development of sociolinguistic approaches to English around the world, which took the lead from work in the sociology of language. These approaches (e.g. Fishman et al., 1977) were also committed to the study of variety, but were not focused exclusively upon features of language difference but also upon how such variety occurs in relation to social circumstance and position. Within the global English disciplinary history, the work of Braj Kachru in particular (e.g. 1986a, 1986b) has broadened the object of study by adopting this more explicitly sociolinguistic framework, and by including within the analytic scope the sociopolitical and ideological issues that accompany formal variation. His critique of Quirk (discussed in Chapter 2) is illustrative of many of the concerns he introduced in response to the less sociopolitically reflective 'English studies' approach pursued by the Survey of English Usage. And his insistence on the importance of the 'sociolinguistic realities' of speakers in diverse world contexts has done much to instil within the discipline a political awareness about the actualities of English language use around the globe.

The 'world Englishes' approach that is associated with Kachru's name offers a pluricentric model of the English-speaking world which accords legitimacy to stable varieties in diverse contexts, and combines a descriptive linguistics with an analysis of the politically inflected discourses of the language. This approach has been hugely influential, not least in pedagogical contexts and with TESOL theoreticians (Jenkins, 2006). The English as a Lingua Franca research project is one notable example of this influence, involving as it does the application of a sociopolitical awareness to the description of world English use.

It is the third major subset of approaches to the study of English in the world that introduces overtly politico-ideological issues into the picture. These are approaches which have a 'critical' agenda, and aim to situate English language practices firmly within their historical context. In doing so, they have shifted the focus of debate to a critique both of the role played in the global English situation by the international policy ventures of the dominant Anglophone countries (Pennycook, 1994, 1998; Phillipson, 1992), and of the ethical responsibilities of the applied linguistics community (Pennycook, 2001). Phillipson, in developing his argument about the linguistic imperialist practices of the West, employs a Marxist framework to analyze the role played by English and its promotional organizations in maintaining an Anglo–American hegemony within the world system. Ideology, of an expressly neo-Marxist complexion, is thus central to this approach. And while counter theories such as the work of Brutt–Griffler (2002), which aims to revise the linguistic imperialism thesis by emphasising the agency of non-native speakers in the worldwide spread of English, have challenged some of Phillipson's contentions, the influence of his line of argument, and of Pennycook's (1994: 9) assertion that the 'natural, neutral, and beneficial' attitude toward the spread of English is at best distorted, at worst propagandist, has been immense and has set an agenda which places political awareness at the centre of the discipline.

It is the opinion of some commentators, however, that the political sensibilities of this third stage in the history of global English studies have come to occlude linguistic concerns, and that debate is now centered more around political philosophy than sociolinguistics. Bolton (2005: 75), for example, suggests that Pennycook employs in his recent scholarship 'a brand of critical linguistics with little linguistics' and '[t]he rhetoric of Pennycook *qua* critical linguist... shifts the object of study almost entirely from language data and linguistic analysis to that of activist pedagogical politics'. Furthermore, there appears to be a danger with such approaches that the political agenda of the researcher can have a determining effect on the research project, and that *a priori* assumptions about the place, purpose and impact of English language practices in the world can lead to theorizing which is not suitably sensitive to the actual practices of the diverse contexts in which such practices occur (Seargeant, 2008).

The history of global English studies has drawn little on linguistic anthropological approaches, which is a surprising omission given the seeming consonance of concerns between the linguistic context that global English invariably involves and the analytic apparatus that linguistic anthropology has developed. For a context such as Japan, where canonical sociolinguistic concerns (with their concentration on the form, evolution and social affordances of a native variety) are of relatively minor relevance, the traditional world Englishes approach has certain limitations. As Berns (2005) notes, Expanding Circle countries such as Japan have received noticeably less attention within the research literature than Outer Circle countries.[1] This is doubtless in great part due to the existence of distinct varieties and established sociolinguistic functions in countries such as India and Singapore. But as was noted in the Introduction, Japan exhibits a great fascination for the English language *despite* the lack of official status and the absence of a discrete 'Japanese English' (Yano, 2001).

Kachru's (2005, Chapter 4) own analysis of English within the Japanese context exhibits certain of the limitations of the traditional world

Englishes approach, and as such he has been criticized for overestimating the likely emergence of a distinct Japanese English variety (Yano, 2008). He does, however, touch briefly on ideological attitudes toward English in his summary of work by Lummis (1976) on the *eikaiwa* or 'English conversation' industry. Lummis's essay, which is over three decades old now, is an intriguing analysis of how culturally essentialist assumptions about American–Japanese relations structure the way in which this English conversation industry operates in Japan. Based upon Lummis's autobiographical experience of working within this industry, the essay offers a somewhat polemical account of how a post-Occupation ideology of cultural inferiority is enacted within the language classroom, and of how the English language is perceived as a fundamental mark of cultural, if not racial, difference. In putting forward this argument, the essay raises several interesting issues about the politics of English within Japan. However, its framework for analysis is rather undeveloped, its purpose more polemical than theoretical, and its focus on what it describes itself as a 'subculture of *eikaiwa*' (p. 13) considers only one area of society in which English plays a prominent role. Other studies of English within Japan have concentrated predominantly on educational questions (see Chapter 4), or on language contact issues (and especially the role of loanwords in the Japanese lexis (Stanlaw, 2004)). But as yet there has been little attempt to analyze the broader significance of the place that English occupies within the social landscape of Japan, and the multiplicity of forms and roles it assumes in everyday social life. And it is in this that a language ideologies approach can assist with, as it takes as its object of analysis both linguistic form and sociopolitical function (and the dynamic relations between the two), and examines the patterns of belief that bind language to social existence. In the following section, I will provide an overview of this approach and some of its theoretical components, before suggesting how it may productively be employed for the purposes of this study.

Language Ideologies

As has been intimated above, the central focus of the growing body of research which constitutes language ideologies study is the interface between language beliefs and language use. In his paper on 'Language structure and linguistic ideology' Michael Silverstein writes 'ideologies about language, or linguistic ideologies, are any sets of beliefs about language articulated by users as a rationalisation or justification of perceived language structure or use' (1979: 193). The importance of this observation is that such rationalizations act as the mediating dynamic between language form and language function, and that language use is thus reliant for its efficacy on the ways in which such rationalizations operate and on the cultural presuppositions with which they interact.

This 1979 paper marks the inauguration of 'language ideology' as a distinct field of study (Blommaert, 2006b), and it is here that Silverstein first formulates the equation which lies at the heart of this approach to the analysis of language use. In simplified terms this can be expressed as follows: ideology creates function which enables speech (ideology → function → speech). In other words, language use always occurs within an ideological context (a complex of sociocultural presuppositions about the nature and purpose of that language use) which facilitates the inference of meaning. Analysis of the 'code' itself is inadequate for explaining how the situated social work of language operates, and thus 'to understand how speaking (or other similar uses of language) is effective social action... we must systematise the description of relationships of coexistence... that holds between elements of speech and elements comprising the context in which speech elements are uttered' (Silverstein, 1979: 205).

Other definitions of the concept of language ideology offer a slightly altered emphasis on the relation between self-reflection and linguistic practice. Woolard (1998: 3), for example, characterizes language ideologies as '[r]epresentations, whether explicit or implicit, that construe the intersection of language and human beings in a social world'. The act of rationalization is downplayed in this definition, with the corollary that language ideologies are not necessarily seen as agents of change in the development of linguistic structure in the way that they are in the Silverstein model. Heath (1989: 393) likewise conceives of language ideologies as 'self-evident ideas and objectives a group holds concerning roles of language in the social experiences of members as they contribute to the expression of the group', while Kroskrity (2006: 498) offers a metatheoretical definition of the term as one that is used 'to circumscribe a body of research which simultaneously problematises speakers' consciousness of their language and discourse as well as their positionality (in political economic systems) in shaping beliefs, proclamations, and evaluations of linguistics forms and discursive practices'. For Kroskrity, it is the ways in which linguistic practices are embedded within social practices that constitutes the object of analysis for a language ideologies approach.

Generalizing from these different characterizations, language ideology can be defined, in broad terms, as the structured and consequential ways in which we think about language. The countable form (*a* language ideology) is employed to identify a distinctive pattern of beliefs affecting language, which, for convenience, either within folk conceptions or scientific discourse, is considered to have a certain conceptual stability (the paradigm example is the standard language ideology). The generality of this definition reflects the diversity of theoretical research concerns that the term covers, and it is worth cataloging these in further detail in order to consider their suitability for the analysis of the topic in hand. Before this, however, a word on the central notion of 'ideology' is in order.

The Concept of Ideology

The literature on the concept of ideology, and on the genealogy of the term within the history of ideas, is extensive (e.g. Eagleton, 1991; Hawkes, 2003), as are surveys and discussions of the relationship of this genealogy to the language sciences (e.g. Blommaert, 2005: Chapter 7; Harpham, 2002: Chapter 2; Woolard, 1998). In this section, I will provide some introductory remarks about how the term might most usefully be employed for the current purpose, and this usage can then be refined throughout the course of the book in order to provide precision and shape to the overall debate.

Ideology in the context of linguistic anthropology can be defined as a system of entrenched beliefs about aspects of the lived experience which structure one's relationship to that experience. A central division in ideology studies has been between negative and neutral valuations of these systems of entrenched beliefs: between the traditionally Marxist approach of ideology as a 'false consciousness' which provides a distortion of the actual or truthful nature of experience, and a 'total concept of ideology' (Mannheim, 1936) which comprises socially situated systems of thought that are collectively shared by every member of the community. In terms of ancestral lineage, it is the latter paradigm that feeds into the field of study that is constituted by language ideologies theory. The line from neo-Kantianism through Boas and Whorf to contemporary linguistic anthropology develops this 'neutrally' defined conception, and will, on occasions, elide the concept with similar notions such as culture, worldview, belief or *mentalité* (Woolard, 1998). This 'total conception' highlights the way that beliefs about language (in the form of self-reflexivity) are an essential (i.e. ever-present) part of the linguistic process (Lucy, 1993) and are not overtly political in an either/or way (we cannot get *beyond* the political). However, in so far as ideologies are classifications of the world according to a specific system of values shared by a community, they reproduce hierarchies within society and thus are, in the final instance, determined by and productive of power relations (they are the habitual cognitive behaviors that enable the reproduction of such power relations (Bourdieu, 1991)). That is to say, given that social life is at its base political, so too is ideology, and thus there exist ideologies (such as that of the standard language) which do, in effect, privilege the interests of certain sectors of the community. Ideology thus conceptualized is an entailment of two factors: firstly that ideologies are omnipresent and that they are the ideational (and behavioral) matrices which enable signification; and secondly that social organization is always politically effected, and thus the belief systems of dominant or influential groups are afforded greater prominence within social debate. Thus it is that the 'total concept' of ideology does in fact lead to something like the neo-Marxist view of a vehicle for the promotion of the interests of particular social groups. In other words, the neutral view of ideology only remains truly neutral for as long as it stays theoretical. Once it is applied to specific historical event it absorbs the political specificity that is the nature of all historical events.

A final point worth making is that ideologies should not be seen as primarily mentalist, but also as behavioral, as practice-based, and, in a sense, prereflective, in that they need not involve explicit rationalization. Here Bourdieu's (1990: 56) concept of *habitus* is relevant. Bourdieu writes that '[t]he *habitus* – embodied history, internalised as second nature and so forgotten as history – is the active presence of the whole past of which it is the product'. In other words, it is learned behaviors and dispositions which produce expectations about ways of being in the world which are considered both natural and ahistorical. The behavioral and embodied nature of ideology is an important factor to bear in mind in that it means that beliefs are to be read not only in verbal articulation, but also in social practice and the arrangement of the social environment.

With respect to language, therefore, to speak of ideologies is to say that there exist sociopolitical (that is, historically specific) conceptions of what constitutes language and of how it functions as part of social existence. These conceptions can be both implicit and explicit, but in either case they constitute a shared (though continuously disputed) belief system that influences the way in which we interact with language (Seargeant, 2009).

The issues incorporated in the field of language ideology range from the regulation of micro-level details of communicative interaction and their iterative impact on the development of linguistic form to broad concerns about the role played by language in both culture and civilization. Within this continuum, Woolard (1998: 4) identifies three main areas of study as follows: (1) metapragmatics and concepts of language in use; (2) language varieties and language contact; and (3) the historiography of public or scientific discourses on language. As she stresses, however, in any particular instantiation it is important to note that ideologies of language are never solely about language, but instead about the ties between language and other social factors (such as gender, class or nationality).

And it is this symbiosis of linguistic and extra-linguistic concerns, and the associations that the concept of (a) language accrues, which is the nucleus of our object of study.

Indexicality and Symbolic Meaning

In his 1979 paper, Silverstein develops a theoretical framework centered around the interrelation between language ideology and linguistic form. Of central importance to the way in which this interrelationship operates is the concept of 'indexicalities' – that is, marked aspects of language that function as indicators of specific presuppositions about usage. Silverstein here draws upon the semiotic terminology of Peirce,[2] and posits that the symbolic (that is arbitrary) relationship between signifier and signified (the traditional focus of formal linguistics) needs to be supplemented by an awareness of the indexical relationship between aspects of language use and the belief systems to which they point. Language thus has an 'indexical layer' which, when articulated as discussion of language function, results in a 'metapragmatics' of language use. In this way, language use (the form–function relationship) is always linked firmly to culture, as it is the sociocultural context in which one speaks which determines the way in which that speech will be interpreted. This sociocultural context provides the 'world view' (in Whorf's use of the term (1956)), to which language makes reference in generating pragmatic meaning. As Silverstein puts it, this world view 'constitutes the natives' ideology of the way their language serves as a propositional system representing and talking about what is 'out there' (1979: 201). He goes on to show how this has often, at least in Western conceptualizations of language, privileged a referential ideology of language, establishing a specific relationship of 'reference-and-predication' (p. 208) between linguistic utterance and experiential sense data. This referential ideology is 'enacted' in patterns of use. The attitude assumed by the parties involved toward an act of communication asserts by implication or by explicit metapragmatic comment this general belief system about the function of language. It is this process which comprises the first of the three objects of study which Woolard identifies in her classification of approaches.

Language ideology can also be expressed in talk *about* language and in more general language-related cultural practice. Thus we can say that there is both internal conceptualization of the language (the *in situ* organization and negotiation of meaning, or the metapragmatics) and external conceptualization (a discourse of the language or its symbolic citation). My interest in this book is in the latter: that is, the way in which a particular language accrues specific cultural meaning within a society, and how this then acts as a determining cultural force in its own right, while also creating the context within which people approach that language in that society.

It is worth at this stage adding a word about the nature of the relationship between sign and object as it operates in the context of language conceptualization. The object (that is the concept of the language) can be signaled both by use and citation of the language, producing in each case a different type of relationship with the sign. In other words, when English is *used* within Japanese society, such use is *indexical* (in Silversteinian terms) of characteristics associated with the social group which is typically thought of as using the language (its use *points to* affiliations with the US or UK, for example). Alternatively, the *citation* of the language, which draws on a similar complex of ideological beliefs about the language, stands in a *symbolic* relationship to these beliefs, as there is no existential relationship between the two. Culler's (1975: 17) example of the Rolls-Royce which is an index of wealth because one must be affluent to afford one, but then becomes a conventional symbol for wealth within social use is a useful analogue for the relationships between sign and object in the case of English (see Chandler, 2002 for the interpretation of this example within a Peircean semiotic framework).[3] We can say, therefore, that the concept of the language itself has a symbolic value, and that its use, in any form, is indexical of the beliefs and debates that constitute the value of this symbol. As a symbol, the language is overdetermined, and a tidy relationship between sign and object will only exist in a reductionist synopsis of its symbolic value (in assertions such as English = Western outlook). Thus, the symbolic value is tied to the place and circumstance of the semiotic act in which it is used, and an interpretation of this value must begin with an understanding of this context.

To complete the Peircean triad, we may suppose that an ideology of iconicity also exists (Gal & Irvine, 1995), whereby the lexico–grammatical structure of the English language is viewed, in a contrastive relationship with Japanese, as embodying features which have a correlate in the cultural characteristics of the nation(s) with which English is associated. Thus, for example, the 'straight-forward' grammar of English, stripped of an elaborately hierarchical honorific system, is seen from the perspective of Japan as an iconic reflection of normative social relations in the Anglophone West. In this view, linguistic form is not merely an index of a particular social group, but is considered to be a representation of the distinctive characteristics of a language community. Thus, for example, when a commentator in the media describes 'Japanese [as being] a deep, profound, at times esoteric language [which is] very different from the shoot-from-the-hips English', (*Mainichi Daily News*, 19 May 2002) there is a transference of cultural stereotypes onto the perceived structure of idealized national languages.

The different dimensions of signs are, as this outline suggests, interrelated, and they combine in a process of continual generation (Keane, 2003: 413). So, for example, the symbolic meaning of the language is also a part of the ideology that guides metapragmatic usage. There have been a number of important studies that examine the relationship between sociolinguistic use and indexical-symbolic language ideology, especially within the context of group or national identities. Heller's (1982) research in Quebec, for example, explores the indexical strategies that constitute codeswitching, where the choice of which language to use (French or English) can operate as an index of allegiance to a particular political agenda. Likewise, Woolard's (1989) study of Catalan in Barcelona explores language use and linguistic allegiances (Catalan versus Castilian Spanish) within the context of regionally inflected European politics. Studies of this type constitute the second of Woolard's categories of language ideological research.

In bi- or multilingual situations of this sort, the conceptualization of language typically begins with an ideology that views a particular language as a bounded entity, something distinct and self-sufficient (what Blommaert (2006b: 512) calls the 'artefactual' view of language). There are thus two process co-occurring here: the first is that the specific language ('English', 'French', 'Catalan') is being conceptualized – mainly in terms of its function and cultural associations; in addition, language in general is being conceptualized, both as a particular form of human practice and in terms of its relationship to contemporary ideas of the self within (global) society. Furthermore, as suggested above, this conceptualization takes place on two levels: both in the act of linguistic practice and also in discourse about the language.

Analysis of the nature, construction and influence of this symbolic meaning can therefore lead to two distinct avenues of inquiry: one that considers the way in which this meaning results in specific strategies of regulation for the language and how these relate to other social and cultural contestations; and another that considers how the ideologies of the language influence the way that it is spoken and thus result in the metapragmatics of a contextually specific sociolect or variety. My focus here is predominantly on the former of these, on the relationships that people take toward the (idea of the) language, and the way in which it operates within society as a determining cultural force. I am interested therefore in how the language is *used* in the broadest sense of the word: in how its name is invoked (as in the example in Chapter 2 of the comments by the Education Minister), in how its ornamental trace is displayed and how its cultural connotations are mobilized (as in the McPal example).

An understanding of this is important because this symbolism often *prefigures* usage in terms of speech. That is to say, it prefigures the indexical complexes that constitute the metapragmatics of a particular contextually specific language practice in that it positions that language practice within society, organizing the conceptual routes by which people approach the language. This is particularly the case for bi- or multilingual societies, where there exist hierarchies of languages that are regulated both institutionally and as part of the everyday environment. It is an analysis of these regulative practices, both as they are articulated in 'official' discourse (in applied linguistics doctrine or policy statements, for example) and also inscribed within the lived environment, that will form the substance of this book, and that can, it is hoped, then be used to provide a more complete view of the concept of a global language.

The Historical Ontology of Language

To reiterate, therefore, my specific focus is the way in which the English language is conceptualized, both in Japan as well as in the wider context of applied linguistics research and theory (and how a detailed look at the one can enhance our understanding of the other). The key focus, then, is to be on the relationship between the English language and social, cultural and political concerns. Underpinning both these perspectives, however, is the more fundamental issue of how language is conceptualized as a feature of the human experience, and what existential form it is understood to take within the world. This ontological question is of key importance as it sets the parameters for any subsequent discussion of the language, and can play an influential role in determining the direction of research and debate (to paraphrase Heidegger – science presupposes ontology (1962 [1927]: 30)). The debates referred to above, as well as the various conceptualizations of the language that I wish to explore within the context of Japan, all begin with specific assumptions about the nature of language itself. As such, it will be helpful to formulate a methodology that will allow us to critique the ontological assumptions from which we work and to scrutinize both the evidence upon which they are based and the implications to which they give rise. For while an investigation of the specific cultural associations that comprise the conceptualization of English within Japan takes as its primary object of study the inter-relation between language and social practice, the nature and function of the linguistic system itself (the scientific study of which is the focus of the third category in Woolard's taxonomy of language ideological research interests) are determining factors in this interrelationship.

In the late essay 'What is Enlightenment?', Foucault uses an analysis of Kant's answer to this same question ['*Was ist Aufklärung?*'] as a contrastive device for delineating his own conception of the modern intellectual project: an understanding of our own subjectivity. He writes that

> if the Kantian question was that of knowing what limits knowledge has to renounce transgressing, it seems to me that the critical question today has to be turned back into a positive one: in what is given to us as universal, necessary, obligatory, what place is occupied by whatever is singular, contingent, and the product of arbitrary constraints? (1991: 45)

The focus, he proposes, should not be on perennial or universal questions of being, but on the distinctive nature of our present situation: 'What is our *actualité*? what are we as part of our *actualité*? what is the target activity of philosophy as far as we are part of our *actualité*?' (1983). This, he suggests, is the key issue for modern philosophy. And to facilitate the process of offering an answer he promotes his archaeological and genealogical methods, by means of which we might investigate the 'historical ontology of ourselves' (1991: 45), with the ambition of understanding the human subject through an investigation of its social relations as historically situated events.

This methodology has been a productive force in the analysis of the nature of knowledge and social practice, and can be valuably turned toward a critique of the role that language plays in the social existence of humankind. By using an historicist framework to examine the ways in which language has been conceptualized in terms of its existential form within the world, we are able to make explicit the types of assumption upon which more specific linguistic debate is founded. Drawing upon an ethnographic epistemology (Blommaert, 2006a) – that is, the examination of beliefs as they occur within their historical and cultural context – we can narrow in on what is singular, contingent and arbitrary in any specific conceptualization of language, and use this information both as an important variable in the self-reflexive analysis of our own research methodology, and also as part of the analysis of the role that beliefs about language play in the use of language.

As was mentioned above, this question has recently been addressed by Blommaert (2006b) with his identification of an 'artefactual' view of language which is prevalent in many contemporary commonsense linguistic beliefs. In this, language is seen as a 'manipulable, bounded artefact consisting of (grammatical) "structures" with a clear function, denotation'

(p. 512). Here, then, ontology and function are closely linked, with the mainstream referential ideology (Silverstein, 1979) privileging certain features of linguistic behavior and promoting these as essential to language's existence. Given the importance of this general view to contemporary studies of language it is worth highlighting a number of its specific features. These will then be dealt with in context-specific examples later in the book.

One technique available for making explicit the ways in which people conventionally think about the nature of language is to identify patterns of representation within discourse, and the types of metaphoric association that are made as part of such representations. A key conceit in this respect for the ontology of language is what, in the terminology of conceptual metaphor theory (Lakoff & Johnson, 1980), would be expressed as LANGUAGE IS A POSSESSION. That is to say, the entity that is language is often conceptualized as an object that can be possessed by a person or group of people, and has a range of properties compatible with such an action. It is this conceptual framework which enables narratives of language 'loss' (Block, 2008), the debate about 'ownership' (Widdowson, 1994; see Seargeant, 2008 for discussion) and, more recently, ideas of 'consumption' (as employed in the McPal example referred to in Chapter 2).

Another key issue related to the understanding of the ontology of language is the relationship between the concepts of language in general and a particular language. As discussed above, it is often the case that a named language (English in this case) is considered to be a discrete and bounded entity in its own right, at least in popular understanding. In linguistic anthropology, however, it has long been acknowledged that such a view is simplistic and fraught with problems. Duranti (1997: 70), for example, notes that

> Every time we subject a language (e.g. 'English,' 'Swahili,' etc.) to systematic investigation, we discover that it displays a considerable variation across speakers and situations. This means that we cannot be sure that what we are describing for a few speakers or even for an entire group of people will have a social distribution larger than the group.

Such a view, however, is not reflected in the mainstream 'artefactual' view of language, nor is it encoded in the demotic of most languages. The practicalities of linguistic usage in many speech communities designate a single lexeme to the combined linguistic behaviors of particular communities, and it is only through elaborate qualification that alternative conceptions of language can be expressed. The result is the view of any particular language as a single and complete system existing alongside many other such singularly complete systems. The ontology of each is something akin to a Platonic ideal, only ever complete and perfect in the combined competence of its collected users.

One consequence of such a view is that discussion of any particular language often falls prey to what we might term the totalizing fallacy, whereby a single, stable variety, usually presented as noncontextual (that is to say, with universal valency), is posited as the proper object of investigation (Blommaert, 2003). The existence of such a stable variety is considered self-evident, despite the fact that the details of its actual nature are a source of constant dispute. (In the field of English as a global language, for instance, there is a struggle between the monocentrists and the pluricentrists for the heart and soul of a totalized concept of the English language, with neither side entertaining the full implications of linguistic variation and often not incorporating within their model issues such as register and genre.) Again, the vocabulary of the demotic configures this view in its hierarchical distribution of terminology centered around the unmarked term 'language', and branching off into 'variety', 'dialect' and so on. This general template then generates the same hierarchical relationships for the specific: for example, English, British English and Cockney.

A further result of this view is that the categorial relationship between 'language in general' and 'a particular language' ends with the two becoming virtually synonymous in terms of their basic existence. Rather than 'language' being the more general class, and *a* language being a specific, real-world instance, any given language can act as the archetype for the complete linguistic system; and 'language' becomes simply an abstraction of different complete systems. Each individual language then is viewed as identically complete, but with a slightly different pattern of internal organization (an enigmatic 'flaw' in the overall design of this human faculty which allows for conundrums such as the popular version of linguistic relativity [different lexicogrammar = different world view], and the *traduttore, traditore* imponderable).

Such assumptions about the ontology of language, encoded in the logic of arguments about or explicit references to language, also lead to the question of what does (and what does not) count as language, and this also can be an instructive factor in the development of theories about language. An investigation, therefore, of the bounds between 'language' and 'non language', or what is legitimated as a part of a named language and what is not, can help delineate such fundamental ontological assumptions, and also expose the motivations for such beliefs. Here again, the key relationship is the one between function and ontology, and the way in which preconceptions about the purpose of linguistic behavior (what role language is meant to fulfill in human interaction or existence) will color an understanding of the nature of that behavior.

Culture and the Context for Analysis

Before making the transition from theory to methodology, there is one final terminological complication to attend to. This is the term 'culture' as it is used to refer to the circumscribed context which comprises the focus for the study. As was noted earlier, within certain anthropological traditions the use of the terms culture and ideology are elided, while in other traditions the concept is a close equivalent of 'society' in that it refers, in Raymond Williams words, simply to 'a particular *way of life*' (1976: 10). There is a particular reason, however, for retaining 'culture' as a term of reference in the present study, and this is that it is frequently deployed within the (popular) discourse of global English to refer to group-specific behaviors and symbolic practices, amongst which language is traditionally included. Because of this, however, we are, when talking of *Japanese cultural practices*, in fact working with two slightly different concepts of culture with differing provenances and differing functional remits. One of these relies on the contextual determinacy of its intended site of reception, and is a vernacular usage which appeals to commonsense or mainstream ideologies, particularly those concerned with national identity. The other works at an analytic level, and is a term belonging to the scientific register used for anatomizing social practices and group behaviors. The use of the second as an analytic term in this study is prompted, therefore, by the pre-existence of the first in the discourse which is to be analyzed. Thus when, for example, Japanese policy documents write 'the Japanese language, our mother tongue, is the basis for perpetuating Japan's culture and traditions' (CJGTC, 2000a: 10), the referent is a set of established beliefs within Japanese society about identity issues as they relate to specific practices. In analyzing the constituent features of these beliefs, we can retain the term culture which is used here as part of the vernacular, and replace commonsense presuppositions about its meaning with certain theoretical tenets. These theoretical tenets are as follows: the term 'culture' is being used in the book to refer to shared patterns of learned or symbolic behavior, the aggregate of which constitute *a* culture, in so far as they are promoted as being essential for (or linked to an essentialist understanding of) group identity, and are seen as distinct from the behaviors of others. This definition therefore includes within itself the act of self-promotion (which thus makes it a complement of the commonsense use of the word in discourses of national identity), while also positing the existence of mainstream practices which provide the matrix for significant behavior (be it conformist or nonconformist) within the social group. Such a usage is similar to what Bauman (1999: 13) refers to as the 'differential concept of culture', which is

employed to account for the apparent differences between communities of people (temporally, ecologically or socially discriminated). This usage locates the differential concept of culture among numerous 'residue concepts', contrived frequently in the social sciences to explain away the sediment of deviant idiosyncrasies unaccountable for by the otherwise universal and omnipotent regularities (where it shares the ascribed function with ideas, tradition, life experience etc.).

Yet while for Bauman this concept is an 'intellectual frame' (p. 14) imposed upon human experience as part of the analytic apparatus of the researcher, the usage in the present book is also a reflection of the self-promotional activities of those who align their identity with the concept.

The ready-made categorization that language provides us with – in this case, the concept of 'Japan' and the 'Japanese' – while suggesting a monolithic group and possibly implying conformity – is not meant to conceal the obvious diversity of conviction, predilection and attitude that exists in any community. Instead, its use employs the stereotype in the way that mainstream cultural practice employs that stereotype – as a touchstone against which diversity and individual opposition attains significance. Reference to 'Japanese culture' within my analysis, therefore, is to aggregate and salient behavior, either promoted explicitly ('this is what Japan is like') or forming part of the way that social relations are tacitly organized within a community which accepts the label 'Japanese' as being a significant part of its identity.

In summary, then, we have a body of theory which traces the ideational and behavioral presuppositions which have a bearing upon the nature and functional efficacy of language, and on the consequential relations between language and social practice. It does this by considering how language is positioned within the ideological matrices which structure symbolic involvement in particular social networks. These ideological complexes can be signaled in various ways: either by the diverse uses of the linguistic code itself or by citation of the language as concept. They are also related to structured beliefs and practices organized within communities which are rationalized as part of a network of circumscribed groupings (e.g. regional, national, ethnic and generational), and which are often referred to in terms of discrete cultures.

The advantage of this body of theory is that it is able to extend the traditional world Englishes concerns about context-specific language practices. It considers not only the canonical sociolinguistics of discrete varieties or the communicative functions played by a lingua franca, but also the various other uses and existences of language within society, and how such uses relate to and are organized by established patterns of thought about the idea of (a) language.

Methodology and the Objects of Analysis

Having outlined these key tenets, we come now to the question of how we can bring this body of theory to bear on the analysis of the conceptualization of English within Japan. The methodology that will be employed involves reading the meaning that is attributed to the language in sites of social significance. In order to trace and illuminate the ideologies of the language it is necessary to examine how English is positioned within society, and interrogate the assumptions about the meanings associated with it that explain the nature of this positioning. It is the articulation of this positioning by means of the wide palette of semiotic resources which constitute the cultural organization of society which will be taken as the *discourse* of English within the country (Blommaert, 2005). The language's conceptual equivalence with other cultural or political factors is rarely, if ever, expressed in an explicit or direct equation. Rarely in the discourse do statements such as 'English = international outlook' occur in any overt form. Instead we are confronted with problematics such as the existence, social acceptability and relative commercial success of an English language teaching establishment such as McPal. Within the book it is sites such as this which are taken as objects of study, in so far as they exist as instantiations of the ideologies of the language which are structuring social practice. The challenge then is to address them as objects of investigation and read from their existence, functioning and influence the ideologies that support them. This can be achieved by interrogating the structural logic which sustains them, and examining the role played by the concept of English within this structural logic. By structural logic what is meant is the logic (that is the cohesive set of assumptions) which is the structuring principle behind a set of social practices or the establishment and functioning of an institution. In so far as it is the significance accorded to elements within these social practices that provides their structure, it is this significance which can become the target of investigation.

In practice, what this involves is excavating the patterning of assumptions that produce the specific positioning of English within a given scenario. In the McPal case, for example, this requires inquiring into what the motivating factors are for the marriage of multinational fast food corporation and preschool English language educational establishment. In considering the role that context-specific ideologies of the language play in brokering this union, we can consider the assumptions about English that are expressed within the promotional material for the school, in the social practice that comprises its curriculum, in its business practices (e.g. its staff recruitment policies), and so on. These various practices combine to produce a discourse of the language, and thus it is an analysis of these combinatory practices and the meanings that they connote which becomes the working method for an investigation into the ideology of English within Japan.

Given that language ideologies theory contends that the entrenched beliefs that provide the interpretative matrix for social signification are shared across a community (indeed, they are one of the factors which maintain the cohesion of a community (Silverstein, 1998)), we should suppose that the assumptions that underpin one instance of social practice should contribute to the structural logic that governs other such instances. Such a supposition can thus become a target of empirical investigation that can be used to map the distribution of ideologies. It is for this reason that an extended range of objects of study will be used. Thus, both similarities and differences in the conceptualization of English across the social landscape can be gauged, and beliefs (both contested and promoted as self-evident) can be analyzed from the function they perform in a situated context. The guiding principle for the selection of the objects of study is that the language ideologies which create the idea of English in Japan are to be sought in arenas in which the subject of English is of consequence and where it exists as a focal point for social practice. As was intimated in the introduction, the sites for such investigation can be various, and lead, in the current study, to the following objects of investigation:

- officially articulated statements on the topic of English, especially those related to policy (at both the recommendation and legislative stages);
- the academic discussion contributing toward and analyzing such policy statements and their practical implications;
- curriculum design, and the practice and personnel issues associated with it;
- the promotional discourse of both public and private educational institutions;
- the structural organization and operational models of institutions involved in English language education;
- the responses and rationalizations of those with an investment in English language practices;
- instances of artistic and popular culture which draw upon English language practices or English language culture.

Other possible objects of analysis which act as sites for ideological contest and transmission would be pedagogical resources such as dictionaries and textbooks, as well as tests and assessment instruments, but these have not been included in any substantial form in the current study.

The range of objects of analysis that are included embrace both 'official' discourse on the language (policy statements and curriculum design), popular representations of English (in the media and in the private education market) and critical engagements with the language and Japanese culture (in the work of artists and writers). They have been selected for both their centrality in the discourse (e.g. policy statements) and the peripheral nature of their status (e.g. the private language schools) as the intention is to consider the extent to which cohesion exists across such diversity and how far certain structural paradigms govern the meaning that English has within 'Japanese society'. The study also offers interview data from participants who have a specific engagement with English language practices in the course of their everyday lives and who are the object of the promotional campaigns and policy initiatives that involve English. Finally, the book examines both the ontological and ideological presuppositions about global English that structure contemporary applied linguistics debate and theory-generation, and this is used as a cross-referent with the data from the Japanese context.

It is worth here drawing out some specific methodological concerns as they relate to certain of the types of data. Issues relating to the individual scenarios under investigation will be described in the introductory sections of the chapters in which these scenarios are dealt with, but a word about the general analytic to be applied to texts, to talk, and to social institutions is in order here as it forms a part of the wider theoretical approach.

Much of the data that constitutes the object of analysis is written texts. The working principle behind the examination of this data follows the methodological model outlined above. The principle is that assumptions about the language that are encoded within the discourse can be expressed in both implicit and explicit terms, and yet there is a coherence to such assumptions within and across texts, reflecting the fact that they are both systemic and habitual (Verschueren, 1995). Using the working definition of an ideology as being any entrenched system of beliefs which structures social behavior, the analysis is therefore dedicated to identifying the ideologies which create a meaningful context for the discourse of English in Japan within a particular context or genre. These ideologies are conceptualizations of the language which have become normalized, which are 'taken for granted', and thus the analysis is looking for premises upon which arguments are based within the discourse, or for connections between concepts which need not be expressed in explicit terms because the discourse community to which they are addressed is already conversant with the significance of their citation or juxtaposition. Of importance is the fact that these assumptions should occur in what Verschueren has termed 'patterns of recurrence' (p. 143), and the analysis is thus committed to mapping such recurrence as a means of exposing the implicit structure of the discourse.

Other texts that feature as objects of analysis are of a more multimodal nature, combining images and visual composition with verbal text (in the case of magazine articles or adverts) or the moving image (in the case of television programmes). In the analysis of these texts, the use of modes such as composition, color, typography and spatial design are considered to be semiotically significant, and the significance of the text as a whole is understood to reside in the combination of these modes (Kress & van Leeuwen, 2006). The same analytic approach of identifying salient conceptual patterning, the use of metaphoric schema and the association and juxtaposition of key assumptions, is used here also, with the same focus on patterns of recurrent presuppositions that produce the coherence of the text's message. The context, in terms of genre, social function and intended audience, is also an important factor for consideration when applying this general analytic approach to the specific texts under investigation.

The textual data are, in a number of instances, supplemented by interview data. This provides an opportunity to engage certain individuals, whose daily life has orientations to the English language, in discussion about their beliefs and rationalizations about language use. Of interest here are the ideas about English language practice and its significance that are held by these individuals. The object of analysis here is the expressed attitudes of the participants toward English, and also the manner of the articulation for this in terms of the associations, juxtapositions and explicit conceptualizations that are made. Such data can be read as indicative of the trend of received wisdom within the community, and for this reason it is surface features of the discourse which are of particular interest. That is to say, viewed from the perspective of a language ideologies framework, one would expect participants to rationalize their behavior (either retrospectively or in projections about future action) according to beliefs they hold concerning language. Such metalinguistic rationalization will be filtered through the semiotic resources available to them, and this thus gives us two aspects of their response to analyze: the rationalizations themselves, and the resources they use to articulate these rationalizations. These explicitly articulated rationalizations need not accord with their actions or linguistic behavior (an issue I will discuss in more detail in

Chapter 8), but they are of significance nevertheless in that they are likely to be consequential in some form or other (Preston, 1998). As with the analysis of textual data, therefore, it is ideas that are treated as self-evident, and which are not accorded special justification, which can be gathered inductively and assembled to suggest the outline of how English is being collectively conceptualized within Japan.

Given the diverse and dispersed nature of these various objects of investigation, some organizational framework is needed for the sake of analytic cohesion. For the bulk of the research, therefore, I have grouped the analysis around key concepts which recur within the discourse, thus producing 'conceptual case studies' (see Chapter 5 for the more detailed introduction to this approach). The rationale for this is the desire to examine patterns of recurrence as they exist in the wider community rather than in isolated settings. Having said this however, I will begin with an examination of a specific site rather than a specific concept – a site in which these discourses about the language are at their most visible, and where they arguably have the most impact on society at large: this is in the debate and articulation of educational policy.

Chapter 4
English in Japan: The Current Shape of the Debate

The State and Status of English Language Teaching in Japan

In the current social climate (the era of globalization), to ask why someone, or indeed why a whole nation, should wish to learn English may seem a redundant question – the answer would appear to many to be self-evident. Yet an exact answer to this question, tailored to the circumstances and beliefs of the individual, is liable to provide insights into both the cultural and social beliefs of that individual, as well as the role that English plays within the individual's society. To this extent, the question is one that transcends the narrow confines of TESOL research and involves also the sociocultural context in which the language is being taught and used. The reasons why someone wants to learn the language relate to how they perceive the language, to what they think its nature, function and affordances are. And while this response is in part personal construction (the product of the historically-situated individual biography), it is also framed by public discourse about the language. It is for this reason that an analysis of how the English language is conceptualized in pedagogic and policy documents can offer an initial reading of the way in which the language operates as an influential cultural force within Japanese society. Insights from this can shed light on the stance that Japanese policy is taking toward globalizing trends in the international community, while also providing an important step in the analysis of how educational policy transfers into curriculum and classroom practice, and why it is that English Language Teaching (ELT) in Japan exists in the state that it does.

The purpose of this chapter is to examine the way in which the English language is framed within the debate about language education in Japan, and in so doing, to identify and analyze the ideologies of the language that structure both mainstream applied linguistics research in this area and its complementary thread in educational policy. The contention is that these ideologies create a particular shape for the debate, and thus their identification and subsequent analysis allows us to reflect critically upon the assumptions that provide the epistemic matrix within which discussion of this topic is conducted.

Before moving ahead with this though it is worth making explicit two points about the parameters of the examination. The analysis in this chapter constitutes one particular perspective on the way in which English is conceptualized within Japanese society, and Chapters 5–8 will provide alternative perspectives. Despite the fact that the academic accounts examined in this chapter draw upon empirical research in their surveys of the situation, and that policy is partly motivated by this as well as other research, the perspective presented here is one that views the situation from above: it is the discourse of institutional regulators of the education system rather than that of its participants or of collateral sections of society. Furthermore, although it is context-specific in that it is responding to the particulars of the Japanese situation, it exists also as a part of the wider international discourse of general applied linguistic theory, sharing a theoretical history and language with scholars working in very different contexts. There is, then, a sense in which this is the 'official' version of events – it is how the twin poles of institutional regulation (legislation and academia) characterize the situation – and thus provides the basic architecture around which discussion of the topic is most often framed in general public discourse.

The specific method of this chapter is to engage in a critical survey of a number of key studies within the applied linguistics literature on English in Japan, and discern from these the ways in which the language is most prominently conceptualized. The chapter reviews a selection of the academic literature that has studied ELT debates relating to Japan, and examines the ways in which the subject has, over the years, been presented. It discusses the nature and provenance of the issues most often identified, and cross-references these with an examination of the policy reforms that have been proposed and enacted by the Japanese government in recent years. Consideration is also given to the way in which these twin spheres of academic research and education policy influence and interact with one another, and how the nature of this relationship contributes to a wider discourse of the English language within Japan. The intention throughout is not simply to summarize the genealogy and objectives of any of these texts, but to draw out the ideologies of the language around which they structure their critiques and recommendations.

The selection of policy documents as the focus for the study is straightforward, as these are the key statements by successive governments on how the English language should be regulated within society. The choice of applied linguistics research and debate requires more in the way of qualification. The studies chosen are those published in key international journals, and those most frequently cited in the development of the English-language discourse on ELT in Japan. An initial point of note, however, is that the studies surveyed here are written in the English language itself (though by scholars from a variety of national backgrounds), and as such are but one strand in a far wider field of academic discussion on the topic. One motivating factor behind this choice is the common perception that, as Block (1996: 66) notes, '[t]he applied linguistics centre is above all in North America and the UK', and the journals often perceived as being the most prestigious vehicles for the presentation of such research are published in the English language. A similar point is made by Makoni and Meinhof (2003) in their review of applied linguistics in Africa. There are, of course, several other places where the production and reproduction of knowledge for ELT specialists in Japan is based (in publications, conferences, professional associations and government organized ad hoc committees, for instance) on all of which operate in Japanese. The UK and North American context does not, therefore, necessarily operate as the primary influence on English language educationalists in Japan. It is, however, still *perceived* as the 'center' in much of the discourse. Holliday (2005: 6), for example, notes that there is 'an established belief that "native-speaker" teachers represent a "Western culture" from which springs the ideals both of the English language and of English language teaching methodology'. Thus, while a study of articles published solely in English cannot be taken as a complete picture of the ideologies present in Japanese educational policy and practice,[1] it still offers a compelling opportunity to analyze the way in which ELT in Japan is discursively represented in one important and influential domain.

Identifying the Issues

In 1978, the editor of *The Teaching of English in Japan* outlined the purpose of his book and summarized the state of foreign language education in Japan at that time in the following terms:

> In general, reading comprehension skills are fostered, while hearing and speaking skills are less stressed. This can be partially explained by the history of Japan's relative isolation from English-speaking peoples... English usage within Japan was largely limited to the translation and critical study of foreign works. Even today, because university entrance examinations require English reading comprehension, high schools often neglect the development of hearing and speaking skills. Recently, however, there has been growing concern that Japan must actively exchange ideas and culture with other

nations through international communication...Japanese teachers of English especially recognise their lack of communication with teachers, linguists and school administrators of other nations. This communication gap stems partially from the dearth of English publications that deal with English teaching trends inside Japan...It is in order to help correct this shortcoming that this present collection of criticism and scholastic analysis of TEFL in Japan by Japanese and foreign contributors is being published. (Koike, 1978: iv–v)

This 917 page volume, comprising 82 essays on subjects ranging from history and culture to methodology and linguistics and with contributors from universities in Japan, the USA and England, was the first substantial survey in English of the general state of ELT in Japan. In the thirty years since its appearance there have been countless English language publications which have revisited this area, and there exists now a very considerable body of literature written in English examining the many issues that comprise ELT theory and practice in Japan. Journals such as *World Englishes* (Kachru & Smith, 1995; Sakai, 2005) and *Language, Culture and Curriculum* (Lessard–Clouston, 1998) have devoted whole issues to the subject, while specialist titles such as those published by JALT (Japan Association of Language Teachers),[2] now exist for the sole purpose of promoting such research. Where 30 years ago Koike might have found the subject badly underrepresented in English language publications, today the situation is much changed.

What Koike (1978) has to say about the methods and effects of ELT in the late 1970s, however, does not appear so very different from similar appraisals of the state of language education in the country at the beginning of the 21st century, and this thematic continuity provides one form of structure for the development of the debate. Articles on the subject still comment on the priority given in the education system to reading comprehension and grammar-translation, and on the neglect of listening and speaking skills, while the need for a more communicative-based approach has been a constant refrain over the last three decades. For example, Honna (1995: 57) appraises the situation thus

> People have not developed proficiency in English as a language for international communication... The late Edwin O. Reischauer, former US ambassador to Japan, seriously listed Japan's miserable performance in English teaching as one of the seven wonders of the world. Many government, industrial, and educational leaders expressed concern and proposed reforms. However, no significant change has been witnessed. What is wrong?

According to this prominent strand in the discourse, the hope expressed by Koike that his edited book might have a direct impact on ELT in Japan and promote a different educational model appears not to have transpired. Many papers on the subject in fact take as their main thesis the intransigence of the education system and its perceived failure to produce communicative competence in its students. Reading the emergent literature in this field one can easily be led to conclude that although those thirty years have seen an ever-increasing interest in language learning in Japan, as well as an increase in research dedicated to the monitoring and guiding of this expansion, there are certain fundamental issues that seemingly remain almost completely unaffected by the times or changes in society.

The result of viewing the situation from this perspective is the installation of what we might term the 'problem frame' for the debate. Through Reischauer's comments in *The Japanese* (1977), studies such as Koike (1978) and Honna (1995), and up to the present day with Aspinal's examination of 'policy failure in the case of foreign language education in Japan' (2006: 255), discussions of the subject foreground the presence of a 'problem' within the current system and this becomes, in effect, the default position from which arguments are built, a generic convention for addressing the issue of ELT in Japan. Echoes of this can also be found in the wording of policy documents themselves: 'Today's Japanese are lacking...basic skills. Their English-language abilities as measured by their TOEFL scores in 1998 were the lowest in Asia. The Japanese themselves are painfully aware of the inadequacy of their communication skills' (CJGTC, 2000a: 4). And while this is not an ideology of the English language itself, it is of significant importance as being the matrix by which discussions of the teaching and learning of the language in Japan traditionally need to be plotted.

Creating an Historical Context

Strategies for explaining and providing a solution to this 'problem' take various forms. Many of the earlier studies of ELT in Japan are satisfied simply to recount to their English-reading audience how language education is organized in Japan, without the need for any explicit critical evaluation. The essay 'Teaching English in Japan' by Kitao and Kitao (1995 [originally written 1985]), is a good example of this. The abstract states that, 'In this paper, we have discussed some reasons why Japanese people study English, a brief history of English education in Japan, and the state of English education in elementary schools, secondary schools, universities, English language schools, and companies' (p. 5). And this, without recourse to critical commentary or contextualisation, is precisely what they do. Even as late as 1998 Lessard-Clouston introduces the special edition of *Language, Culture and Curriculum* by saying that, 'To many Westerners, Japan, along with the Japanese language and Japanese society in general, appears to remain something of a mystery' (1998: 1), and thus it is that the specific details of the system and its unfamiliarity for a Western audience are considered substance enough for many introductory essays. Again, this is representative less of an ideology of the language itself than an implicit belief in universal strategies of language pedagogy which necessitate access to the 'center' of applied linguistics thought. There is a suggestion that segregation from such a center will result in a form of intellectual isolation which will be detrimental to teaching practice in Japan. The corollary of this, then, becomes that the pedagogic strategies developed in the 'applied linguistics center' (Block, 1996: 66) are sought out as a solution to a local problem.

Often, a review of key dates in the history of ELT in Japan over the last four hundred years is also considered a necessary context within which to view the current situation (e.g. Morrow, 1987). Again the volume edited by Koike (1978) sets the precedent by following its introductory section with two essays glossing the chronology of English education in Japan from the early 19th century (from the 'Phaeton Incident', in which a British warship arrived in the port of Nagasaki prompting the Tokugawa government to start training Dutch interpreters in the English language), up until the 1970s and the formation of the several regional English Language Education Associations that were established to improve teaching within the country (Hoshiyama, 1978; Omura, 1978).

The most commonly cited paper on this subject is Ike (1995), which begins its chronology with the first recorded contact between the Japanese and the English language when, in 1600, the Englishman William Adams, was washed up on the shores of Kyushu. Despite the two and a half centuries of self-imposed isolation that the Tokugawa government embarked upon soon after this (the *sakoku* period), Ike records a small number of disparate incidents which can loosely be related to ELT during this period, before moving to the main section of his essay and a detailed exposition of the two major transitional periods in modern Japanese history which came with the Meiji Restoration of 1868 and the American occupation after the Second World War, both of which had important ramifications for the teaching of English in Japan. It is in this discussion that the development of the grammar-translation method (*yakudoku*) and the importance of the exam system in Japanese education policy are introduced, both of which are constant features in all the future debates about ELT and its effectiveness in Japan.

Though Ike's final sentence, in which he hopes 'a greater emphasis on communication and on cultural sensitivity in English education will contribute to a deeper understanding, and in turn will eventually help Japanese to learn English' (p. 10), does prescribe the type of policy developments he would like to see, his essay has as its primary purpose the chronicling of the history of English education in Japan. In the same issue of *World Englishes*, Koike and Tanaka (1995) also employ a historical review of ELT (again revisiting the Meiji Restoration and the implementation of a new education system based on foreign models), and they are even more explicit in linking historical precedents to issues in current practice: 'By examining this brief history, we could say that the purposes of teaching foreign languages in those early days [of the Meiji period] were practical and cultural.... What has been described so far is very important if one is to grasp the unique characteristics of foreign language education in Japan, as well as their impact on Japanese society' (p. 16). These ideas then form the conceptual foundation for their discussion of contemporary foreign language education policy, and the challenges with which late 20th century educational reforms are faced.[3]

One of the main effects of this repeated use of a historical context is to link the English language with key incidents in the chronology of Japanese international relations, creating a narrative that tracks the pattern of contact between Japan and the West. This narrative is itself a particular history of the nation, which begins as an entirely insular province and then, in incremental steps, is opened up to the wider international community. While the English language is not cast as being directly responsible for this political history, it is presented in such a way that its status becomes an index of Japan-international relations, with each significant incident of language contact or educational innovation being associated directly with a major political landmark.

A further product of this approach is to give a particular explanation for the type of language teaching that is so prevalent in the Japanese school system. The grammar-translation method is explained in functional terms within this historical narrative as an enabler of the modernization process that followed the Meiji Restoration as it allowed for the importing and deciphering of Western technology and expertise in the late 19th/early 20th century. In a sense, then, this attitude toward the language (as a code that needed to be mastered to unlock the knowledge of the West) plays a valued role in the development of modern Japan, and thus has a significance beyond that of pragmatic language pedagogy.

Another consequence of this discursive approach to the subject is that it positions the language as being something brought from outside. This may appear a self-evident point – English has never been a native language of Japan – but the fact that it is reiterated in several of the accounts creates a very particular meaning for the language in current political thinking. For while English may now be the language of the world ('owned' by all who use it and so forth), in the history of Japan – a history which is here being presented as an 'explanation' of the current 'problem' in ELT practice – it is associated at every stage with a very specific chronology of foreign contact, political coercion and even invasion; and it is this context which contributes to the connotations for the language which were employed in the statement by the former Education Minister that was quoted in Chapter 2.

The Communicative Approach

While a truncated history of international relations may figure as a key framing device in much of the discourse, the most prevalent ideology is that of English as a means of international communication. This is, of course, *the* mainstream language ideology in applied linguistics of the last 30 years, and has promoted the exchange of ideational meaning between parties as the chief purpose of language education in a great deal of policy and practice recommendations. To an extent, studies of the Japanese situation are simply rehearsing these arguments, but what is of particular interest for our context-specific investigation are the particularities of the juxtapositions that occur in the debate: that is, how the idea of English as a means of communication is framed by associated or conflicting notions in the discourse.

In the traditional chronology of the subject (outlined in Ike, 1995), the reforms to the education system which were first proposed during Yasuhiro Nakasone's premiership in the mid-1980s are considered to be the third major transitional period for ELT in Japan (after the Meiji Restoration and the American occupation). These have been introduced over the last two decades, most noticeably in the *Course of Study* documents which lay out the national curriculum for primary and secondary education as prescribed by the Ministry of Education [*Monbusho*].[4] Issued at intervals of about a decade since first being introduced in 1947, it is the Reform Acts of 1989 and 2002 that are considered to contain the most important innovations for English language education. Coinciding with the rise in importance of Communicative Language Teaching (CLT) in the wider TESOL environment (Brumfit & Johnson, 1979; Littlewood, 1981), *Monbusho* begins in these documents to stress the need for communicative language practices, and in doing so there is here a perceived break with the grammar-translation method favored by the mainstream system for the previous 100 years. The juxtaposition of this 'traditional' method with the innovations which are in keeping with the new global orthodoxy is the dynamic for much of the research work in this area, which has as its expressed aim an assessment of the success of the transition to a more communication-based language curriculum.

Browne and Wada (1998), for example, conduct a survey of Japanese English-language teachers to record their attitudes to the new regulations. They examine how factors such as preservice and in-service training, textbook development and the effect of the JET Program (Japan Exchange and Teaching Program) have influenced the state of ELT in Japanese high schools. They present their findings as pointing to an intransigent and highly centralized system where the rhetoric of the new guidelines is rendered close to meaningless by deeply entrenched institutional practices:

> When one considers that the vast majority of English teachers in Japan receive no formal teacher training... and that every Mombusho-approved textbook comes with a teacher's manual that has detailed lesson plans emphasising translation and drill-focused teaching techniques, it is not surprising that a wide gap exists between the communicative goals of the guidelines and actual classroom practice. (p. 105)

Implicit in this is the idea that past and present systems are incompatible, that it is an either/or choice for practice and, more tellingly, that government policy in this area is a true index of educational intention. As was discussed earlier, language ideologies are never about language *in vacuo*, but also a complex of other social factors. Yet for the most part these other social factors are not addressed. Browne and Wada do later display a moment of scepticism about whether the focus of their study is entirely valid when they speculate as to whether, 'Mombusho truly believes that the new Course of Study Guidelines' emphasis on developing a student's communicative ability is an important goal' (p. 109), yet otherwise they take the government rhetoric at face value and posit this policy-practice conflict as the major issue for ELT in contemporary Japan.

Several other studies have explored similar ground. Gorsuch (2001) canvasses high school teachers to assess the current state of Japanese EFL (English as Foreign Language) education 'during a period of time in which sweeping, nationally applied policies have been instituted,' and her conclusion is very similar, with her findings giving 'empirical evidence suggesting that teachers mildly approve of communicative activities, yet the data also suggested there are potent impediments working against teachers actually using such activities in their classrooms'. Sakui describes the ramifications of implementing this new policy as resulting in 'a dichotomous curriculum realisation' (2004: 158), while LoCastro (1996) comments that although the reforms are seemingly of great importance for Japan's fuller participation in the global community while also being in line with recent thinking on curriculum design around the world, on closer examination there is 'a gross mismatch between the supposed aims and the sociocultural context' (p. 45). She considers that there are three major impediments to change: (1) other aspects of the education system which have not been reformed are in conflict with these new guidelines (most noticeably the system of entrance exams); (2) the fact that the teachers and students who are being affected by the changes have not been consulted with regard to the reforms; and (3) that the language of *Monbusho* documents is likely to be affected by sociocultural variables, and that concepts imported from abroad may have a very different meaning in Japanese culture.

Certain of these impediments are presented as being extremely deep-rooted. The exam system, considered incompatible with practices normally associated with CLT, is central to the education system in general and plays an important structuring role in society in enabling the reproduction of hierarchies in university and company status. Indeed, Honna and Takeshita (2002) suggest that although by the beginning of the 21st century there has been an apparent shift from exam-oriented teaching to more communication-based skills, in practice this has simply meant that certain universities and companies no longer require the traditional university entrance exam qualification but instead are willing to accept TOEIC or TOEFL[5] qualifications instead. This is meant to signify a loosening up of the traditional system, but as anyone who is familiar with the TOEIC exam knows, despite the fact that it has the word 'communication' in its title, it is still very much an exercise in orthodox grammatical knowledge. As such, the forecast for a successful transition to more effective communicative language teaching practices in the Japanese education system is repeatedly presented as being distinctly bleak.

LoCastro, however, also voices slight doubts which match the sentiments expressed by Browne and Wada (1998) over the validity of this debate, when she says that, 'these problems do raise questions, both concerning the likely success of the recent innovations and about the extent to which change is really desired' (LoCastro, 1996: 45). Again, this is not developed to any great extent in her paper, suggesting that mainstream ideologies of policy as an educational blueprint for practice and of traditional methods as the converse of modern innovations still act as the implicit structure for her argument despite this one anomaly. She also, however, introduces another influential line of argument by questioning the way that certain key terms employed by the *Course of Study* guidelines should be read. Thus, for example, she notes how ' "communication" itself may not be a universally shared concept; that is, it may have different meanings in different cultures' (p. 45). She further reflects on the fact that the hierarchical way in which Japanese society, and its language, is structured means that interpersonal relationships dictate the way in which the concept of communication operates within the society, and ensures that it is something qualitatively different from the concepts of communication of the 'avowedly more egalitarian Anglo–American societies' (p. 45). The ramifications of this suggestion are considerable. The idea that the concept of 'communication', which is at the very center of the debate about the current state of ELT in Japan, is being misinterpreted – and that it is being misinterpreted by the academic community researching and working within the field – would suggest the presence of a major fault line lying just beneath the surface of this well-established debate. There is a parallel here, of course, with the totalizing fallacy that governs much of the treatment of the English language itself, as discussed in Chapter 3. Communication too is often treated as an unproblematized notion, and the implicit understanding is that its meaning is considered self-evident, that is has universally applicable value, unless statements to the contrary are foregrounded. This view has further parallels in the strand of discourse which looks to the "native speaker" countries as the oracle for orthodox English teaching practice, thus promoting a particular culturally determined practice as universal.

Internationalism and the Ethnocentric Debate

The fact that at the beginning of the 21st century the same issues to which Koike (1978) was directing attention are still high on the agenda and seemingly unresolved suggests that there are others concerns that need to be taken into account. Back in 1979 Hayes wrote that:

> The inward nature of the Japanese, the periods of ethnocentricity, ultranationalism and xenophobia all augur against the teaching of English. It may very well be that the Japanese do not want to learn English or, for that matter, any foreign language, as the bilingual and those having spent any time abroad are 'deviant' in the Japanese eye, not to be entirely trusted ... [they] may be 'contaminated' and no longer 'pure' Japanese. (1979: 372)

In the following decade, Reischauer and Jansen (1988: 392) also raised this as a possibility: 'Ridiculous though this may seem, there appears to be a genuine reluctance to have English very well known by many

Japanese. Knowing a foreign language too well, it is feared, would erode the uniqueness of the Japanese people'.

This kind of cultural stereotyping does not figure so overtly in more recent accounts, and yet it is a theme that can still be perceived on both sides of the debate, and that is used to explain or justify certain aspects of the status quo. The idea of Japanese ethnocentrism, and its possible consequences for English language education, is closely connected to *kokusaika*, which has been a concept of great relevance for the perception of the English language in Japan over the last two decades. *Kokusaika* (literally translated as 'internationalization') came to prominence in Japan in the 1980s and is often considered by social historians to have been a response by the government to foreign pressure for Japan to open up its markets. Official rhetoric publicized the importance of international communication for Japan's status within the global community, yet, according to Itoh (1998: 12), 'the primary goal of Japan's internationalisation was to enhance its national economic interest, and thus the more Japan became internationalised, the more nationalistic it became. Although the two notions were antithetical to each other, they were inseparable in the Japanese case'. This neonationalist agenda can also be perceived in education philosophy (Kubota, 1999), and, according to Okano and Tsuchiya (1999: 216), the *Course of Study* curriculum of 1989 was meant 'to enhance "national integration among people" by nurturing belief that Japan is an influential state in the global community and by cultivating an "ethnic identity". It involved developing "self-awareness of being Japanese"'. The recently proposed changes to the 'Fundamental Law of Education' (see Chapter 2) have brought these issues to the forefront of national debate once again, and indeed comments by the education minister Bunmei Ibuki about the 'homogenous' nature of Japan (*Japan Times*, 26 Feb. 2007) are a direct echo of statements by former Prime Minister Yasuhiro Nakasone from 1986.

Itoh ascribes Japan's unwillingness to open up to its two and a half century isolation from the rest of the world during the *sakoku* ('closed country') period that preceded the Meiji Restoration:

> That combination of natural [island nation] and voluntary [sakoku] isolation created a uniquely homogenous culture and parochial mentality. The sakoku mentality still lingers and underlies the modern Japanese way of thinking and behaving. This mind-set is not only ubiquitous in the business sector but is also prevalent in Japan's cultural, education, and societal systems. (1998: 13)

A similar theme finds its way into the ELT debate. In his paper 'Internationalisation – As If It Mattered', Dougill (1995: 70) relates this particular political and psychological heritage to the education system: 'The grammar-translation and memorisation methods so popular in Japan are further evidence of the tradition of insularity, for they reflect the one-way importation of knowledge and information which characterized Japan's desire for modernisation while retaining its own identity'. His thesis is that a history of insularity undermines the talk of internationalization within the country, and that the promotion of the English language is thus a specious and superficial act. This argument builds upon the aforementioned historicist ideology, as well as what Dougill sees as a deeply ingrained form of cultural conditioning which means that the Japanese insist on their uniqueness, and therefore have no interest in actually integrating with the international community. The continued patronage of the grammar-translation method by the exam system, the use of 'decorative' English in advertising and popular culture and the oft-voiced suggestion that English is too difficult for Japanese people to learn are all taken as evidences to support this line of argument. McVeigh (2002) has also dealt with a similar range of themes, taking as his starting point the enigmatic suggestion from Befu (1983) that, 'It is as if ineptitude of foreign language instruction and learning is maintained (though, needless to say, unconsciously) for the very purpose of convincing millions of Japanese of their separateness.' In this conception of the social politics of Japan, the English language itself is the divisive tool of a separatist nationalistic ideology.

Kawai (2007) also focuses on this as a determining cultural force in popular attitudes toward the language. She sees in Japanese social history a strong essentialist view of the national language; that is to say, for an ethnically unified group, the single language is viewed as intrinsic to the 'nation' and national identity. Within Japan this ideology was forged in the development of the modern state in the post-Meiji Restoration period and then further and repeatedly articulated in the *nihonjinron* genre after World War Two.[6] This is a version of the common Romantic ideology of the concept of a national language, with the added embellishment that in this discourse English is directly juxtaposed to the national language, and the values associated with the national language are transferred in negative form to the 'foreign' language. Evidence of the prevalence of this belief can perhaps be read in the way that a key government policy document felt the need to explicitly challenge this view by stating that 'It is a fundamental fallacy to believe that cherishing the Japanese language precludes studying other languages or that caring for Japanese culture requires rejecting foreign cultures' (CJGTC, 2000b: 20). The comments quoted in Chapter 2 from the education minister about the threat that English education can cause for traditional Japanese values (*Japan Times*, 3 Oct. 2006) again reverse the official position, but in doing so indicate that this is a key axis around which debate is structured.

One consequence of relating the concept of Japanese ethnocentrism to foreign language learning is that it prioritizes the role of culture in ELT practice (Shimizu, 1995; Stapleton, 2000). The language becomes not so much a tool for international communication, but a living artifact belonging to a foreign culture. Likewise, native speaker teachers become specimens of that foreign culture, their role as instructors of specialized knowledge overshadowed by their status as foreign nationals, so that it is the emblematic presence of a foreign culture in the classroom that is the defining factor in their appointment in schools. As Hall (1998: 105–106) writes in his study of what he terms 'academic apartheid' in the higher education system in Japan, for many the term 'internationalization' merely means 'having pure and unacclimated aliens on campus – the two-dimensional presence of the linguistically incapacitated, culture-shocked foreign newcomer as exotic ambience'. And though this is perhaps not as commonplace as it was two decades ago, a recent example of a language school in Kofu, Yamanashi Prefecture, whose recruitment poster advertised specifically for teachers with 'blond hair, and blue or green eyes' (*Japan Times*, 13 Feb. 2007) indicates that this strand of the discourse still has some currency.

Practice and Policy

The majority of the literature on the subject of ELT dwells on issues of policy and practice and the chances of their productive convergence. The policy reforms that have been introduced over the last decade and have generated so much debate over the issue of 'communication' are a result of initiatives first taken by the Nakasone administrations of the mid-1980s (Hood, 2001). As prime minister, Nakasone is remembered for embodying many of the conflicting attitudes that structure the discourse of internationalism in Japan. It was during his administration that the rhetoric of *kokusaika* found official sanction and began to make regular appearances in the wording of policy, while practical initiatives in international cooperation and understanding such as the JET Program were also begun. Yet in positioning Japan as an 'international' power Nakasone was insistent on the need to promote and define Japanese values, and his premiership was punctuated by highly publicized acts of nationalism, many of which were interpreted by the international community as being overtly racist.

He left power in 1987 shortly after the final report by the Ad Hoc Council on education that he had created was submitted. Two years later the new *Course of Study* was published, and the 'Overall Objectives' of this document reflect the trends in political thought and the public rhetoric of this era. The curriculum is intended: 'To develop students' abilities to understand a foreign language and express themselves in it, to foster a positive attitude toward communicating in it, and to heighten interest in language and culture, deepening international understanding' (Monbusho, 1989). The rhetoric of *kokusaika* and the recent innovations in applied linguistics theory are thus blended in a vision of the role that foreign language learning is to play in contemporary society.

In recent years, there has been a growing literature that analyzes English education policy (Butler & Iino, 2005; Gottlieb, 2001; Hashimoto, 2002; Honna & Takeshita, 2002; Kawai, 2007). As well as the *Course of Study* documents, this has focused upon the *Action Plan* drawn up by the Ministry of Education in 2003 which was intended to cultivate 'Japanese with English Abilities' (MEXT, 2003), and involved additional financial resources for teacher training and the promotion of schemes like the 'Super English Language High Schools'. Another key document is the proposal commissioned by the Obuchi government in 2000 to explore the possibility of introducing English as a second official language in Japan, published under the title *The Frontier Within: Individual Empowerment and Better Governance in the New Millennium* (CJGTC, 2000a).

Before looking at these documents in greater detail, it is worth first discussing the nature of them as cultural artifacts. 'Policy' in this book is used to refer to the statements of intent issued by the administrative authority of a country concerning goal-orientated procedures of action. It is in contrast in this respect with 'practice', which is the way in which such proposals are enacted within the classroom. It is worth adding, however, that policy is an ongoing process, engaging with and contested by public opinion, and one that is open to interpretation and thus never an entirely stable blueprint for practice. Policies are in dialogic relation with educational practitioners as well as with media commentary and public opinion, and thus are addressed to multiple audiences. The interpretation of these texts can therefore also be multiple, and it would be foolish to suggest that a discourse analysis of them (uncovering the discursive nature of their construction) can show us what they are 'really' about. What is of interest, therefore, is the way in which concepts implicit in the structure of these documents find parallels in the other forms of public discourse which we have been examining, and how this can be read as the dynamic context in which the English language exists within Japanese society.

As has been noted, the most remarked upon aspect of the reforms is the stress put upon 'communicative ability' in the curriculum. In practice, this meant the introduction of a new subject at the Upper Secondary level entitled Oral Communication, in which the focus was upon the 'use' of English rather than 'knowledge' about the language, and though 'use' had been mentioned in previous *Courses of Study* this was the first time a specific subject had been devoted to it. The emphasis on the importance of communicative competence in the language teaching curriculum follows a general worldwide trend dating back to the beginning of the eighties and the work of scholars such as Breen and Candlin (1980). The wording of the 1989 *Course of Study* (and indeed the 2002 version) does not differ in any great respect from similar curriculum documents across the globe. However, as has been discussed above, certain commentators have registered occasional unease about Japan's belated embracing of 'concepts developed in the Anglo–American applied linguistic context' and whether these 'can be adopted uncritically in [the] very different situation [of Japan]' (Coleman, 1996: 19). As has also been noted though, such qualms are the exception rather than the rule.

In their seminal paper on the essentials of a communicative curriculum, Breen and Candlin (1980: 90) posit, 'The communicative curriculum defines language learning as learning how to communicate as a member of a particular socio-cultural group'. Immediately, such a statement raises problems for the possibilities of *inter*cultural communication, and also implicitly seems to recognize that 'communication' is not a single or universal concept, but one that depends for its exact definition on the sociocultural group that is practicing it. They go on to state that

> the communicative curriculum seeks relationships between any specific target competence and relevant aspects of the learner's own initial competence. We need to ask: What communicative knowledge – and its effective aspects – does the learner already possess and exploit? What communicative abilities – and the skills which manifest them – does the learner already activate and depend upon in using and selecting from his presently established repertoire? (p. 93)

Breen and Candlin are here careful to advise that a language syllabus based around communicative ability will necessarily need to build on the type of communicative competence already practiced by the student. It is here that LoCastro's suggestion that communication 'may have different meanings in different cultures' (1996: 45) can be seen to be of great significance. Kerr (2001: 105), in his study of contemporary Japan, quotes a Japanese academic on the conflicts arising from the clash between two discrete ideologies of communication that exist within Japan today:

> When people say 'There's no communication between parents and children,' this is an American way of thinking. In Japan we didn't need spoken communication between parents and children. A glance

at the face, a glance at the back, and we understood enough. That was our way of thinking... It's when we took as our model a culture relying on words that things went wrong. Although we live in a society replete with problems that words cannot ever solve, we think we can solve them with words, and this is where things go wrong.

Often, though, recognition of the different cultural norms that constitute 'communication', and their implications for the adoption of the CLT method in the English language classroom, are neither acknowledged nor addressed in the literature. One of the results of this can be to segregate the type of communication taught in the English language class from that practiced in general Japanese society. It is in this context that the notable change in emphasis on the Overall Objectives for the foreign language curriculum in the 2002 *Course of Study* takes on a particular significance. In the earlier document, the aim was to 'To develop students' abilities to understand a foreign language... and foster a positive attitude toward communicating in it' (Monbusho 1989), but in its revision it has become 'To develop students' practical communication abilities... and foster a positive attitude toward communication through foreign languages' (MEXT 2002). The rearrangement of the word-order here thus promotes the concept of communication above that of knowledge of the language. We then begin to get a gradual shift away from the concept of language as a general tool of communication to the idea that certain languages represent particular types of communication, and thus the communicative curriculum becomes not simply about learning a particular foreign language, but learning the specific values and ideologies of interpersonal interaction that are associated with that language. With English being promoted as the global language however, these culturally specific values are presented as universal, and subsumed under the single signifier 'communication'. The logical conclusion of this uncritical embracing of a 'communicative approach' becomes that the deficit problem outlined by the TESOL community (Honna's [1995] rhetorical interpellation of 'What is wrong?') now relates not merely to unsuccessful second language acquisition, but to a lack of proficiency in the fundamentals of human communication according to a perceived world-standard.

We come to a point therefore where, perversely, the situation that Befu (1983) identified, whereby the learning of English in Japan is purposely hamstrung to assist a nationalist agenda, finds an inverted parallel in the way that parts of the academic community erect, albeit inadvertently, a barrier between their conception of the English language and a reading of present day Japanese society. In a sense, one could say that the discourse of Japanese uniqueness is reproduced in this type of critique of the current situation. In its anatomy of the state of ELT in Japan, much of this literature would seem to posit that the 'problem' lies in the history of Japanese society (a chronology of fractious international relations), in its current infrastructure and organization (a hierarchical society with a language which explicitly encodes such social stratification in its politeness codes) and in the way it structures and enacts education (built around a critically important exam system), all of which are incompatible with successful English language teaching strategies. There is a danger that in pursuing this approach the suggestion becomes that English is something for which Japanese society itself will have to alter before it can be properly adopted and effectively taught. The pedagogical significance of this is that the 'foreignness' of English, as both code *and* cultural practice, is foregrounded.

A similar coexistence of mutually inconsistent ideologies also occurs in the formulation of the functional nature of language in policy documents. In the *Action Plan* (MEXT, 2003), English is described as playing 'a central role as the common international language in linking people who have different mother tongues', while in the *Frontier Within*, it is referred to as 'not...simply a foreign language but as the international lingua franca' (CJGTC, 2000b: 10). Elsewhere, however, English is regularly discussed within the context of 'foreign' language education (MEXT, 2002; Monbusho, 1989), a characterization which corresponds with the traditional functional distinctions which categorize Japan as an EFL country. The distinction between 'foreign' and 'international' – of such importance in much of contemporary applied linguistics – would seem, on this evidence, not to have entered the consciousness of policy in Japan.

Not only, though, is this an ambivalent use of terminology, it also reflects a confusion in the approach taken to the language. The *Frontier Within*, in which English is referred to as the 'international lingua franca' is advocating the adoption of English as an official language in Japan, and thus has a vested interest in stressing the language's purported freedom from specific affiliations. Yet, both the old and new *Courses of Study* explicitly make the connection between language and culture, the 1989 version outlining its purpose as being 'to instil an interest in language and culture, thus laying the foundation for international understanding' (Monbusho, 1989); while the more recent version is intended 'to deepen linguistic and cultural understanding through a foreign language' (MEXT, 2002).[7] The implication here is not that English is simply a functional lingua franca for the exchange of ideational meaning between any members of the international community, but that it is also a heuristic tool through which to access foreign culture.

Conclusion

Due to the highly centralized nature of the Japanese education system, the *Course of Study* policy documents affect the whole breadth of society. The framework detailed in these texts and other policy initiatives such as the *Action Plan* provides the basis for all school curricula in the country and is mandatory in both public and private institutions. In combination with the choice of textbook – which again must be sanctioned by the Ministry of Education – this creates the context in which the vast majority of children in Japan from the age of 13–18 learn English.[8] Thus, the conception of English education expressed within these recommendations has a great impact on the way the English language is viewed within the whole of society.

The prominence given to the concept of communication and the way this is debated and interpreted in both the policy documents and the academic literature highlights the way in which the English language operates as a site for ideological struggle. As policy reforms reflect changes and anxieties within Japanese society while also embracing the rhetoric of global politics, so too does the academic discourse reflect social issues specific to the academic community within Japan while also responding to trends within the global applied linguistic community. And it is in the disputed areas between these plural discourses that the cultural meaning of English in Japan is created. The ideologies identified here are those at the center of the public and institutional discussion of the language, and the majority of mainstream research in this area draws upon the shared assumptions and generic language of these in constructing its own contribution to the debate and thus, as we have seen, many issues recur with frequency and are implicitly positioned as fundamental to the topic in general. It is in this way that the generation of knowledge in relation to this subject is predicated around a few key coordinates. One effect of the dominance of these particular ideologies in the mainstream treatment of the topic is that, in effect, the predicate is included in the subject. That is to say, the way the discourse is normatively modeled around these ideologies creates an element of determinism in the generation of its research findings. By positing that there is a 'problem' in need of solution – in using this as the narrative arc of the research presentation – the research needs to establish the existence of a problem before being able to move on to the possibility of a solution. The details of the solution can then be illuminating and instructive, and much important work has been carried out in this field, yet the debate is still argued within the confines of this particular perspective. These are the guiding principles of thought for this subject and, given certain institutional conventions and coercions (the power of the journals to withhold publication or the power of the press to ignore 'irrelevant' critique), these are the constraints that form the shape of the debate. It is for this reason that it is important not only to be aware of them and the significant epistemological influence they have on research and policy, but also to cross-reference them with other possible interpretations. To move beyond the conventional parameters of knowledge generation in this context, therefore, we need to consider the ways in which the language is conceptualized from different perspectives within society, and it is to this that I turn in the next three chapters.

Chapter 5
Globalization: 'Enriching Japanese Culture Through Contact with Other Cultures'

Conceptual Case Studies

That English language practices have, over the second half of the last century, come to operate as an extremely effective means of international communication within certain fields and geographical contexts seems beyond dispute. Yet a unitary form of English is still not quite the lingua franca for the whole world in the way some suggest, and certainly does not encircle the entire globe in either influence or access. For vast portions of the world's population English remains a foreign language – often an obscure and unnecessary one – despite the prominent discourse which promotes its global reach.[1] David Crystal's oft-quoted definition that 'a language achieves a genuinely global status when it develops a special role that is recognised in every country' (1997: 2) suggests that it is more the concept of the language than its actuality as a communicative tool that has gained real global reach, so that even in those countries where a negligible fraction of the population are properly fluent in a form of the language, the concept may still have attained a pre-eminent status in the popular imagination. It would seem, therefore, that when speaking about English as a 'global' language, the use of the term has prefigured the actual existence of the phenomenon to which it would refer, and this use is predicated to a great extent on the terminology chosen to define the language.

One motivating factor behind the choice of this particular adjective is the echo it has with the contemporary fascination with globalization, and certainly there is much mutual influence between the two concepts to justify a morphological symmetry. As a concept, globalization covers a wide range of social changes, referring to both a politico-economic movement, as well as to immense cultural transformations. It is also linked to a revolution in communications technology, and it is this, in enabling ideas to move with rapidity across the globe, that has acted as facilitator for the diverse changes in the social dynamics of human life. The study of English relates directly to this source point in the process, and is thus implicated in the many consequences of the increased flow of information (and the capital, power and people who follow in its wake). The result of this relationship is that English is often seen as a symbol of globalization, while globalization becomes a key motif in the symbolic meaning that the English language attracts.

It is this combinatory concept (high-profile language plus rapid reorganization of social relations) that has motivated much of the work in EIL/world Englishes, positing a challenge which educationalists and applied linguists have attempted to address in the search for productive regulation of the English language around the world. Yet the combination of the two concepts also has an impact in the wider society beyond language professionals, and results in the symbolic meaning of the English language being dispersed throughout a diverse range of sectors of society. And while the 'official' discourse of language professionals might have a crucial impact on the way people orientate themselves toward the language (the attitudes they take toward it and the uses they make of it), this wider distribution of symbolic meanings also plays a significant role in the process and is an index of the spectrum of ideologies which contribute to the character of the language within society. As Kroskrity (2006: 497) notes

> language ideologies are not merely those ideas which stem from the 'official culture' of the ruling class but rather a more ubiquitous set of diverse beliefs, however implicit or explicit they may be, used by speakers of all types as models for constructing linguistic evaluations.

To this end, it is necessary to look at the situated nature of this conceptualization of the English language, and at how the issues involved in the discourse surrounding it are related to other pressing concerns within the sociopolitical environment. In other words, to understand how English might operate as a global language, we need to take the measure of its impact in the world, and this necessitates an examination of the way in which it is perceived in context-specific situations. It is this that will be the substance of the next three chapters.

Rather than structure this study around particular communal or physical sites where English language use is a prominent activity (the higher education sector in Japan, for example, or a number of selected classrooms or business environments), I will create instead conceptual case studies, anchored around salient concepts or motifs within the discourse. Whereas a traditionally conceived case study will look at a single 'unit of human activity' as it occurs within its real-life context, and will draw upon the analysis of this both for insights into that specific case and as an exemplar for more widely generalizable phenomena (Gillham, 2000: 1), a conceptual case study can begin with the phenomena themselves and track their real-life instantiations in various social contexts. In other words, by extracting specific motifs and using these as the structural center for the discussion, it will be possible to range across different and diverse sites, taking a measure of the way meanings for the language are dispersed across the horizon of the social environment. With the field of investigation for this book being Japanese society *in toto*, evidence of the idea of the language needs to be sought across multiple sites rather than in one bounded arena, and the device of conceptual case studies makes this possible. Such an approach also allows us to contextualize the key structuring motifs with reference both to their relations to other forms of cultural practice within the situated environment (to discourses associated with other conceptual schemata) and to wider 'universal' debates (sociological theory, applied linguistics theory, etc.). In this way, it will be possible to consider the axis between the universal and the historically contingent, and use this to inform the critique of general theoretical principles about English within a globalized context.

This, then, is the structural scope and focus for this part of the study. The method itself is predicated on the intention to consider the way in which the language is presented and used at the symbolic level within the lived environment. Rather than concentrate solely on the narratives of informants, I will consider the way in which diverse aspects of the social environment project an image of the language, creating the matrix of symbolic meanings within which people approach the language. This will in part be supplemented by the views of participants in language-related social practice (those who study, teach or work with the language), but it is the contention of the book that the discourse is not simply a conceptual channel in the minds and utterances of citizens, but an ever-present part of the physical and social environment, and is inscribed within society in ritual, practice, physical organization as well as in verbal and visual semiotic behaviors. This concept of discourse is thus not restricted to verbally articulated utterances, but includes a broader range of semiotic practices (Blommaert, 2005; Gee, 1999), and ideologies of the language are to be sought in the configurations of various forms of cultural practice – in print and broadcast media, in advertising, in product and package design, in fashion, in art and in general processes of social organization. (In this way, the method is not as narrow as that of the previous chapter, where textual articulation was the primary focus, and the 'case' being studied consisted of language education policy and the genre of academic research which paralleled it.) The result is a necessarily eclectic method, drawing upon discourse analysis techniques to examine the semiotic properties of a range of different forms of cultural display. As with traditional case study approaches, the data will be abstracted and collated according to the central concerns of the research (Gillham, 2000: 2), and are then to be contextualized within a cultural–historicist discussion of the nature and genealogy of the key motifs.

A word needs to be added about the 'motifs' around which I will organize the conceptual case studies. In order to examine the way in which the language is conceptualized in Japanese society and to explore the significance of this conceptualization, I will divide the enquiry into three more specific questions, and ask the following: How does English relate to Japan and Japanese culture; what counts as English within this context; and, why do people take an interest in the language. This division attends to how the language is positioned, to what the language is understood to be, and to what value the language is understood to have within Japanese society. The motifs that are associated with these three areas of investigation in the following chapters of the book have then been applied retrospectively; that is to say, their exact character has emerged from the investigation into the way the three areas identified above are expressed within the wider discourse of English within Japan.

A salient motif in the discourse of what counts as English is the issue of 'authenticity', and it is this, therefore, that will become the structuring device for Chapter 6. In Chapter 7, I will explore the relationship between 'aspiration' and the current status of English within the world, as this is a concept that figures especially strongly in discourses centering on why individuals are attracted to the language. Both of these, I shall argue, are key nodes of conceptual meaning for English in Japan. I shall begin, however, with what functions as the über-motif in this discourse, the concept of globalization itself. For in the last two decades or so, it is within the context of globalization that English is most often discussed, and it is within this context that the relationship between the English language and Japanese culture is most often discursively negotiated.

It is often said that Japan has historically had a problematic relationship with the rest of the world – a relationship characterized by a process of regulating contact with the West – and that this process has perpetuated an insular self-image and led to an internationalization programme which has more to do with absorbing foreign influence than interacting with the international community (Clammer, 2000; Itoh, 1998). By tracing the development of this situation and examining certain key points of contact that Japan has with the international community, from the tourist industry to study abroad programmes, I wish to articulate a theory of Japan's response to globalization that can be used as a framework with which to analyze the positioning and functionally inflected conceptualization of English within the country, and consider the way in which the two are dialectically constructed.

The Future as a Foreign Country

> In the future, power will belong to those peoples with no origins and no authenticity who know how to exploit the situation to the full. Look at Japan, which [has managed] to transform the power of territoriality and feudalism into that of deterritoriality and weightlessness. Japan is already a satellite of the planet Earth. (Baudrillard, 1988: 76)

It is one of the popular images of Japan in the Western imagination that the country offers an alternative view of human social evolution. This image is one of exoticism, but not the exoticism of an alien culture rooted in centuries of separate history so much as a perverse corruption of much of what constitutes contemporary Western culture. Whereas popular images of other cultures might stress fundamental contrasts, or even conflicts, with the values that comprise Western society (a 'clash of civilizations'), this image of Japan focuses more on similarities in the superficial environment, yet looking always for signs of excess and of the defamiliarized. So the image is of a highly modern, technologically advanced society, yet one unfettered by the values and meanings that have shaped and licensed modernity in the West. As a fantasy image, it still subscribes to concepts of the mysterious, the bizarre and the vaguely immoral that characterized the Orientalism of many 19th-century writers (Said, 1979), yet it does so within the context of a society founded on principles recognizable to the West: principles of rampant consumerism and endless technological possibility.

This image has been co-opted by writers and film-makers, most especially those working in the genre of Science Fiction, and has encouraged them to use Japan as a locus and motif for their fiction. Yet by setting Japan up as the 'global imagination's default setting for the future', to use William Gibson's (2001) much quoted phrase, the image of contemporary Japan is stripped of geographical and historical (and thus political) specificity. Japan is removed from time and place, annexed from the rest of the modern world, and thus it is that it becomes, in the Western imagination, weightless and deterritorial. Reflected in this formula is the reality of Japan's relationship with the rest of the world represented in terms of the high profile of its strong economy and the proliferation of Japanese-made products across the globe, contrasted with the relative lack of influence the country has in any of the traditional political arenas. The exact nature of this relationship with the wider world has long been something that has troubled the Japanese government (Takahashi, 2001), and the ambiguities displayed in the Western characterization of this relationship have parallels in the way that Japan itself debates the same divide. For if the West looks upon Japan as a vision of the future orbiting the real world, then Japan perhaps considers itself as an island nation clearly separated from an international mainland.

On 20 March 2003, the day the Iraq war began, the Japanese government published two small initiatives aimed at enhancing the country's status as a global player. The first of these was a directive to estate agents that they do their best to combat discrimination toward foreigners who wish to use their services. The second was an announcement by the Ministry of Education of a plan to improve English skills amongst Japanese by having 10,000 high school students go overseas on yearly exchange programmes.[2] Though plucked almost at random from the several similar announcements that appear regularly in the media, both of these are illustrative of contemporary Japanese attitudes toward the challenges of globalization. The former, while giving lip service to the need for a racial tolerance that would encourage multiculturalism (though crucially not backing this with any form of legislation), exposes the type of impediments in the present social and political infrastructure that prevent such a society developing.[3] That the prejudice highlighted here is in the housing market gives some suggestion of how difficult it can be for foreign residents to put down the most basic roots within society. The latter, meanwhile, is the latest in a lengthy list of initiatives to improve the country's English skills, a goal which has long been one of the key tenets of their internationalization programme, yet which over the last 30 years has continually been viewed as problematic and mostly unsuccessful (see, for example, Gorsuch, 2001; Honna, 1995; LoCastro, 1996) – a point that seems to be tacitly admitted with this new initiative, as it moves to export the problem of language education abroad. Both of these are responsive measures, a reaction to the way the shift in global politics is likely to affect Japan. Put crudely, on the evidence of the directives referred to above, Japan's internationalization programme simply requires its citizens to be politer to foreigners and to travel abroad more often. What neither of these measures attempts to do is fundamentally alter Japanese culture to accommodate an evolving world model, or in any sense take an active role in shaping global culture.

Dejima Mentality

The last time the government operated a dedicated policy of sending scholars abroad in the interests of a form of internationalism was in the immediate aftermath of the Meiji Restoration of 1868.[4] As a response to the pressure exerted by the West to open itself up to foreign trade and in an attempt to avoid the fate of its Chinese neighbors (namely, semi-colonial dependence on the Western powers (Storry, 1990: 106)), Japan embarked on its rapid modernization programme which involved emulating the West in its technological developments and social infrastructure. This policy of *Wakon yousai* or 'Japanese spirit with Western learning', advocated by the educationalist Yukichi Fukuzawa, was also therefore a responsive measure intended to preserve Japanese cultural identity and national sovereignty, while adapting to the global challenges that were reshaping the world at the end of the 19th century.

Prior to this, Japan's national identity and indigenous culture had been protected by a policy of almost complete isolation from the rest of the world. As a response to the spread of Christianity at the beginning of the 17th century, the government moved to eliminate Western influence from the culture, first by banning overseas travel for Japanese nationals in 1635, and then ordering the creation of an artificial island protruding from the mainland in Nagasaki Harbor to intern all Portuguese residents of the town. In 1639, the government decided to expel all Portuguese residents, thus enforcing the period of national isolation, known as *sakoku*, which lasted from 1640 to 1853. The artificial island, however, was occupied by the Dutch, who had had trade relations with Japan ever since one of their ships ran aground on the shores of Oita prefecture in 1600. Despite the policy of self-enforced isolation, these relations did continue in a limited capacity, but for the following 218 years, the small artificial island, *Dejima*, connected to the mainland by a narrow footbridge and home to a handful of Dutch merchants was the only contact that Japan licensed with the Western world.

The symbolic significance of this tiny satellite island representing for Japan its only contact with the outside world, and the highly-regulated conditions by which Dejima's foreign population were able to interact with the general population of Nagasaki, refines the widely-held theory that a *sakoku* mentality still influences the way Japan relates to the world 150 years after the policy was swept away by Commodore Perry's arrival in Tokyo Harbor with his fleet of warships (Itoh, 1998).[5] Though the years since feudal Japan was rapidly reconfigured to operate within the modern world have seen significant interaction with the international community, including the creation of a colonial empire and the backlash of occupation, the protectionist and ideologically regulated character of this contact is deeply rooted within this history of self-isolation.

The Theme Park of the World

Illustration of the way this relationship is managed can be sought in the way foreign cultures are often presented within Japan. On the outskirts of the small village of Maruyama (population 6000) in Chiba prefecture, located about four miles by train from Tokyo, can be found the Maruyama Shakespeare Country Park. Opened in 1997, the park – one of a number of foreign country theme parks [*gaikoku mura*] in Japan – consists of an Elizabethan formal garden, a 'Physic' Garden, a farm yard and orchard as well as an 'authentic Elizabethan landscaped environment', including a village green, the Stratford Market Cross and a working windmill, all of which complement the detailed replicas of several of the famous buildings in Stratford-upon-Avon associated with Shakespeare, including his birthplace and Mary Arden's house. These have been built with materials imported from England and by observing traditional methods of craftsmanship, thus aiming, where possible, for authenticity,[6] and to this same end the Japanese staff all wear Jacobethan costumes. The park even has a replica of New Place, the large house Shakespeare bought for his retirement on his return from London. In this respect, the Maruyama Shakespeare Country Park can even claim to be something of an improvement on Stratford-upon-Avon, as the original New Place no longer exists, having been burnt to the ground in 1759, and tourists in England will be disappointed to find nothing but its foundations there today.[7]

Despite the obvious international complexion of this project, the park is aimed almost exclusively at Japanese visitors. The website is entirely in Japanese, and publicity material from the local tourist association stresses: 'The atmosphere of 16th century English life has been so faithfully re-created, that even people who are not familiar with Shakespeare can enjoy [it].'[8] Furthermore, although authenticity has been pursued, and the park offers both a cultural and educational experience (the interiors of the houses operating as museums), the reasons for building the project in this particular location can be categorized as whimsical at best: the idea came from the fact that Maruyama is famous for its rosemary shrubs, and due to there being a few isolated references in Shakespeare's plays to this herb ('Doth not/rosemary and Romeo begin both with a letter?' *Romeo and Juliet* II, iv, 202–203), the prefectural administration decided to combine the two themes in creating a garden that could act as a tourist attraction for the area.

Yet, the existence of this theme park in such a small village in rural Japan, though wildly incongruous in many respects, is also the product of distinct trends in the spread of global culture, and illustrative of the way in which Japanese society processes images of international culture. Hendry (2000a: 217), writing about the trend for *gaikoku mura* in Japan, suggests that one of the attractions of such places is that they offer to the local tourist 'all the pleasures [of travelling the world] with no need to practice another language, apply for a visa, or make a long and tedious journey'. To this we might also add that in recreating famous sites from world heritage improvements can be added, and that which history has harshly or foolishly neglected can be resurrected. The Japanese tourist traveling from the capital can have a glimpse into the architecture and horticulture of Early Modern England, enjoy the natural beauty of Maruyama's rosemary bushes and experience a piece of world heritage that exists nowhere else on the globe, before returning home on the evening of the same day.

Such foreign country theme parks, though having counterparts elsewhere in the world (Ritzer, 1999), have come to be seen as something of a Japanese phenomenon (Hendry, 2000a, 2000b; Yoshimoto, 1994), and can be found scattered across the country. Some of these are dedicated to individual countries (for example, the Parque España in Mie prefecture, or the New Zealand Village in Hiroshima prefecture), others to famous figures from one particular country (the Maruyama Shakespeare Country Park, or the Glucks Konigsreich in Hokkaido with its many references to the Brothers Grimm), while occasionally they have more general international themes, as with Little World in Aichi prefecture which comprises a collection of traditional buildings from 22 different countries and uses the advertising slogan: 'A one day trip around the world'. The intention is always to fulfil an educational brief and offer an authentic cultural experience, yet at the same time the lack of any traditional or historical relevance for the locations in which they are built makes them rootless and two-dimensional. What is being recreated is the world according to the tourist brochure, with great attention paid to the look of the landscape (and specifically how it will photograph), while also offering the chance to experience traditional food and shop for traditional goods (Clammer, 1997). Occasionally, the interactive experience is enhanced with the opportunity to try on local costumes (one of the major attractions, for example, of the Little World theme park) or even talk to local people (who are employed specifically for this purpose). The effect is of the whole world being absorbed and idealized in these constructions as a tourist attraction, and in the process being stripped of its distance, its context and its political reality.

In one respect, the development of such attractions is simply an extension of a type of foreign tourism also popular in Japan. Kerr (2001: 369) writes that

> One of the most remarkable phenomenon of the 1980s and 1990s is the creation of special worlds abroad made just for the Japanese. Most Japanese tourists travel in groups, and their itinerary consists of a 'package' – including attractions, hotels, and restaurants that cater only to them.

Here too the sights of the world are seen from within the security of one's own culture, which is transported along with the tourist by means of a highly organized network of commercial services. Like the *gaikoku mura* there is no need to struggle with another language or unusual customs, and a predetermined path is navigated through the foreign culture to provide an experience that conforms to the expectations that have been cultivated by media representations back in Japan. In this way, the existence of such package tours allows Japan to regulate its image of the outside world even when actually traveling abroad. In this context, the *gaikoku mura*, which symbolically position a simulacrum of the world within Japan and in so doing are able to refashion the image of the world according to subjective, home-grown standards, can be seen as symptomatic of Japan's attitude to international relations. The discourse of *kokusaika* which has flourished since the 1980s and is thus largely contemporaneous with the boom in theme park construction (both being prompted in part by the bubble economy) can itself be seen as a similar process of simulation (Baudrillard, 1994), of recasting the concept of internationalism according to specific Japanese needs and of presenting an internationalist image to the international community while still managing to adhere to a nationalist or even isolationist agenda (Itoh, 1998).

It is of interest to note that such a theme-park mentality also extends to Japan's own cultural heritage. For example, down the road from Little World is Meiji Mura, a complex of recreated buildings from late 19th-century Japan now transposed to a remote hill in the countryside, while at the moment the artificial island of *Dejima* is also being rebuilt on its original site as a tourist attraction. Due to land reclamation in the century and a half since it was last used, however, it no longer protrudes from the mainland but exists now several hundred meters inland in amongst the office blocks of downtown Nagasaki, and the city council is planning to reroute a river to act as a moat to restore the semblance of its previous surroundings. Thus the offshore island that symbolized for Japan the outside world for over 200 years will soon exist once again, but this time symbolically withdrawn well within the main body of Japan, and recalibrated according to the needs of contemporary tourism.

Local Variations of Globalization

Robertson (1992, 1995), in his discussion of theoretical patterns of social globalization, has introduced the term 'glocalization' to describe the way in which global pressures are made to conform to local conditions, and whereby the local culture does not act merely as a passive recipient, but absorbs and reprocesses global forces. He traces the concept back to the Japanese sociological term *dochakuka*, which is based on the agricultural principle of adapting farming techniques to local conditions and which has traditionally been translated as 'indigenization'. Such a process obviously has direct relevance for a Japan which has historically taken great pains in managing the borders, both geographical and cultural, between itself and the world. The phenomenon of the *gaikoku mura*, where world culture is absorbed into a pattern of Japanese social expression and where it is removed from its own political context and placed instead within a national political agenda, is a prominent example of the way local concerns can adapt globally promiscuous cultural imagery, and rather than creating a hybrid culture separated from the mainstream of Japanese social practice, produce something that is rooted firmly within an indigenous cultural tradition. In fact, Yoshimoto (1994: 193–4) sees local concerns as the very *raison d'être* of this phenomenon:

> conceived as showcases for advanced technology and newly acquired wealth in the age of the 'bubble economy', the 'foreign villages' are constructed to attract the tourists from neighbouring prefectures and sometimes from all over Japan to boost the local economy and, no matter how strange it might sound, to re-establish the specificity of regional culture.

That this principle is in origin Japanese can perhaps be taken as modestly significant given the appositeness with which it fits the cultural practices discussed above. Yet, there is a strand of discourse within Japanese society which claims that *dochakuka* is a specifically or even uniquely Japanese concept. One of the consequences of the *kokusaika* process has been to encourage a large body of literature promoting the idea of nationalist uniqueness. Known as *nihonjinron*, these tracts make exhaustive use of example and precedent from all disciplines of human learning in an attempt to argue for the distinctiveness of Japanese identity (Yoshino, 1992), and amongst their many claims is an insistence on the idea that all foreign culture is 'Japanized' on entering the country, and that the indigenization process itself is indeed specific to Japanese culture:

> The presence of the alien, rather than undermining the thesis of indigenous purity, merely sustains it.... If the native language was flooded with foreign loan words, this only shows that there must be a predisposition in the national character, or some specific character in the language which facilitates the adoption of foreign words. Indeed, we are told, the very expression 'intake of foreign culture' is itself particularly Japanese. (Dale, 1986: 52)

In this conception, Japanese national identity remains entirely untainted by outside influence, and globalization is a process that happens elsewhere.

Intriguingly, the *nihonjinron* thesis, which contends that the uniqueness of Japanese culture is an extension of the distinct ethnic identity which constitutes the Japanese nation, provides an alternative theoretical model for the differential concept of culture that Zygmunt Bauman has outlined. In the *nihonjinron* thesis, we have a racially determined concept of culture, where specific cultural practices (language being numbered among them (Carroll, 2001: 139)) are considered to be products of ethnic origin. Such a deterministic view of culture rescinds what Bauman considers to be the seminal assumption of the traditional differential concept of culture: the assumption that because different cultures produce different patterns of fundamental beliefs, this is an argument against absolute innate standards that govern human behavior (Bauman, 1999: 15). This post-Lockean interpretation is somehow turned on its head by the *nihonjinron* writers. For them, difference between cultures is an argument for national difference being a reflection of genetic difference along ethnic lines.

The *nihonjinron* preoccupation with Japanese uniqueness is, of course, an extreme nationalist argument, and yet it is one that has received much popular interest and as such does play some part in the image that Japan has of itself and of its relationship with the rest of the world (Stanlaw, 2004: 274). For Robertson, however, glocalization is neither a way of denying the influence of global culture nor of insisting on the integrity of indigenous culture. He sees it as a phenomenon that will lead to distinctly unique national cultures rooted in tradition but operating within an ever more interconnected world. And, he argues, the process by which local cultures absorb and reprocess foreign influence breaks down traditional proprietary relationships so that 'seemingly "national" symbolic resources are in fact increasingly available for differentiated global interpretation and consumption'. Thus, for example, 'Shakespeare no longer belongs to England. Shakespeare has assumed a universalistic significance', (1995: 38). Another example of such a glocal force, severed from its proprietary national origins and available for differentiated global use, is, of course, the English language. And in the same way that we need to be wary of the totalizing fallacy with the concept of English, and instead execute a nuanced analysis of the shape that English language practices take in a specific environment, so too the word 'global' within the formula 'global language' requires reference to the specific context within which it is used and understood. It is thus that this conception of globalization as it is configured in Japan provides for English language practices a very particular reception.

The Absorption of English: Loanwords

Other than in the specialized area of education there are two main ways in which English influences Japanese society: through loanwords, and in terms of its emblematic use in the media, advertising and popular culture. In each of these, it becomes absorbed within native social trends. I will look at both of these in order to analyze them further.

Loanwords from English are a significant and ever-growing part of the Japanese lexicon (Miller, 1967; Morrow, 1987; Stanlaw, 1992, 2004), and the way they are absorbed within the language show signs of distinct naturalization (Honna, 1995; Kay, 1995). If we take, for example, the collection of words used for dwellings we can see the variety of patterns of English influence on Japanese. The main word for 'house' in Japanese is *ie*, a term that nationalist writers of *nihonjinron* claim as an indigenous concept with a dense complex of connotations that render it impossible for translation into foreign languages (Dale, 1986: 57). Most people, however, especially in urban areas, will live in apartments, and in keeping with the provenance of the concept of such dwellings, the Japanese language uses the loanword *apaato*, derived from the American English word. As with a great number of loanwords however, not only has the phonology been altered to conform to the Japanese syllabary (resulting in what is known as 'katakana English'), but the word has also been morphologically contracted, here by a process of back clipping. This type of loanword, which in Japanese is called *gairaigo*, produces a uniquely Japanese lexeme, though one which, in both provenance and semantic meaning, is directly related to a word in the English lexicon. There is another type of loanword however, known as *wasei-eigo*, which performs a further act of naturalization by significantly altering the semantic meaning of the original. An example of this would be the Japanese word *manshon*, phonetically derived from the English word 'mansion' but having a meaning far closer to 'apartment'. Such words are the direct result of English's global influence, and yet rather than strengthening the case for English as an international language (i.e. a single code to unite the peoples of the world), they are an exemplar of the way local cultures can refashion foreign influence to produce something unique. Stanlaw (2004) demonstrates how loanwords are used in conjunction or contrast with native terms to achieve particular sociolinguistic ends. Indeed, he suggests that 'English loanwords are not really loanwords at all, as there is no actual borrowing that occurs' (p. 19). Rather, these lexical items are original to the Japanese language, and just inspired or motivated by English vocabulary.[9]

In practical terms, the perception of loanwords and their relationship to Japanese culture is ambiguous. Former Prime Minister Junichiro Koizumi spoke out with some force about the problematic nature of having so many foreign imports in the language, mobilizing the conventional arguments that this was not only a barrier to communication (the underlying assumption being that the primary function of language is the unimpeded exchange of precise ideational meaning), but also detrimental to the Japanese language (the ideology here being that of distinct linguistic systems correspondent to equally distinct national communities).[10] At the same time, however, Koizumi's own government frequently made use of English-motivated linguistic resources. For example, the much-publicized campaign intended to alter social norms concerning codes of dress in the workplace during the summer was given the name 'Cool biz' [*kûru-bizu*], a fine illustration of *wasei-eigo*. The intention of this campaign was to reduce the use of air-conditioning in office buildings by persuading salarymen to relax their strict conventions concerning appropriate dress, and dispense with jacket and tie during the hot summer months, and thus the lexical resources that were drawn upon were the English words 'cool' and 'business'. Use of English-derived vocabulary was not limited to this particular neologism, however. Among the slogans used during the campaign were, for example, complex stylistic formulations such as the following: ストップ・ザ・温暖化・たいそう (*sutoppu za ondanka taisô*; translation: 'stop [the] global warming exercises' (see Figure 5.1)).[11]

Figure 5.1 Global warming campaign: *Sutoppu za ondanka taisô*

Globalization: 'Enriching Japanese Culture' 77

What is of interest in this example is that it is the imperative of the verb 'stop' and the definite article which are English derivations, whereas the substantive concept itself is a Japanese lexeme. For the concept of 'global warming', both the calque 地球温暖化 (*chikyû ondanka*) – often shortened simply to *ondanka* – and the transliteration グローバル・ウォーミング (*gurôbaru wômingu*) are in use in Japanese, and thus the choice to retain the vernacular lexeme in this particular slogan despite use of English-derived vocabulary elsewhere in the phrase appears marked.[12] The inclusion of the definite article is also especially enigmatic here, as it is not a grammatical feature that exists in the Japanese language, and furthermore, this particular syntactic structure would not require a definite article in Standard English. The article is, however, an index of typical English construction (the type of grammatical pattern drilled into the school child), while the use of *sutoppu* is an intertextual link with the generic language of campaigns. Indeed, the whole construction is quite common in government or public organization advertisements (e.g. ストップ・ザ・交通事故死 *sutoppu za kōtsū-jiko*; translation: 'stop [the] traffic accidents'). The result is a text that positions itself in the minds of the local society as part of the global environmental movement by drawing on local patterns of indexicalities.[13] What is also of significance is that even within official and high-profile government texts, the absorption and manipulation of English-derived linguistic resources is commonplace and becomes a semiotic tool in the construction of local political discourse.

That Koizumi should have issued a directive warning his ministers against the overuse of English-derived vocabulary while elsewhere in the government texts such as the above were being produced is not unusual. It is not, after all, uncommon for overtly expressed discourse to be contradicted by patterns of social activity. This is a typical example of divergence between ideas about language and the constraints and deterministic nature that characterizes language and language use itself – in this case, the tendency for the lexicon to expand and adapt according to the needs and motivating influence of contemporary social reality.[14]

The Absorption of English: Ornamentalism

The other way in which English is absorbed within Japanese society is through its ornamental use in advertising, the media and popular culture. The extent to which English words and phrases, written in the Roman alphabet rather than the katakana syllabary, appear on posters, adverts, clothes, signs and a whole range of pop culture artifacts is often remarked on by visitors to the country, and is indeed quite remarkable in comparison with other non-English speaking societies (Hyde, 2002). Mostly this use of the language has no overt denotational function, and is primarily for ornamental effect, yet its prevalence is such that rarely, for example, can one see a billboard advertisement that does not have a strapline or slogan in English. Such fragments of language will often have little regard for the rules of standard grammar and can incorporate a vocabulary that is frequently obscure if not idiosyncratic, and the result is that the majority of the general public is unable to decipher their meaning. This is a use of the language for its general cultural connotations rather than its specific denotation. Though often causing a defamiliarized bewilderment in English-speaking spectators, the process does accord with aspects of language use in Japanese which differ from those in the West. One of the cultural traits so often identified with Japan is the importance given to surface and appearance. It is a culture of ritual and wrapping, and one in which communication is governed by concepts such as *honne* and *tatemae* [one's truthful intent in contrast to one's public expression of opinion], and *menboku* [saving face], where meaning is purposefully divorced from overt expression by linguistic means. The written language itself, supremely visual in its variety of form, also doubles as decorative art (Shelton & Okayama, 2006). Within this context, the existence of an ornamental English in Japan can be seen not as the ignorant or willful misuse of the original language, but rather a strategy of using the language as an expressive tool which need not be dominated by the strictures of core semantic meanings. As such, it is often a pure visual motif, which may have certain cultural connotations – Takashi, for example, suggests that such usage is meant to create 'modern and cosmopolitan images, rather than to meet lexical needs' (1992: 133) – but is motivated as much by specifically aesthetic concerns.

In both these forms of absorption, therefore, the English language is not imported wholly as a communicative tool, but unpacked and its component parts reconfigured in unfamiliar contexts. Though the education system may promote English as a way of developing a positive attitude in students toward communication and 'deepening international understanding' (MEXT, 2002), the language itself has a prominent alternative presence within society which does not conform in any sense to ideals of universal linguistic communion.

The Promulgation Function

In its promotion as a tool for linguistic communion, however, we can also see a process of culturally specific positioning. One prominent strand in the discourse of the relationship between globalization and English is the concept of 'appropriation' (Kramsch, 1998b: 81), whereby the native community adopt English language practices for their own specific cultural purposes, and in the process adapt them to their own needs, thereby 'owning' the language rather than trespassing on the rights of others whenever they use it (again, the possession metaphors are on active service here). This is often related to cultural identity, and when it involves drawing upon stylistic elements of language behavior it leads to practices such as 'crossing' and 'styling the other' (Rampton, 1995, 1999) whereby indexicalities associated with particular group membership are drawn upon by those from outside the group for a variety of strategic and identity management purposes. Though English usage in Japan does become a site for such activities, especially within popular culture contexts (Pennycook, 2003), the function I wish to draw attention to here is one where identity is not indicated through patterns of codeswitching, crossing or other forms of stylistic marking, but is instead meant to be articulated ideationally via the transparent medium of international communication which English represents. In this case, use of the language ('English') is not a statement about cultural identity in its own right, but is understood as a means of facilitating the articulation of a verbalized statement about cultural identity.

The appropriation involved in this process, therefore, is not one of claiming or adapting the language or style of the other (as with 'crossing' or 'writing back' (Pennycook, 1994)), but of utilizing this particular language as a tool for the widest possible dissemination of a message. In practices of this sort, English is assigned a promulgation function, and in the era of globalization this attitude toward the language is becoming increasingly common, with instances of such behavior often drawing specifically upon the *concept* of English's global status, and in doing so symbolically linking local issues to global values (to universal concepts of political or human rights, for example (Toolan, 2003)). In Japan, however, the prevailing use of the practice is specifically linked to cultural identity, and results in an interesting paradox whereby promotion of a nationalist sentiment requires the embracing of a 'foreign' language.

The proactive promotion of distinct cultural identities, and the emergence in some territories of separatist movements and local nationalisms is considered by some social theorists (e.g. Giddens, 1999) to be a consequence of globalization, of course. And Japan's amalgamation of nationalist/internationalization agendas can be seen as part of this trend. As Kubota (1998: 300) explains

> [In the 1980s] Japan as a world economic power experienced a need to communicate better with its international partners in order to ensure

its economic prosperity while maintaining its own identity. A strategy that Japan employed in order to fulfil this need was neither to subjugate the nation to the West nor to seek a counter-hegemony against the West; it was to accommodate the hegemony of the West by becoming one of the equal members of the West and to convince the West and other nations of its position based on a distinct cultural heritage. The discourse of *kokusaika* thus harmoniously embraces both Westernisation through learning the communication mode of English and the promotion of nationalistic values.

Hashimoto (2000: 45) makes a similar point based upon her reading of policy documents for education reform: 'A crucial point is that the promotion of internationalisation seems to aim to re-educate Japanese citizens to reassert their collective identity as Japanese'.

The promotion of English is then drawn directly into this discourse. The Ministry of Education's *Frontier Within* document, for example, argues 'If we treasure the Japanese language and culture, we should actively assimilate other languages and cultures, enriching Japanese culture through contact with other cultures and showing other countries the attraction of Japanese culture by introducing it in an appropriate fashion in the *kokusai gengo* [the international language]' (CJGTC, 2000b: 20).[15] This same sentiment can be found in advertising campaigns for English language schools, such as the one for the Gaba chain which asked Japanese citizens what they would do were they able to speak English, and solicited answers such as: 'I would introduce the traditional Japanese arts of ceramics and knitting to the world'.[16] A practical example of this mind-set can be seen in a contrast between the ways the national language is promoted in Japan and in France. Like France's *Académie française*, Japan has a central regulatory agency responsible for overseeing the national language and, like its French counterpart, it has been involved in recent years in a process of attempting to stem the tide of what it perceives as the anglicization of the lexicon.[17] Yet whereas the strategy executed by the *Académie française* is overtly francophone in every respect, the *Kokuritsu Kokugo Kenkyūjo* (or *Kokken* for short: The National Institute for Japanese Language) uses the English language as a medium for self-promotion in combination with Japanese. Compare, for example, the two bodies' respective web presences (Figure 5.2).

The *Académie française* makes no concession to an anglophone audience, presenting itself entirely in the national language. The Japanese equivalent, however, allows the English translation of its title to overwhelm the Japanese both in spatial positioning and size upon the page, while also defaulting to English for the legal coda about copyright.[18]

Globalization: 'Enriching Japanese Culture' 81

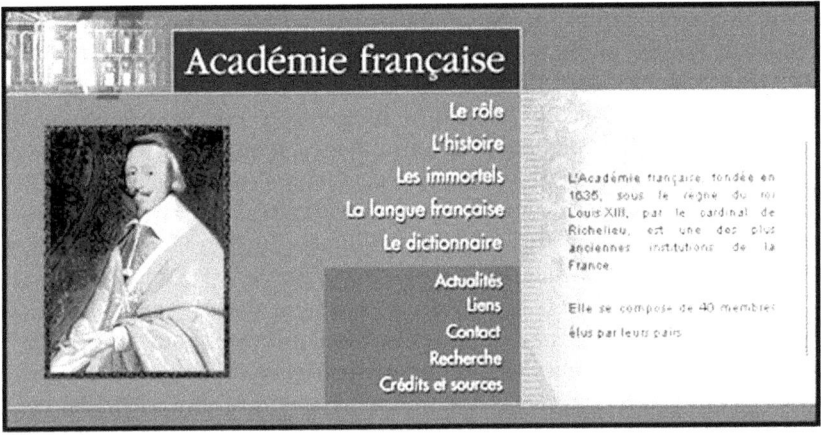

Figure 5.2 L'Académie française and The National Institute for Japanese Language

Literary and Artistic Reconfigurations

The extent to which English has influenced a foreign culture can further be examined by the use made of it by those involved in acts of cultural production. In Japan, despite the high profile of the English language, there is no tradition of native literature written in English. It does make token appearances in pop songs (Moody, 2006) as well as some contemporary literature however, where it operates, as Ono (1992) phrases it, as part of a 'style repertoire', mostly using nonce borrowings to create a variety of rhetorical effects. Stanlaw (2004: 102) suggests that 'The English words used [in pop songs] are often creative and critical Japanese (not American or British) poetic devices which allow songwriters, and even some poets, an access to a wider range of allusions, images, metaphors, and technical possibilities than is available from "purely" Japanese linguistic resources', and Pennycook (2003: 517), with reference to Japanese rap lyrics, suggests that English is used in this context indexically 'to signify identification with certain cultural affiliations'. Again then there is a process of nativization with the borrowings, especially in terms of the phonetic alteration they must undergo to fit in with the scansion and rhythm of songs which use the Japanese syllabary as their template. And nativization also occurs in terms of the cultural cachet the words have within this particular context, giving them an allusive meaning which will differ considerably from the substantive meaning of the American or British English lexical item. Their use in this way is therefore a continuation of the 'loanword' process, practicing similar techniques of nativization for similar, albeit more pronounced, purposes. Kachru (2005: 81) sees such usage as part of what he terms the 'bilingual's creativity' and comments that whereas this selective usage of English 'may be off-putting to native speakers [it] is actually a very creative productive linguistic process in acculturalization of English lexical items in Japanese'. What is not occurring here, however, is a specific critical or self-reflexive engagement with the cultural implications of the English language for Japanese society. There is no metalinguistic critique – the purposeful and self-reflexive reconfiguring of the language seen in writers such as Salman Rushdie and Chinua Achebe, and that has been discussed by Pennycook (1994) under the rubric of 'writing back'.

There are certain artists, however, who have dealt directly with the influence of the language on Japanese culture, and used a critical examination of this process as a central theme for their work. Muneteru Ujino, for example, drawing on the tradition of text as an art form in traditional Japanese calligraphy and the premodern *sumi-e* genre of painting, but also with a nod toward contemporary Western artists such as Edward Ruscha, creates sculptures which spell out words or phrases. He often uses words of English origin which have become mutated in meaning as they are absorbed into Japanese. To understand the use he makes of the specific character of English in Japan we need to return again to the concept of loanwords in Japan, and the variety called *wasei-eigo* ['English made in Japan'].

With *wasei-eigo* we can see a process based upon what Hymes has called 'second language relativity' (1966). This contends that while the form of an utterance might travel well, the function does not, ideologies that govern meaning in one community being significantly different from those in another community, thus altering the results of the form–function equation (Blommaert, 2003). It is for this reason that the same utterance can have different effects (be interpreted as having different meanings) in different cultural contexts. In the case of *wasei-eigo*, such relative disjuncture has become ossified in the lexicon, so that a whole corpus of lexical items appear to be 'English' derivations, but the passage from motivation to final form is attenuated to the extent that there is little semantic relation between the original English and the newly coined Japanese: for example, terms such as *baikingu* ['Viking'] meaning a smorgasbord, or *bâjinrôdo* ['virgin road'] for the aisle in the church down which the bride walks.

When the issue of proprietorialism is added to the mix, the result is not simply one of incommensurable meaning, but of hegemonic views of the validity (or value) of nonstandard usages. Based upon the foundational conceptual metaphor LANGUAGE IS A POSSESSION, and the refining ideology that equates linguistic practice with nation, the proprietorial view promotes the idea that not only are other cultural uses of English form is incorrect, but that they are a violation of the orthodoxies that represent the culture (and cultural identity) of the self. A key example is an internet site such as www.engrish.com, which lightly ridicules instances of Japanese 'misuse' of English, focusing upon discrepancies between the norms dictated by standard (US) English usage and those on display in Japanese society.

It is this issue that Muneteru Ujino has addressed in his work. Thus, for example, the work 'One Room Mansion' (ワンルームマンション) is constructed like the advertising board of an estate agent, yet has carved within it the title's phrase in katakana (see Figure 5.3).[19] This is a phrase that has its etymology in English, but is now an established part of the Japanese lexis. In fact, the term is naturalized to such an extent that as English it would appear to be semantically illogical – the idea of a one-room mansion is an oxymoron, whereas in Japanese it has the meaning 'studio flat'. And yet, by being written in katakana it is indecipherable to the non-Japanese speaking spectator and thus for him or her, this semantic anomaly goes unnoticed and the work appears as merely ornamental – a display of typography for aesthetic functions in the way that much English exists within Japan. For the Japanese viewer without proficiency in the English language, the anomaly is also indecipherable, and the work simply seems to be an oft-used phrase of seemingly English origin.

Ujino's work then plays directly on the influence of Western culture for Japanese society, and not only do his sculptures use phrases that are indicative of the Japanese language's consumption of Western culture on

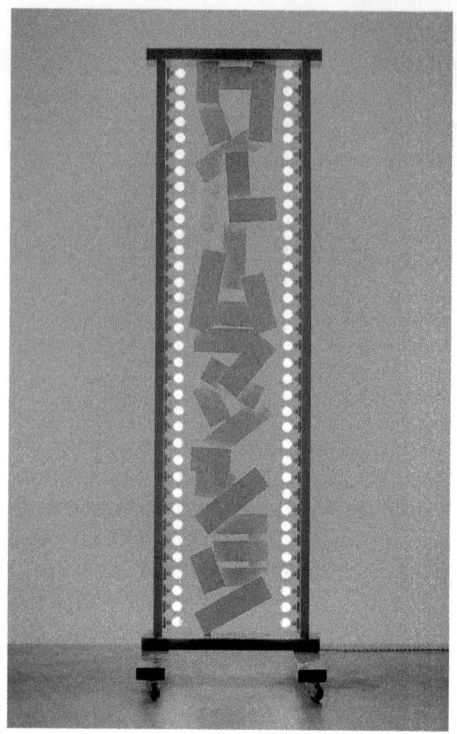

ワンルームマンション

⇩

WANRUUMUMANSHON

⇩

One room mansion

⇩

Studio flat

Figure 5.3 Muneteru Ujino's 'One Room Mansion'

its own terms, but he foregrounds themes of linguistic segregation and in doing so transforms the process into an artifact of Japanese culture.

A similar theme has been explored by other contemporary artists. Makoto Aida, for example, held a performance-art piece in New York around the katakana pronunciation of English words, while Hiroko Ichihara's work 'Please Teach Me English' involved soliciting English translations for a number of short phrases that she posted to a Japanese Web site, and then exhibiting the unpredictable results alongside the original texts.[20] In prose fiction, the work of the author Yoshinori Shimizu (1993) often deals with linguistic themes, and in his short story *Kotoba no Sensô* [*The War of Words*], he tries to conceive of a Japanese language stripped firstly of all English influences, and then of all Chinese influences,[21] with absurd results. The narrative is a parody on the 'purity' ideology of the Japanese language, which is linked to the cultural uniqueness paradigm that finds voice in the *nihonjinron* genre. By pursuing a rigorous policy of attempting to expunge all 'foreign' influences, Shimizu creates a *reductio ad absurdum* to satirize the ideology of distinct national language practices.

In each of these cases, then, English motivated vocabulary items do not merely contribute to a style repertoire for poetic expression, but they interrogate the ways in which English has become a part of both Japanese life and language; and in doing so, they also reify this process as part of modern Japanese culture. It is not the language itself that is being appropriated within the native culture here, but the ideological debates over English usage, and the social implications that the influence of English linguistic forms have for concepts of the native culture. And in doing this, these writers and artists are producing something that is specifically Japanese; that is to say, its appreciation and even interpretation is predicated upon knowledge of the Japanese language and Japanese social history. Shimizu's short story, for example, could not possibly be translated into English because it makes symbolic use of the different writing systems and the different visual character they have upon the page, as it dismisses English influences (written in katakana) and Chinese influences (written in kanji) in its search for a purity of the 'Japanese language'.

Conclusion

In summation to his study of the impact of globalization on Japan, Clammer (2000: 164) writes

> If globalisation has in fact contributed to the diversity rather than the homogenisation of cultures, then it does make sense to explore it in its manifestations rather than from the level of totality. The sociology of modern Japan has suffered from being largely pursued from within a set of pre-existing abstractions; a return to the study of actual cultural practices would both clarify what contemporary Japanese culture is, and how, if at all, it relates to tradition.

English can be seen as both prism and catalyst for such practices. It reflects the dynamics at work within society in the way that it too is absorbed and adapted to the native culture, and it also becomes an active site on which the negotiation of relations with the international community takes place. For by absorbing English into the Japanese language, by managing shifts in semantics and co-opting it for purely ornamental purposes, the language is, in effect, made foreign to the global community, and could thus be said to act as a further boundary between Japan and outside world. Certainly the discourse addressing the place and status of English in Japan is structured around a concern for national and cultural identity and the distinctions that need to be drawn in order to define this. In the conceptions voiced at various levels of society about the promulgation function, in attitudes toward loanwords, and in the work of artists such as Ujino and Shimizu, this is a key axis around which the significance of the language is debated. Here, it is the *idea* of the language that becomes a site on which the processes of social reconfiguration that are subsumed under the term *globalization* are assimilated. In one way, the use of the symbolism of English in this process has a completely nonlinguistic function, as it draws on the many ideological meanings associated with the status of the language and utilizes these as part of a general (and constant) reorganization of the wider political discourses concerned with the nation state, national and cultural identity and the challenges of globalized social change. Yet, there is never a total disjunct between ideology and practice, and just as ideas of the English language become a site for the negotiation of cultural identity, so too does the opposite hold true, and discourses concerned with cultural identity have a significant effect on the way that English itself is positioned within society. It is this positioning, especially as it affects language education practice and the type of English that is privileged by this, that is the next subject for investigation.

Chapter 6
Authenticity: 'More English than England Itself'

Alternative Visions of 'Realistic' Language Practice

In the mountains of the prefecture of Fukushima can be found British Hills, a leisure complex which aims to recreate within the mainland of Japan a fully realized simulation of what is promoted as an authentic English-language speaking environment. The publicity for the complex describes it as 'a small British countryside village complete with castle, British style guesthouses, English speakers, country gardens and surroundings. Even the weather seems British!'[1] British Hills is another in the tradition of the *gaikoku mura* which were discussed in Chapter 5. As noted, places of this sort recreate famous or architecturally typical buildings along with the physical and cultural landscape of foreign countries, always with great emphasis given to the authenticity of design and construction. Eschewing the rides and attractions of the more typical theme park, they offer instead a glimpse of a foreign culture, of the architecture, dress and food, all of which can be experienced without the inconvenience of traveling abroad (Hendry, 2000a).

The case of British Hills, however, is slightly atypical, in that it is owned by the Sano Educational Foundation which also incorporates Kanda University of International Studies and Kanda Institute of Foreign Languages, and as such does not refer to itself as a theme park but as an 'Education and Cultural Resort' or 'school with hotel-like facilities'. To this end, it shares its leisure brief with an educational one, running a series of classes, having an in-house educational staff and loaning the facilities to a variety of other institutions and organizations. As well as providing educational opportunities for its two sister institutions, it attracts visiting groups from high schools and business programmes nationwide; even the Japanese Association of Language Teachers (JALT) has held symposiums there.

In conception and promotion, a great deal is made of the authentic nature of the place. The slogan boasts that the complex is 'More English than England itself', and both in terms of its setting and the learning experience, much effort has gone into creating a simulation which will allow students to feel fully immersed in an English-speaking environment resonant with an exotic culture. Not only have the buildings been constructed in and then shipped over from the UK, but the furniture and fittings are all imported, as is the merchandize in the souvenir shop (Cadburys chocolate, teddy bears or tea). In addition to this, both teachers and hospitality staff are native speakers, and the complex's own promotional literature, as well as third-party publicity in the media and by the educational establishments that make use of the place, all point out the realism of the 'British-style atmosphere [but] without the danger and expense of overseas travel'.

Although within the context of the English language's presence within Japan, and indeed within the specific context of ELT in the country, British Hills is something of an extreme example, the prominence given in both design and promotion to an idea of 'authenticity' is symptomatic of a more general trend within language establishments across the country, and, as will be argued, this operates as another key motif for the way in which English is perceived within Japan. The use of this motif has far-reaching ramifications for the organization of language-related social practice in the country, from the hiring of teachers, through the characterization of the language in advertising and promotion, to the method and type of language teaching employed in a variety of institutions. An analysis of this motif, therefore, can go a long way toward mapping out the meaning the language has in society and the functions to which it is put. If one of the consequences of globalization is an expression of what constitutes 'Japanese' cultural identity within a changing social structure, a related and consequential phenomenon is what constitutes the identity of the English language in this new global society; what, that is, should be understood as 'real' English.

Just as the culture of a particular country will construct a unique conceptual meaning for the language, so also will other discrete cultures, not least that of the applied linguistic academic community. In the world of foreign language teaching, 'authenticity' has often figured in recent years in theoretical debates about practice and method, with a specific and relatively narrowly defined reference of meaning. The technical use of the term in this context is rather different from the concept as illustrated by the British Hills example. Emerging as an issue contemporaneously with the move toward a communicative approach to language teaching in the late 1970s, 'authenticity' in this perspective is related to the desire for more 'realistic' language to be used in the classroom, and to how the learning experience can best be framed to reflect the learner's language needs in the outside world (e.g. Breen, 1985; van Lier, 1996). In this context, the concept of authentic English, true to the actuality of contemporary communication needs and not simply to tradition and traditional practice, has developed to incorporate the more politically inflected arguments about ownership, allegiance and cultural identity in ELT theory that have been discussed in earlier chapters. To define what is to be considered as authentic English for the purposes of teaching and language promotion, then, is to enter the debate about the cultural politics of the language and pose fundamental questions about the exact nature of what is taught and learnt. The contested construction of a concept of authenticity within the culture of mainstream applied linguistic academia influences teaching practices that are adopted around the world.

The remit of this chapter, therefore, is to examine these debates with the intention of contrasting the theories about authentic language practice alluded to above, with examples of the various ways that issues of authenticity within the context of ELT in Japan actually manifest themselves. In the wake of the many influential studies in the last decade and a half that have examined the role of English within the world context in terms of postcolonial and multicultural discourse (e.g. Holborow, 1999; Pennycook, 1994, 1998; Phillipson, 1992), it has been impossible to conceive of the language as a politically neutral form of international communication. Again, the point I wish to argue here, though, is that different cultures construct their own profiles and purposes for the English language, and that in certain contexts these profiles can in fact obstruct the easy adoption of the language as a form of international communication while still allowing it to fulfill other significant functions within society.

What Is Authentic?

Before moving to concrete examples, I will first outline some theoretical details. 'Authenticity' is a concept which cuts deep through contemporary debates about the perception and state of social existence. Having stood as a central motif in the modernist construal of human knowledge, it then became a site of dispute and revision for postmodernism, with its promotion of the idea of a reality mediated by simulation and substituted by a representation of itself (Baudrillard, 1983; Jameson, 1984). For Giddens (1991) and his conception of late modernity, authenticity is accorded a similar importance – though with a substantively different significance – and acts as the moral foundation upon which self-identity is reflexively constructed. In broader cultural terms, the concept has emerged in discourses of national identity and cultural integrity in response to the forces of globalization. In each case, the paradigm around which social understanding is stretched locates authenticity as a touchstone, and the circumstances and nature of its employment are pivotal to the respective models of social reality.

Leaving aside for the time being the philosophical use of the term as it relates to subjectivity and self-realization, what 'authenticity' usually denotes is a sense of an object or experience being genuine or original. However, in common usage it is also often employed to mean the *appearance* of genuineness or originality. One can speak of experiencing an authentic home-cooked taste from a processed meal purchased at the supermarket, or of authentic battle scenes in a film rife with special effects. In neither case is there the suggestion that one is experiencing the genuine article – what you buy in the supermarket is not really home-cooked, and what you see on the screen is not a real battle – rather, they contain some quality that allows one to believe in them as convincing representations.

This usage of the term is in part due, no doubt, to the conflation of actual and represented experience that increasingly defines our age. In an environment where so much of our knowledge and interaction with our social surroundings is mediated by television or by the virtual reality of computer-based communication, it is not surprising that the gap between the genuine and the convincing representation should be elided in discourse in the same way that it so often is in experience, so that calling something 'authentic' merely becomes shorthand for saying it 'appears authentic'. Indeed, often the use of the term, especially when employed by advertisers, indicates that the object so described is *not* in fact genuine. Yet the semantic core of the word (in the codified language) does contain two discrete concepts which allow it to straddle or vacillate between the poles of actuality and representation. The *Oxford English Dictionary*, for example, records two trends of usage: the first 'as being authoritative or duly authorised', and the second as 'being what it professes in origin or authorship, as being genuine' (*O.E.D.*, Second edition, 1989). While the idea of 'genuine' is central to its meaning, therefore, it also implies 'authority', and, depending on the balance between these two, the sense can differ distinctly. Thus, 'authenticity' need not necessarily equate with genuineness itself but with a quality that allows one to believe that something has the authority to truthfully represent the genuine.

These are, then, two distinct meanings in common usage: the one suggestive of genuineness, the other of the authoritative simulation of genuineness; and yet because they both share the same signifier, there is the possibility for elision and for the attributes of the one to be imparted to the meaning of the other. It is the ambiguous nature of this double meaning that holds the attraction for so much contemporary cultural theory. Subjects living within an increasingly simulated world where traditional social structures no longer define social roles and relationships so explicitly, where local culture is swept along on the tide of global change, turns perhaps to the concept of authenticity for consolation and a sense of stability. The fiction of an authority that is not necessarily genuine itself but inherently persuasive in its close (though undisclosed) relation to genuineness can anchor the perception of 'reality' and become a secure and grounded point from which to judge experience. In this sense, 'authenticity' has a certain iconic value, and its frequent use in advertising would seem to tap into the contemporary desire for a counterbalance to the perceived 'artificiality' of modern life, leading to what popular sociologists such as Boyle (2003) identify as an 'authenticity movement' battling against the synthetic and the virtual, for example, by buying organic food at the supermarket.

Yet, if authenticity is not of necessity based on an essential genuineness but can simply be based on belief predicated on authority, this stability quickly disappears. Rather than being an objective truth (in so far as such a thing can be discerned), 'authenticity' in this context relies instead on being perceived as such by its audience. If it is a matter of belief, then what is authentic for one person need not be so for another, and authenticity becomes not an innate characteristic but an evaluation bestowed from outside, a process relying on an act of authentication by the perceiver and to a great extent on the claim to authenticity by the subject. This claim to authenticity and the authority it bestows have implications that can range from the commercial to the moral to the political.

The Authentic Text and Authenticity of Interaction

Within applied linguistics and language teaching theory, this claim to authenticity can be seen in these terms as working to validate the type of English that should be adopted in policy and teaching practice. Discussion of authenticity here has paralleled the development of the discourse about English as an international language, which grew from the desire to teach a language directly relevant to the daily experience of the learner and from the 'reality' of a world in which it is estimated now that the majority of English speakers have it as an additional language (Crystal, 1997). Rather than claim that a single model of standard English should be promoted as authentic, the trend has been to authorize a plurality of native varieties, or different Englishes, while also suggesting that international communication via English as a lingua franca is the authentic experience of the language for the majority of the people in the world and that this should thus be reflected in the type of English authorized by policy and practice (Jenkins, 2006).

As a technical term referring to the teaching of natural or 'realistic' language behavior in the classroom, 'authenticity' emerged as an issue in the 1970s (e.g. Jakobovits, 1981; Savignon, 1972) and was a key tenet in the development of the communication-based, or communicative approach to the theory of teaching (Brumfit & Johnson, 1979). The 'authentic' text is contrasted with one designed specifically for instructional purposes where its primary function is to illustrate particular linguistic constructions rather than to communicate a meaning. In this case, the word 'authentic' is used in contradistinction to 'artificial' or 'prefabricated', and the motivation behind the choice is the implication of a reliable relationship with reality.

When Widdowson introduced the distinction between the use of the terms 'genuine' and 'authentic' with reference to language used in the classroom, the former referring to an actual text taken from the mainstream of social communication and imported untouched into the classroom, with the latter being seen not as 'a quality residing in instances of language but... a quality which is bestowed upon them, created by the response of the receiver' (1979: 165), he brought to the debate the question of perception. Authenticity shifts here from being a property of the text itself to being an act of interpretation on the part of the user. Thus, the possibility is opened up for contesting claims as to what is to be considered as authentic.

For many, the assumption has long been that authentic language behavior is based on the way native speakers encounter English in everyday communication (e.g. Johnson & Johnson, 1998; see Widdowson, 1996 for criticism of this position). Kramsch (1998a: 16) observes, '[a]s a rule, native speakers are viewed around the world as the genuine article, the authentic embodiment of the standard language'. Yet as the number of non-native speakers grows, the relative nature of authenticity can allow for a shift in authority, and the desirable model need not be that of the L1 user but of L2 speakers using it as a lingua franca. In such cases, what is authentic to the native speaker is likely to be contrived and inappropriate for the non-native. In recognition of this, the hegemony of the native-speaker model has been repeatedly problematized in the last two decades (Jenkins, 2000; Rampton, 1990), and there has been a concerted call for new paradigms to be universally recognized which reflect the actual contemporary status of the language. There is now a trend in TESOL theory which argues that 'authenticity' in such a climate should mean effective communication via English as a lingua franca (Seidlhofer, 2004).

By the time we come to the re-evaluation of the centrality of the native speaker to paradigms of authentic communication, the term begins to refer not simply to a type of text but also to the interaction between speakers. This shift from an essentialized view of the language (the 'genuine' text) to one more concerned with the status of the user moves the debate about authenticity into a much more overtly politically marked arena where the question shifts from 'what English?' to 'whose English?' The range of viewpoints that have developed over the years around this subject all concern the type of language that should be employed in the classroom and how this can either be modeled on the outside world (and a descriptive interpretation of the 'real-life' communication that takes place out there) or how it should influence the outside world (and take a prescriptive or utopian approach based on the 'reality' of the role of English as an international language that is 'owned' by all). In either case, 'authenticity' is used to refer to the way in which it is imagined that language is normatively used in society for communicative purposes. And while the theories are both pragmatically motivated, in as much as they try to find a workable model for classroom practice, and also ideologically motivated, in that they would impose upon language use a particular view of society, in both cases the use of the term confers the suggestion of an objective authority.

The differing perspectives on 'authentic' language use described above give the appearance of being a development rather than a conflict, and this is possibly because the debate has been carried out based on the hypothetical classroom within TESOL theory, which has its own mainstream unitary culture specific to the discipline. As Pennycook (2000: 89) points out, 'so much of what we read about in TESOL and Applied Linguistics... tends to view classes as closed boxes' thus ignoring the 'complex interplay between classrooms and the outside world' (p. 92). It is when we step beyond the classroom and examine the presentation of ELT in society that we encounter further alternative and conflicting constructions of the concept of 'authenticity' which can offer a very different perspective on the role English plays in an international context.

A number of critics have noted that the native-speaker model often receives less criticism from non-native speakers themselves and is still considered highly desirable as a norm in many societies. For Cook (1999: 196), the intractability of the native-speaker argument can best be explained as the 'product of many pressures on [students] to regard L2 users as failed natives', whereas for Kramsch (1993), it is a matter of fragile confidence in the learner. Matsuda (2003: 484) has investigated the issue by surveying a group of Japanese secondary school students about their attitudes to English as an international language, and she finds that they 'still seem to hold a view that English belongs to native speakers of the language and that they are only marginal participants in the use of EIL'. This she sees as a problem that handicaps the students from active and equal linguistic engagement in the global community, and she proposes that the development of this type of attitude be combated by action taken within the classroom:

> Careful decision making about the selection of instructional model, cultural topics addressed in class discussions, types of interaction introduced in the classroom, and forms of assessment can help English learners better understand the pluralism in English today and realise the crucial roles they may play in defining English as an international language. (p. 494)

While such measures may indeed raise awareness of debates about the use and varieties of English in the world, and Matsuda's research offers an admirable insight into the attitudes of Japanese high school students to their relationship with the concept of English, what is missing from this account is an acknowledgment of the social situation within which the learning process takes place. If the students' attitudes are considered only to be a direct result of the teaching they receive in class and the various limitations this teaching exhibits, then alterations to the syllabus and teacher training would be expected to have profound effects. Yet this leaves no place for other sources of information which might influence the students' views in conflicting ways and which might also relate to why teaching practice takes the form that it does.

ELT in Japan: The Commercial Sector

Chapter 4 discussed issues about the relationship between policy and practice in institutional education, but the focus, as in many studies, was on government-run or accredited institutions which constitute the official mainstream. The most visible context in which the actualities of language learning within Japanese society clash with current trends and recommendations in contemporary TESOL theory is that of the commercial language school, or *eikaiwa* industry. Given that these organizations are first and foremost commercial businesses, the promotion of their services is likely to tend toward the saleable rather than the pedagogically sound. If the image of academic excellence appeals and is believable, it is probably of little concern how orthodox or effective it is. Yet these establishments occupy such a prominent position in society that the image they promote of successful language teaching will both reflect what is perceived within society as being correct and desirable practice (and for this reason most likely to appeal to the widest population) while also influencing the way in which the language is viewed. Their commercial popularism means that they are the propagators of stereotype, drawing on pre-existent attitudes within society and then molding these into a cohesive and influential narrative of the aspirational benefits of education. In terms of the shaping of the concept of the language in society therefore, their influence is likely to be great.

Within Japan there are a handful of major chains of commercial language school (e.g. Geos, ECC, Aeon, Berlitz and Nova/G.Communications) with branches in cities and towns throughout the country, as well as innumerable smaller independent outfits. Foreign language schools represent a 670 billion yen industry, of which the large chains account for 25%.[2] These operate extensive and aggressive advertising campaigns in both print and television regularly featuring major Japanese and international celebrities in their promotions, and have a very high profile and strong brand recognition. Specializing in communicative English, or 'conversation classes' [*eikaiwa*], these establishments draw students from all geographical, social and age groups, including those who are enrolled elsewhere in secondary or higher education English language programmes (McVeigh, 2002). Their popularity and brand image relies heavily on their ability to provide language instruction that differs from that based on the grammar–translation method that is traditionally used at school. To do this, they stress an idea of 'real' communication which is achieved by authentic interaction with the language.

Promotional literature from the Nova Group,[3] for example, outlines a proprietary teaching system ('The Nova System Concept'), which had as its two key selling points the fact that 'the teachers are all native-speaker foreigners' and that class sizes are kept small. The publicity goes on to explain

> To become able to speak a foreign language the most important thing is practice. For example, for skiing theoretical knowledge is of course important, but unless you actually ski down the slope you will never become good. The more you ski the better you become, and so also the more you actually speak a foreign language the better you become at it. At Nova we use the 'direct method' style of teaching, where our native-speaker teachers never speak a word of Japanese and you get into the habit of thinking about a foreign language in that foreign language.[4]

The assumption here is very clearly that real practice requires that the interlocutor be a native speaker. It ties the idea of communicative practice to the native speaker as if they were logical equivalents, an effect which is further enhanced by adorning promotional pamphlets, adverts and Web sites with photographs of Caucasians enacting the role of a well-dressed instructor (Bailey, 2006). The 'authenticity' stressed here refers to interaction rather than text, demoting the language to being of secondary importance in comparison to the teacher's cultural status.

At this stage, it is worth briefly discussing the definition and use of the term 'native speaker'. The scrutiny that the phrase has attracted in applied linguistics literature in recent years (e.g. Cook, 1999; Davies, 2003; Paikeday, 1985) has drawn attention to the ambiguity and problematic nature of the concept, and the complex questions it poses about the relationship between 'native' status, language expertise and language loyalty. For many, the term is regarded as offensive – Jenkins (2000) describes it as an anachronism now – and various terminological and conceptual alternatives have been suggested. Within publicity such as that quoted above, however, the term is, as Davies (2003: 7) puts it, 'not intended to be exact, rather it is an appeal to commonsense, to use a difficult and uncertain concept which is at the same time a useful piece of shorthand'. Despite the claims for the pedagogical effectiveness of the 'method' of the Nova school, such institutions are operating as commercial concerns, and thus their promotion is motivated to a great extent by what they consider to be most saleable. In this context, the 'native speaker' is promoted as a key selling point and becomes a symbol that both represents 'authentic' communication-oriented English while also adhering to the exoticised use of the image of the foreigner that is so widespread in advertising campaigns in Japan in general (Creighton, 1995). It is an image rather than a pedagogical precept, and the implications this has for both the perception of the English language and what happens within the classroom are likely to be considerable. As McVeigh (2002: 167) writes

> The advertising tactics of many commercial English schools rely on superficialities to attract customers (images of 'foreign' blue-eyed and blonde women or smiling, well-dressed, and handsome men). Some commercial schools literally hire non-Japanese off the streets on racial appearances alone.... Such superficialities and images of the English learning business are confused with genuine learning activities in the classroom.

It is in ways such as this, then, that advertising strategy is likely to affect directly the teaching methods within the classroom, promoting a particular image for commercial purposes which then becomes accepted as the pedagogical norm. In this context, therefore, the 'native' part of the formulation would seem to be more important than the 'speaker' part. And the term 'native speaker' in this instance is not being used as a clumsy and unthought-out synonym for expert target language speaker so much as being cited specifically for the person's social or cultural connotations.

The Nova promotional literature, in fact, takes the process one step further. It goes on to offer a 'scientific' explanation for the difficulties that the average Japanese person experiences when learning English and which can apparently be remedied by regular interaction with a native speaker. In doing so, the literature introduces explicit racial stereotyping to the debate:

> The truth is that the English and Japanese languages exist on different wave lengths. For this reason, a normal Japanese person's brain cannot distinguish English which is on the non-Japanese wave length from noise, and thus can't catch what is spoken in English.... It is important to listen repeatedly to and speak with native speakers in order to activate the language field within our brain.

Complete with diagrams illustrating the brain activity of a typical Japanese university student and the difficulties such a person has grappling with unfamiliar wave lengths (see Figure 6.1), this type of campaign is far removed from the utopian EIL project of a truly international language. Statements such as these specifically posit racial differences as fundamental for linguistic ability, and the English language thus becomes not just the property of those born and raised in an English-speaking environment but also a genetic trait; the specific language is here being presented as having an ontic reality in the brain. Arguments of this sort are reminiscent of the assertions that Japanese and Western brains are demonstrably different which were made by Tsunoda Tadanobu in the 1970s and which are related to the aforementioned *Nihonjinron* discourse (Dale, 1986; Kubota, 1998). Nova's campaign would seem to claim that English be considered a specifically foreign entity and not a natural part of Japanese society. Thus, despite the frequent use of the 'international' tag that also decorates such campaigns, what is promoted as being on offer is far more the traditional EFL ideal, the language as representative of a particular foreign culture.

Though campaigns which make such extensive use of the image of the native speaker are most noticeable in the commercial language schools, a similar, albeit less extreme, process can be seen in Japanese higher education institutions as well. Especially in terms of employment patterns, here too it is predominantly native speakers who are hired as language instructors, while very few other positions are open to foreign academics, thus encouraging a professional stereotype on campus (Hall, 1998). Social organization of this sort becomes another mode for articulating the prevailing ideology that is elsewhere expressed in word and image in promotional campaigns such as that of the Nova school. Furthermore, with a large proportion of Japanese universities being privately run, and with student

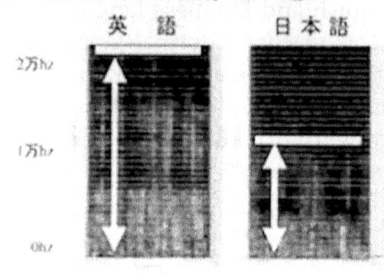

Figure 6.1 Nova's diagram of contrastive 'wave-lengths' for Japanese and English

numbers falling in recent years, advertising campaigns are becoming ever more important for the higher education sector of the market as well, and these are beginning to adopt similar strategies to the commercial language schools, with images of native speakers being featured prominently in promotional literature. The logic of the consumerist society can therefore be seen to be spreading into the mainstream of institutional education. Within this context the idea of English education as a product, carefully constructed and tailored to the needs and expectations of the market, becomes a significant factor in the way the language exists within society and one that vies with pedagogic theory for influence over the way the language is learnt.

The McUniversity and Theme Park Education

The increasingly consumerist nature of higher education within the global context has been memorably cast in metaphor by Ritzer's concept of the McUniversity (1996a), an elaboration upon his theory of the McDonaldization of society (1996b). He identifies the way in which

> [a]dministrators are coming to recognise that their educational campuses need to grow more like the other new means of consumption to thrive... The university... can be seen as a means of educational consumption. These days most campuses are dated, stodgy, and ineffective compared to shopping malls, cruise ships, casinos, and fast food restaurants. To compete, universities are trying to satisfy their students by offering, for example, 'theme housing' – dorms devoted to students with shared special interests. As universities learn more and more from the new means of consumption, it will be increasingly possible and accurate to refer to them as 'McUniversities'. (1999: 24)

Ritzer's research is based on the contemporary United States model, but it is instructive also for a country like Japan which has developed an almost hyper-consumerist society (Clammer, 1997). Again it is the commercial language schools which have been taking the lead in this process of evolution. Ritzer (1996a: 190) suggests that universities will soon be opening up 'small educational satellites' near shopping malls and within easy access of good parking facilities, and already a business strategy of this sort can be seen in the *eikaiwa* industry. The Nova Group called its schools *ekimae ryugaku* or 'foreign study in front of the station', and their branches are always located adjacent to a main transport hub or shopping thoroughfare, while a central strand of their promotion is the convenience and flexibility they offer to students. When G. Communications bought the business it was these features which it retained. Certain branches of Berlitz, meanwhile, now share floor space with Starbucks, and as has been discussed in Chapter 2, the Shogakukan company has held language lessons for children inside McDonald's restaurants, with lesson content taken from the menu. Doubtless many of the employees at *eikaiwa* institutions would also recognize Ritzer's picture of a system in which '[t]heir pay, like those employed in fast-food restaurants, will be low and their benefits few, if any. Also as in the case of fast food restaurants, rules, regulations, system-wide syllabuses and constraints of all types will abound' (1996a: 192). Among the other effects of this process are the standardizing of the 'product' that is on sale (by means of such things as the company-wide use of a particular text book and a regulated 'method' of pedagogy, all of which work against promoting the diverse identities and incarnations of the language) and the importance of positioning that product as a desirable commodity. This is achieved through extensive publicity and, as is the trend in modern advertising strategies, the product sold becomes less the physical (or in this case educational) commodity than the image and the lifestyle fantasy that are projected along with it.

Borrowing Baudrillard's (1994) concept of 'implosion' – the merging of two discrete concepts under the influence of consumption – Ritzer surveys the multifarious ways in which distinct and separate institutions, which would formerly have been perceived as having differing if not incompatible objectives, are now combining to create an environment that places the principles of consumerism at its very heart. As an instance of such implosion, he notes a tendency in higher education whereby 'educational institutions are growing more and more like theme parks' (Ritzer, 1999: 142). This is, in many ways, a logical development of the advertising strategies employed by commercial schools. The aspirational symbolism which is connected with education and so often exploited in advertising for educational institutions is reified by the theme park with its creation of a total fantasy environment. For the study of foreign languages, and the relationship they have with both foreign travel and foreign culture, this implosion seems even more intuitive. Which returns us to British Hills, a fully realized combination of educational establishment and theme park. Whether the Ritzer prophecy which suggests places such as this comprise the future of education will come true remains to be seen, yet this one case does offer a compellingly bold example of the way that a theme-park approach to education, which demonstrates that other Baudrillardian concept of 'simulation' (1983, 1994), contributes to the construction of the symbolic meaning of English.

The Simulation of Authenticity in English Language Practice

As well as its use in the terminology of cultural theory, 'simulation' is another technical term from education practice and is a standard technique in language teaching (Bambrough, 1994; Jones, 1982), again identified with moves in the late 1970s toward the communicative approach.

It involves students imagining themselves in 'real-life' situations in which their English language skills will be exercised. As Sturtridge (1981: 126) says

> Among classroom activities role-play and simulation rate highly as suitable vehicles to use in a communicative approach to language teaching. Used well, they can reduce the artificiality of the classroom, provide a reason for talking and allow the learner to talk meaningfully to other learners.

The theory is that the language behavior of the learner is actually altered by imagining themselves in the role of fluent speaker.

The British Hills model can perhaps be seen as an extreme example of this approach. Though role-play by the students is limited, much is made of the idea that they can experience foreign travel and study abroad without having to leave Japan, so casting them in the role of imaginary tourists. Thus, language learning within the park complex is seen as something that is not restricted to the classroom but spreads to all encounters that occur within the perimeters of the park, thus allowing the organization to offer an experience that is almost the polar opposite of the traditional reading- and grammar-based language class of the high-school curriculum. Yet while there may well be language learning benefits to a system that immerses students in an enforced monolingual environment of this sort – especially in a country where such opportunities are severely limited – there are other effects of the way the language is presented within this controlled context which ensure that this learning experience has a particular ideological bent.

The concept of the 'native speaker' is regarded here, too, as a badge of authenticity for the environment that is being created. As the recruiting guide explains, 'British Hills can employ Japanese service staff at a fraction of the cost we pay our foreigners, but it [is] the friendly foreign faces we are looking for.' The fact that the staff are employed as much for their status as cultural specimens as for their substantive work is further indicated by guidelines in their job description:

> A visit to British Hills for many of our younger students is the first chance they have had to speak with a variety of foreigners.... The following thus also form a central part of all service staff members' duties:
>
> - Meeting buses arriving at British Hills with a friendly hello and lots of waving.
> - Being on the steps to wave goodbye to groups leaving British Hills.

- Taking the time to stop in the passages/ in your department to CHAT to the guests.
- Being sociable and friendly to all guests: whether on or off duty.
- Offering to take and star in hundreds of photographs.
- Basically just going the extra mile to make that personal connection with as many guests as possible.

Elsewhere in the regulations, foreign staff are prohibited from speaking Japanese. Furthermore, despite claims for the authenticity of the English/Britishness of the place, there is a certain ambivalence to the exact nature of the foreign culture that is being simulated. Recruitment is not limited to those with a British passport but also includes citizens of Canada, Australia and New Zealand (US citizens are excluded due, apparently, to visa restrictions); and the overseas recruiting office is in fact located in British Columbia. This amalgamation of all English-speaking countries within the popular imagination is also reflected in the syllabus for the high school/university Global Communication Course that is offered at British Hills and which culminates in a simulated 'Day Abroad, so [as] to test [students] in a realistic way. Thus, evaluating their ability to have a successful homestay in the US the following year.' So while the simulation insists on a monolingual environment that is at odds with the reality of contemporary multilingual Britain, it creates an image of the language as a singular and homogenous entity spoken by a select group of nationalities, rather than one with culturally specific varieties. The totalizing fallacy is enacted here, then, in both curriculum design and personnel recruitment.

As Ritzer has noted, simulation within contemporary society produces an enhanced version of reality, and within the context of the logic of consumerism 'the motivation behind these transformations is that the "real" sites are no longer spectacular enough to attract tourists and tier money.... The increasing demand for a spectacle necessitates greater use of simulations' (1999: 126). The *gaikoku mura* types of theme park justify their existence by claiming to be convenient alternatives to the real tourist destinations (no need for passports or expensive overseas flights) but also often by offering their visitors something better than the original. For example, Hendry (2000b: 15) remarks on how this attitude is reflected at the Maruyama Shakespeare Country Park:

> [The] Japanese park where [there is] a reconstruction of the birthplace of William Shakespeare ... is presented as more like the original home of the 'bard' than the twentieth-century 'real' place in Henley Street,

Stratford-upon-Avon, on the grounds that the house would have been newer and cleaner when he lived in it.

British Hills also attests to this logic in its slogan claiming that the place is 'More English than England itself', and in the several references to the absence of flaws such as crime, graffiti and other forms of antisocial behavior which sadly blight the real United Kingdom. The simulation that comes from the strictly regulated behavior of the staff also produces a more comfortable version of reality. The overall effect is to create an environment which is not necessarily truthful to the original upon which it is purportedly based but is instead an imagined ideal with its own logic and reality. The authenticity upon which British Hills prides itself is not a representation of Britishness as it is currently constructed and enacted in multifarious ways in mainstream British society. Instead, it is an image drawn from aspects of the popular imagination in Japan, from a tourist industry template (which in itself has a complicated provenance, being a mixture of self-promotion by British tourist and cultural organizations as well as Japanese expectations) and also from local protocol for foreign language education. The claim to authenticity then gives it an authority and cohesion in the eyes of the consumer, and the effect is to create an account of English-speaking culture which accords with commercial and ideological interests within the country.

Baudrillard (1994: 6) writes of the new order of reality created by simulation:

> Representation stems from the principle of the equivalence of the sign and of the real. Simulation, on the contrary, stems from the utopia of the principle of equivalence, *from the radical negation of the sign as value*, from the sign as the reversion and death sentence of every reference. Whereas representation attempts to absorb simulation by interpreting it as a false representation, simulation envelops the whole edifice of representation itself as a simulacrum.

The sense here is that the simulation replaces reality, becomes its own reality. A place like British Hills is not merely representing Britishness but reconstructing it, thus presenting itself as a detailed realistic image of something that actually exists only within its own depiction. The use of the concept of authenticity is almost an irony of the process, yet as I suggested earlier, the conflation between the genuine and a convincing copy is a persistent presence within the meaning of the word and thus is often emblematic of the process of simulation. As the concept of authenticity only exists where there is initial doubt about what is authentic, the attempts to convince others of this authenticity are themselves a simulation in that they distort or enhance the original to (im)prove its value.

One of the major consequences of the British Hills simulation is the segregated nature it presents of the existence of the English language within Japan. By suggesting by means of its organization and operational procedures that the authentic nature of English requires this culturally exotic environment and that 'real' language practice can only be achieved in encounters with the 'native speakers' who staff the place, English is firmly positioned here as being separate from the mainstream of Japanese society. It is an attitude that can be seen reflected elsewhere in society. For example, in 2003, the English conversation school Geos announced a plan to team up with the Japan Travel Bureau (JTB) to create another opportunity for students to 'study abroad' without leaving Japan. They could do this by attending the company's 'Tobidase! English Camp', a holiday camp providing a foreign environment and staffed entirely by native speakers of English. Again, the stress is on a quarantined education experience and an ethnically different interlocutor. By symbolically positioning English outside the boundary of mainstream society and creating purpose-built enclaves within which to accommodate it, the perception is created that the language is forever foreign. Kramsch (1998a: 28) writes of the way that '[t]raditional methodologies based on the native speaker usually define language learners in terms of what they are *not*', and this sentiment would seem to be monumentalized by elaborate simulations such as British Hills. Furthermore, by embedding such segregation within the environment of the theme park, the language is presented as one component of a fantasy world and is symbolically stripped of its real-life utility value.

Conclusion

Places such as British Hills and the Nova schools present examples of social practice built around language which produce a very particular idea of that language. Their conception of the language, however, does not in any real sense resemble the ideas that inform the current TESOL debate about the status of English as a global language. Indeed, the cultural meaning of the language as promoted through these schools would seem to pre-empt or prejudice any attempts by TESOL theory to further a workable model of English as a neutral lingua franca. On one level, this situation could be characterized as a straight clash between commercial concerns and pedagogy, yet the use and influence of the images that are employed to further commercial ventures have wide social penetration and thus play significant roles in the way the language as a concept is perceived. The examples here are not, of course, meant to be representative of the whole Japanese foreign language education system, or as being exclusive to Japan. Indeed, it is the ways they differ from what might be called the mainstream of institutional education that makes them of particular interest. Representing alternative perspectives on language-related social practice, they offer an opportunity to examine how issues of linguistic ownership and cultural identification are processed away from the centralized curriculum.

The claim to authenticity as it is used here and in ELT theory, invokes an authority which would stabilize or legitimize its object. Applied to the English language it makes assertions about the validity and orthodoxy of the type of language it promotes, yet the associated process of simulation, rather than deferring to a pre-existing essential concept of the language, reconfigures the meaning of the language within the localized context in which it is operating. The management of this meaning by the local culture is as much a product of domestic cultural, commercial and political concerns as of wider global issues, and thus gives rise not only to a different variety of the language but also to a different conceptual perspective of what English can mean as a global phenomenon. Again, the idea of the language can be a determining cultural force in its own right, but it also predisposes people to approach the language in a very specific way. It is this personal relationship between individual and language that will be explored in Chapter 7.

Chapter 7
Aspiration: 'Enhancing Lifestyles and Living Out Dreams'

A Desire for English

The motifs of 'globalization' and 'authenticity' position English within the world and regulate the shape of the language that is taught and used; they construct its status as a world language and direct the debate about its 'essential' nature and the expediencies of adopting one variety over another. The final motif I wish to examine is one which reflects the relationship that people actually take toward the language. For if globalization is the *where*, authenticity the *what*, then 'aspiration' is the *why*. The popularity of English among the Japanese, be it as a subject of study, a resource to be cited in product design and other forms of cultural display or as a linguistic code for lingua franca purposes, is a topic oft commented upon (e.g. McVeigh, 2002; Strevens, 1992), and in this chapter, I wish to explore the specific characteristics of this popularity and analyze the terms and means by which it is expressed.

As an area of investigation, the importance of the relationship that people take toward the language is twofold. Firstly, the *why* determines the *what*. In other words, the reasons why one is attracted to a language will relate to the beliefs one has about the purpose of that language, and these in turn will influence convictions about the shape and nature of the language. To put this in another way: if I am attracted to a language for some specific reason or purpose, it is likely that I will wish to learn a form of that language that will best allow me to fulfill that purpose. This, at least, is the assumption that underpins foundational statements on global English such as Quirk's (1985: 6) advocacy of a 'single monochrome standard' for the communicative needs of the average learner, or Jenkins's (2000: 11) rationalization that 'ELF emphasises the role of English in communication between speakers from different L1s, i.e. the primary reason for learning English today'. In both these cases, specific functional concerns are cited as the rationale for the form of the language which is then promoted.

The second point is that attitudes toward the language often relate directly to the cultural associations that the language has. Motivation for learning a particular language is likely to be linked both to empirically based observations about the place of that language within society, as well as to mediated impressions about the wider existence of that language. The language desired is never culturally indeterminate, but will instead be viewed as a specific resource situated within a complex of cultural narratives. Indeed, it is the *idea* of the language which will, in fact, be the object of the desire, as the foreign language itself is, by definition, an as yet unknown quantity. A discourse of desire for the language, therefore, acts as a rich index of the symbolic meanings with which the language is imbued.

This chapter will thus explore the relationship between 'aspiration' and the learning of English within the context of its status as a global language, identifying a 'desire for English' as another key motif in the ideology of the language as it attracts the interest of learners in Japan. The focus will initially be on the way a discourse of aspiration is presented in the promotion of the English language in marketing strategies for educational institutions, as well as in the educational policy pronouncements discussed in Chapter 4. This will then be cross-referenced with the narratives and commentary of a selection of Japanese citizens for whom English has been an important part of the academic career. Soliciting their attitudes to the language, and surveying the conceptual vocabulary they use to rationalize these attitudes, can provide an ancillary frame of reference for the discourses in educational policy and promotional literature. As with earlier chapters, the focus will be upon the way in which conceptions of the language are situated within broader discourses both about Japanese society and culture (and specifically the key issue of cultural identity within the context of globalization) on the one hand, and about language in general on the other.

Aspiration and Education

Aspiration and personal betterment can be seen as a general educational precept. David Halpin, in his book on *Hope and Education*, writes of the way 'the process of education... entails working positively with what is initially given in order to realise something that is imminent and wished for' (2003: 15). It is certainly the case that in postcompulsory education, where institutions wishing to promote their services appeal to the agency of the learner, metaphors of hope and aspiration are rife.

A brief look at the advertising slogans of a selection of universities in the UK and in Japan reveals this as a key trope for attracting students (see Figure 7.1):

- 'Yôkoso tôkyô gaikokugo daigaku e [Welcome to Tokyo University of Foreign Studies]. Do you have a dream?' (Tokyo University of Foreign Studies, 2005)
- 'Yume wo mitsukaru haru no ôpun kyanpasu [Find your dream at the spring Open Campus event]' (Nagoya University of Commerce and Business, 2005)
- 'Become what you want to be' (London South Bank University, 2005)
- 'Realise your full potential' (Glasgow Caledonian University, 2005)

These and similar slogans usually appeal to two broad beliefs about personal betterment: the first being that through education one can enhance one's knowledge in order to create more opportunities for life; the second, that education will allow one to discover and draw out one's hidden potentialities. In both cases, the process is seen as a personal project, related to the life course of the individual (rather than being for the benefit of society), and as something that exists on the imaginary plane (in the mind of the prospective student) and is merely awaiting the catalytic input of the educational experience. For broad audiences such as those addressed by the publicity for an entire university, the nature of the aspiration is clearly extremely general, as in these examples. Narratives of aspiration relating to specific forms of knowledge however, while

Figure 7.1 The 'aspiration' motif in university publicity

retaining this individualized and imminent character, are based in much greater detail upon assumptions about the nature of that specific field of knowledge.

Motivation and Language Learning

The most enduringly influential strand of research on the relationship between disposition to a foreign language and language learning has been that conducted since the early 1970s by the social psychologist Robert Gardner and his associates. In his work with Wallace Lambert (1972), Gardner suggested two broad categories of motivational orientation toward a foreign language: the 'integrative' and the 'instrumental'. The former of these relates to motivation which is based upon a wish to identify with a particular group or culture, and to master the language in order to integrate oneself within that speech community. As Skehan (1989: 53) summarizes, 'those people who identify positively in this way would like to resemble the foreign peoples concerned, to understand their culture, and to be able to participate in it'. The alternative is instrumental orientation, which is concerned instead with the benefits that proficiency in the language can bring for the learner's life within his or her own culture, including factors such as access to improved employment opportunities and other aspects of professional development. Within social psychology, which looks to quantify the role that attitudes play in the attainment of linguistic competency, these categories have been the subject of much critique and refinement (see Dörnyei, 2005 for extended discussion), yet as Baker (1992: 31) observes, the broad distinction is one that has been identified in attitudes to language learning by '[r]esearchers across boundaries of time, sample and nation'.

The interest of this current study is not on the extent to which aspirational ideals do or do not operate as successful motivation for language learning, but rather on *how* it is that they are associated with the concept and practice of language learning, both in the marketing strategies of language-linked products and in the rationalizations of language learners. In other words, my interest is in the way that this concept of aspiration is discursively constructed, and in how it informs aspects of the way in which the language itself is perceived.

There is, however, a specific motivation for beginning with the distinction posited by Gardner and Lambert, and that is the almost exact match that the categories have with the major distinction that operates in a traditional understanding of Expanding Circle global English situations. That is to say, there are salient similarities between an integrative orientation and an EFL model of language learning, and between an instrumental orientation and an EIL or ELF model. The integrative attitude to a particular language concerns identification with a particular language group and their cultural pursuits, and in this respect it parallels the traditional definition of English as a foreign language (EFL), where the language is purportedly learnt for the purpose of participating in the life of the community who speak it. An instrumental orientation, which views the language in more utilitarian terms, has similar parallels to the English as an international or lingua franca paradigms (EIL/ELF), where the language is primarily looked upon as a tool for communication in diverse world settings, and not as a heuristic for understanding foreign culture. Given these parallels this initial distinction and its theoretical vocabulary can usefully be adopted as a starting point for the examination of the discourses of aspiration and language learning. What is necessary, however, is to build on these foundations by means of an inductive approach which analyzes the discourses on motivation and desire for language as they actually appear in textual and other semiotic articulation in the Japanese context. In this way, we can attempt to map the patterns of behavior and belief which constitute the ideologies that are formed in the relationship between the individual and the English language. To this end, let us look at a number of examples.

'Audacious Life Goals'

The Gaba company is a relative newcomer in the commercial language school [*eikaiwa*] industry, but in recent years it has become a rival to the major chains (Geos, ECC, Aeon, Berlitz and Nova/G.Communication) and has been expanding from its Tokyo base to open branches across Japan. Part of its expansion strategy has been an intensive promotional campaign, which draws upon a similar rhetoric of aspiration as that used by the higher education institutions discussed above. The company's slogan, for example, is far from modest in its ambition to be 'Giving people the opportunity to achieve their most audacious life goal', while its mission statement extends the claim in the explicit aspirational associations it makes for the English language:

> Gaba [language school] is all about enhancing lifestyles and living out dreams. Learning to communicate in English is only the beginning – as a result of improved language skills people can realise greater potential in their careers, relationships, and themselves.[1]

The statements here are that much more hyperbolic than the university adverts, no doubt because the company resides in the private sector and

Aspiration: 'Living Out Dreams' 111

is thus less regulated in terms of its promotional activities. Of particular note, though, are the three domains in which the transformative influence of English education is claimed to operate: in enhancing *careers* and *relationships*, as well as *the self* in its abstract entirety. Dissecting the life project in this way is characteristic of the genre, and offers us an initial taxonomy of aspiration discourses in the Japanese context. I will expand upon these in more detail below, but before doing so we can look in detail at an example from Gaba's advertising campaign which draws directly on the imaginary relationship with English language ability and some unrealized ambition or flight of fancy, and thus provides a rich illustration of many of the themes and strategies that constitute this discourse.

The advertisement in Figure 7.2 was run in the autumn of 2005. It consists of a self-reflexive question asking 'What would I do if I could speak English?' [*Moshimo watashi ga eigo wo hanasetara!?*], followed by a host of responses from members of the public. Each response is only a sentence long, and is accompanied by a description of the employment status of the interviewee.[2] There are, in total, approximately 100 replies on the poster, which was displayed on public transport and in magazines.

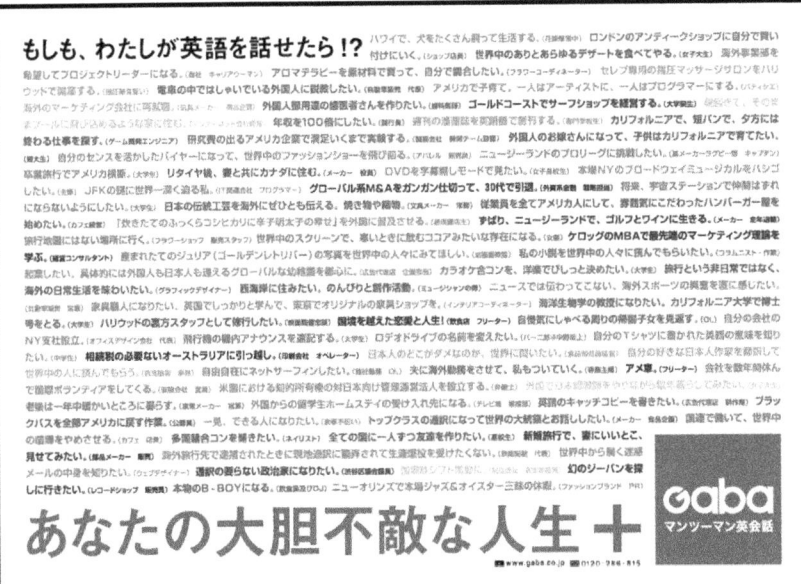

Figure 7.2 Gaba language school advert

Among the many enigmatic responses to the lead question are the following:

(1) I would live in Hawaii with several dogs (*Trainee bride [hanayome shûgyô chû]*).
(2) I would go shopping in London's antique stores by myself (*Shop clerk*).
(3) I would eat all the desserts in the world! (*Female university student*).
(4) I would buy aromatherapy materials and prepare them myself (*Flower arranger*).
(5) I would open a *shiatsu* massage parlor for celebrities in Hollywood (*Apprentice masseuse*).
(6) I would scold noisy foreigners on the train (*Car salesroom owner*).
(7) I would bring up my children in America: one as an artist, the other as a computer programmer (*Pastry chef*).
(8) I would start a dental practice for foreigners (*Dentist*).
(9) I would run a surfing store on the Gold Coast (*Graduate student*).
(10) I would live in a house where I could wake up and dive straight into the pool (*Internet company manager*).
(11) I would increase my salary one hundred times (*Bank worker*).
(12) I would look for a job in California that I could go to in shorts and that would end in the early evening (*Vocational college student*).
(13) I would become the wife of a foreigner and raise some kids in California (*Junior college student*).
(14) I would watch DVDs without subtitles (*Female high school student*).
(15) I would watch one musical after another on Broadway (*Housewife*).
(16) I would become the world-expert on the JFK mystery (*IT company programmer*).
(17) In the future, I would not wish to become isolated from my friends on the Space Station (*University student*).
(18) I would introduce the traditional Japanese arts of ceramics and knitting to the world (*Stationery manufacturer*).

In considering the patterns of association between language and other social or cultural factors, a first general comment about the strategy used here is that it promotes wish-fulfillment as a prompt for language learning. English is positioned as *the* agent of change in people's lives; as the talisman that can effect their dream fulfillment. The second point of note is that several of the ambitions have little or no direct relationship to English ability, but are general desires about lifestyle change. As such, the English language transcends its usual status as a means of (global) communication, and becomes instead a solution to any unspecified Weltschmerz or dissatisfaction with one's current lot.

Examining the distribution of answers a little more closely we can discern certain specific patterns. Common to many of the answers is a general internationalism and the desire for geographical mobility (most often targeted at the United States). In addition, there are frequent associations with various forms of consumption ('shopping in antique stores' (2); 'eating all the deserts in the world' (3)), and with material gain ('increasing my salary one hundred times' (11)) – indeed career ambitions feature especially strongly, and often involve starting up one's own business (surfing shop (9), dental practice (8) and so on). A further noticeable strand is images of freedom and independence, either in everyday activities ('going to work in shorts' (12); 'diving straight into the pool' (10)), related to one's profession ('preparing my own aromatherapy materials' (4)), or as general associations with leisure activities ('watching DVDs' (14); 'seeing shows on Broadway' (15)). Gender-specific answers are not foregrounded to any great extent, but two of the participants express a desire to bring up their children abroad (7, 13), while the junior college student explicitly states her ambition as being to marry a foreigner.

The overall impression, then, appears to be that a lack of English ability is seen to tie one to the expectations and limitations of Japanese society, whereas speaking the language removes these restraints and offers free passage to alternative (Western) futures. Although English features as an ingredient in many (though not all) of the scenarios, the substance of nearly all of them is more to do with social mobility and a desire for an imaginary Western archetype of lifestyle. Two noticeable exceptions are the car showroom manager who would use his English language abilities to 'scold noisy foreigners on the train' (6), and the stationery manufacturer who would 'introduce the traditional Japanese arts of ceramics and knitting to the world' (18). Both of these exhibit a trace of nationalism, the latter being an example of the 'promulgation function' of English that I discussed in Chapter 6, while the former constructs particular negative associations with the English language and its 'foreign' heritage.

To draw on the terminology of Gardner and Lambert's motivation orientations, the majority of the responses in the advert appear to be of the order of integrative motivation, in that they cite specific aspects of international or English-speaking culture as a stimulus for learning. Instrumental motivation features in the desire to increase one's income (11) and to lecture the loud foreigners on the train (6), but mostly the benefits are transposed away from the native culture, and the discourse points in a Westerly direction. In terms of global English classifications, the scenarios would likely best be served by an EFL approach. However, it is the cultural details of the ambitions rather than the general distinction between integrative and instrumental orientation which are of importance for understanding the underlying ideologies of the language, and it is these, therefore, which we will need to examine in more theoretical detail, and to which I will return below. Firstly, though, let us consider a further example.

Language, Travel and Social Mobility

Another genre in which aspirational ideas are linked directly to English ability is the promotion of study abroad or *ryûgaku* programmes. Partly due to the general economic prosperity of the average Japanese citizen (Kobayashi, 2007), services offering short to long-term educational opportunities abroad have been something of a boom industry in Japan over the past two decades. The opportunities for a mixture of travel and education are especially popular among women due to the fact that, according to Kelsky (1999: 233–234)

> many Japanese women are faced with persistent discrimination in the workplace based on gender and age...[S]upported by a deeply entrenched gender division of labour in society, women require an alternative, and travel, study, or work abroad is it.

Magazines such as *Wish* (Figure 7.3) – the title of which itself announces its aspirational credentials – cater specifically to this market, and provide listings of study abroad programmes as well as articles about the experiences of those who have taken part in such programmes. The rhetoric of the articles draws on the same vocabulary as that used in adverts for language schools, with references to 'dreams' and 'life-changing' experiences very much to the fore.

It is not only the verbally articulated content of these publications which contributes to the discourse of aspiration though. Other semiotic resources also assist, as can be seen in the composition of the image on the front cover depicted in Figure 7.3 (*Wish*, Vol. 24, Autumn–Winter 2005). Framed by a list of articles typical of the genre, on subjects such as 'Exciting New York Life' and 'Expand[ing] Your Job Opportunities', the cover shows a young woman on a New York street who is looking purposefully off into the distance. The message encoded here, especially in terms of the social relationship between audience and model, is very much a complement to the attitudes expressed throughout the magazine, as can be shown by an analysis of the image's composition.

In their work on visual representation, Kress and van Leeuwen (2006) draw upon the theoretical framework of social semiotics (Halliday, 1978)

Aspiration: 'Living Out Dreams' 115

Figure 7.3 Study abroad magazine *Wish*

to provide a descriptive 'grammar' of the way in which visual texts are composed of conventionalized relations of form, color and composition in order to convey culturally specific meanings. This 'grammar' makes explicit what is procedurally practiced in everyday acts of visual literacy, in which we 'read' images in a way analogous to the reading of verbal texts. The social semiotics framework in which this theory is grounded draws particular attention to the way in which any act of communication expresses not only referential meaning, but also information about the social relationships between participants. And a number of the conventionalized features of representation that are explicated by Kress and van Leeuwen's theory are present in this cover image, and can thus be used to analyze its meaning.

Firstly, the direction of the woman's gaze is of significance (p. 181), as she is pointing 'forward' within the context of the conventional reading path of the Japanese language. That is to say, although the text on the cover is written in a Western style in terms of its left-right orientation, the magazine structure is in the traditional Japanese format with the binding on the right, and thus the metaphor of backward and forward runs right to left within the composition. The woman is therefore looking 'ahead' in metaphoric terms. Also of note is the angle of the shot, and the resultant positioning of the model in relation to the audience. As Kress and van Leeuwen note, when the represented participant is depicted from a low angle, the impression is one of symbolic power over the viewer (p. 140). The impression created by this composition as a whole, then, is of an individual agent exhibiting a sense of personal empowerment and of direction in life; and this image operates as the abstract for the conventional narrative of the study abroad experience, which is reproduced in the adverts and articles included inside.

Another magazine in this genre is *Ryûgaku Access*, published by ALC (Associated Liberal Creators), a company which specializes in language learning resources. Their products consist mainly of self-study books, the 'Study Abroad Almanac' [*Ryûgaku Jiten*] and their flagship publication, 'English Journal', a twin-text magazine covering current affairs stories composed specifically for the English language learner. Their *Ryûgaku Jiten* series is a set of yearly publications listing worldwide study abroad programmes, with data collated from national surveys such as the RAE in the UK. The company produces several editions of the almanac, each focusing on a different country, level of educational institution or academic specialization (e.g. the *Daigakuin Ryûgaku Jiten* for postgraduate study and the *Gogaku Ryûgaku Jiten* for language courses).

Ryûgaku Access, which is an off-shoot of this series, is something of a hybrid publication, combining both the substantive listings section, as well as a lifestyle magazine section featuring articles focusing on aspects of the study abroad experience. As its name suggests, the magazine is aimed at people who have not yet decided on what sort of study they wish to pursue abroad, and are thus looking for an introduction to the possibilities available. *Ryûgaku Access*, like *Wish*, is a quarterly publication, and therefore positions itself very much within the lifestyle magazine sector, and in this way appeals to a far wider audience than other annual educational listings publications, such as those for university entrance.

Although the articles are about study abroad opportunities in general (touching on subjects ranging from aromatherapy to web design), the learning of English and the rewards this brings is nearly always presented as an essential part of the process. Indeed, the study abroad concept specifically marries the affordances of foreign language competence with the key aspirational motifs of travel and lifestyle change. The imagery of the independent journey, valorized both as a literal and metaphoric goal in these narratives, is seen to be dependent on foreign language expertise. In a country where it is often not financial restrictions that prohibit travel opportunities, one of the greatest impediments to launching out on voyages of self-discovery is the fear of being unable to operate in the foreign culture. If this can be effectively overcome through a period of dedicated study, then the horizons of ambition, it is implied, are endless.

Along with the logic of this juxtaposition of English with other key aspirational motifs, another important factor that contributes to the discourse is the means and modality of the representation. The reading above of the cover of *Wish* suggested that the central narrative of English as a catalyst for empowerment and individual self-realization is not restricted to explicit statements about the benefits of learning the language, but is articulated through a holistic semiotic process. An equally powerful component of this is the use of particular genres of representation to persuade an audience of the truthfulness of the claims being made.

We can examine the effect that genre produces by analyzing a specific example and considering the way in which English is positioned within the narrative of the study abroad experience. Volume 4 from 2006 of *Ryûgaku Access* has, as one of its lead features, a series entitled 'The desired self, and work that that gives satisfaction' [*Akogare no watashi* x *yarigai no shigoto*]. This consists of five testimonials from Japanese natives whose current successful careers are, in their opinion, a direct consequence of the period they spent studying abroad. The first case study is that of Yuka Oishi (Figure 7.4), a young woman who now works in a PR firm in Tokyo dealing with corporate clients in the beauty and fashion industries. Within the genre of women's lifestyle magazines this is considered an enviable career.

The narrative begins with a textbox which summarizes Yuka's educational and employment journey:

> Ever since I was a child I wanted to do something different from other people, so I went to America for three weeks while I was at high school. After I returned I went to junior college [*tandai*], but then went back to study in the US where I majored in PR, and there I learnt the importance of 'communication'.[3]

This is followed by the various 'steps' that Ms Oishi took in order to achieve her current career. The narrative is given a Before-During-After

Figure 7.4 The personal narrative of a successful career woman

structure, beginning with her time at a two-year women-only junior college [*tandai*] in Japan, and then moving on to an English language school affiliated with Central Washington University, and from there being able to transfer to the university's four-year degree in public relations. On her return to Japan, she worked for two years doing PR for a finance company, before moving on to her current position.

The implications of Yuka's narrative are that the Japanese social and educational system would never have allowed her the opportunities to realize the ambitions that she had held ever since childhood. The hierarchy of prestige that ranks Japanese universities means that it is very difficult to transcend the expected career path that comes with the institution one attends (Nakane, 1998). Social mobility is constrained as much by university of graduation as by aptitude or personal initiative. For women, the opportunities are all the more limited (Kobayashi, 2007), and the two-year junior college system is seen more as a preparation for marriage than for a career. For Ms Oishi, then, the dream of a fulfilling job as the centerpiece to an exciting and rewarding life would doubtless have appeared unrealizable within the Japanese social system as soon as she entered junior college. Foreign study, however, gave her access to the type of opportunity for career development she would never have received in Japan. By taking that initial step to go to a language school in America, she was then able to transfer to a four-year degree course, and on the back of this returned to a steady career path which has resulted in her present glamorous position.

This inspirational narrative is constructed around an arc which firstly introduces a seemingly insurmountable challenge (being trapped in the social-determinism of the Japanese education system), but then overcoming these difficulties through hard work and by enrolling on the study abroad programme. In painting this picture, the account includes personal details such as the opposition Ms Oishi initially faced from her parents who did not want her to travel abroad, and the encounter she had with an American professor visiting Japan who first inspired her to search out such an opportunity. In contrast to the fragmentary sentences attributed to the nameless informants in the Gaba advert, the use of a personal narrative which includes dates, place names and photos of the author offers a very high modality for the example, which is presented as the real life experience of a real person. The aspirational associations with English become not just a matter of *what* can be achieved with the assistance of English, but also of *how* such achievement can be attained, and the valuable life-lessons that the process itself provides.

This point is further evinced in the way that Ms Oishi attributes her success not simply to the practical instrumental skills she gained through her studies, but also to a new cultural awareness; as she explains: 'I was influenced by the way that Americans communicate, which is always to be friendly, to say positive things and to praise people. I became able to see that even terrible people have good qualities.' Thus, studying aboard allowed her to benefit not only from the stereotypical cultural values that structure the American education system (a democratic approach to opportunity centered on the potential of the individual), but also from the ethical philosophy of the people she encountered. In this way, the experience was life-changing not only in terms of its external results, but also in the way it changed her on the inside. And this is reflected in the way that her current work is not merely enjoyable and allows her to make full use of her talents, but it is also personally rewarding and gives her the feeling that she is doing something 'worthwhile' [*yarigai wo kanjite iru*].

Examples such as these, then, position English within a wider narrative of social mobility in which an aspirational outlook is expressed through the composition of images, the organization of genre conventions and in the content of the associations made with the language. The result is a discourse of the language which references universal tropes such as the image of the purposeful and empowered woman on the cover of *Wish*, but that also offers a much more context-specific reading of the role that the idea of English plays within contemporary Japanese society.

Aspirational Orientations

We are now in a position to reconsider the issue of categories of motivation orientation as they apply to the context of Japan. Based upon the analysis of the examples above, we can distinguish between two substantive orientations in the discourse of English and aspiration as it is articulated in media texts related to the commercial education sector: the first relates the language to mobility within the job market, while the second sees benefits in terms of social or personal relations. The two strands do correspond in some general respects to the concepts of 'instrumental' and 'integrative' orientation – a career-focused orientation is likely to see English as an important technology that needs to be mastered for professional success in an increasingly globalized working environment; while the role of English in reconfiguring one's social relationships corresponds more to the interpersonal functions of language and its status as an index of culture. Yet for both categories, it is the specific nature of the cultural and sociopolitical contexts which produce the details of the associations that form the substance of the ideology of aspiration, and thus it is necessary to give some theoretical consideration to these contexts.

The first of the two motivational orientations relates English to what Adjoe (2006: 185) has called 'globalised labour identities', and the way in which a change in the individual's perception of his or her place in the world has been brought about by the processes of globalization. As Giddens (1991: 187) writes:

> In conditions of late modernity, we live 'in the world' in a different sense from previous eras of history. Everyone still continues to live a local life, and the constraints of the body ensure that all individuals, at every moment, are contextually situated in time and space. Yet the transformations of place, and the intrusion of distance into local activities, combined with the centrality of mediated experience, radically change what 'the world' actually is.

Within this reconfigured sense of living 'in the world', aspirations about lifestyle choice are constructed from a collage of images from across the globe. Opportunities, especially as they relate to one's identity within the labor market, are measured within a context which transcends local constraints, and English, as the 'global' language, comes to be seen as an essential factor for their realization.

It is worth introducing a distinction here between a *desire* to learn English for the possibility of job prosperity, and a *requirement* to do so. Studies such as that by Niño-Murcia (2003: 121) on the ideology of English in Peru, suggest that for some groups 'English is seen as a requirement *imposed* by globalisation and a global market' [italics added]. Japan presents a rather different scenario, where the socioeconomic context and the political situation mean that English language competency is not a prerequisite for finding stable work and decent wages as it is in some Outer Circle countries or for certain populations where emigration to an English-speaking country is seen as almost the only solution to severe economic deprivation. Yet aspirational discourses within Japan on the benefits of English ability do still invoke the idea of upward mobility within the job market, be it in terms of increased financial reward and responsibility, or, as in the case of the Yuka Oishi narrative, of opportunities otherwise closed to certain sections of society.

As was discussed in Chapter 4, the instrumental argument for English ability is one that has also been made in government policy recommendations. The Commission on Japan's Goals in the Twenty-First Century (CJGTC, 2000a) asserts that 'global literacy' skills (English as an international lingua franca plus IT skills) will be a determining factor in whether citizens in the new millennium can expect to enjoy a better life. At the time of the report, conviction in the validity of this position was such that serious consideration was given to the proposal to make English an official second language in order to ensure the future prosperity of the nation. Yet, as Kobayashi (2007: 63) notes, Japanese society is currently organized in such a way that the social capital gained from English language skills is often more meretricious than material, '[i]n spite of the increasing value placed on English and the governmental endorsement of that trend... English is not the major criteria for career advancement in many corporate sectors'. Instead, factors such as age, gender and university of graduation play a far more significant role, and if English ability does play a part in enhancing career opportunities, it is 'implicitly restricted to those prospective and current professional employees who are already in good standing regardless of their English levels' (p. 64). So, while the assets of English may be of instrumental benefit to a small section of society – namely, those already in possession of secure social capital – it appears that it cannot transcend the social hierarchies that already exist within the country. Any form of 'instrumental' orientation, then, which considers the language to be a necessary tool for success in a job market increasingly influenced by global concerns, needs to be understood in terms of the existing social norms in Japan and the patterns of determinism in much of its labor market.

The importance of this qualification can be seen in the prominence given within the Japanese context to my second category of orientation: that of social mobility. In the examples from the Gaba advert and the *Ryûgaku Access* magazine feature, career enhancement is itself mostly mediated by the necessary prerequisite of social mobility and an emancipation from the strictures of Japanese society. The Yuka Oishi case, for example, suggests that the desired profession was only achieved courtesy of a study abroad programme which allowed her to bypass the traditional Japanese academic career path. In this example, as in many of those in the Gaba advert, social mobility is indicated by images of the West, and this formula is a key trope in the wider discourse. Block, summarizing the conclusions of a number of research studies in this area, comments upon the way 'internationalisation often leads to, or is associated with, what is known as an *akogare* – idealisation or longing – for all things Western (often meaning American or English speaking) and a rejection of all things Japanese' (2006: 105; see also Kelsky, 2001; Piller & Takahashi, 2006). In practice, this means that emblematic symbols of Western culture stand in synecdochically for a social structure founded upon a belief in 'opportunity'.

Given the fact that English is presented in this strand of the discourse as a form of social emancipation and that, as Kelsky noted in the quote cited above, one of the most prominently marginalized sections of Japanese society in terms of employment opportunities is women, the discourse is often specifically gendered. This strand of the discourse can take the following two forms: a romantic or even erotic desire for the West/the Western male (see, for example, Bailey, 2006; Piller & Takahashi, 2006), or a more general wish for what is perceived as a 'global democratic humanism' (Kelsky, 1999: 230) in Western social structures which allows for more gender equality. Both of these trends can be discerned in the examples above: the junior college student (13) in the Gaba advert illustrating the former ('I would become the wife of a foreigner and raise some kids in California'); while the Yuka Oishi narrative subscribes to the latter. Often, desire for the Western male is in part a desire for Western-style social relations. Another feature article in *Ryûgaku Access* (Vol. 4, 2006), for example, asks 200 working women in their twenties about the 'new self' they would like to find [*Anata ga egaku mirai tte nan desu ka?*], and in amongst the customary answers about realizing ambitions to become professional aromatherapists or to uproot to Hawaii, is the outspoken assertion from one respondent, 'I will go out to work and my partner can be a house-husband!' and the desire to get married to someone who will treat her with respect. That this is made within the context of a magazine for study abroad programmes suggests that such a scenario is considered incompatible with this woman's ambitions for her life within a Japanese context.

While the narrative of this gendered discourse, as well as the wider examples of longing for the freedoms and prosperity associated with Western (or specifically American) culture, may appear to align it with some form of integrative orientation, what is of significance is that the identification is with values of the foreign culture that are antithetical to those experienced within one's own life. As such, the impulse is as much a reflection of beliefs or attitudes toward Japanese society as it is of a disposition toward another culture.

We are able, therefore, to offer a modified formula for the two categories of aspirational association that are made with the language in the Japanese context based on this particular data set: an instrumental motivation (mostly career-related) highlights the potential that English will allow *within* given social structures; while an integrative motivation (concerned more with interpersonal relations) foregrounds the potential that English will allow to *transcend* given social structures. In both formulations, the pre-existing social structure is, however, key, and provides the baseline against which the 'transformative' power of English is understood and measured. The result of this is that attitudes toward English are not merely about the impression that one has of English-speaking culture(s) – a desire to mix with and become part of them – but also a way of expressing or exploring attitudes toward the social structure within which one lives. A desire or orientation toward English can thus be seen as a way of expressing ideas of self-identity and social positioning, but is meaningful in this respect based on the following factors: one's current position within the social system, and one's attitude toward this current position. In this way, the discourse of the desire for English becomes, on one level, a narrative about attitudes toward social values in mainstream Japanese culture.

Attitudes to English

In the final part of this chapter, I will use the framework outlined above, and the theoretical issues that it raises, in order to analyze the accounts of a sample of Japanese informants about their attitudes to English. Before doing so, a word needs to be added about the relationship between these accounts and the promotional literature. As has been noted, the texts analyzed above are all products of a particular commercial enterprise, yet this does not mean that the discourses thus produced should be boxed off as merely the hyperbolic rhetoric of the renegade commercialized wing of further education. There is, after all, a partnership with the mainstream education sector in the way that companies such as ALC produce their listings for study abroad programmes. Furthermore, the rhetoric of language education policy has an equally strong voice within the discourse (e.g. CJGTC, 2000a), and one which, it could be argued, shows less concern for the actuality of the benefits of language learning than that portrayed in magazine features such as that on Yuka Oishi. As such, the contribution from informants should be seen as an additional, rather than a countervoice in the discourse. It is not presented as the *reality* of the situation versus the *imaginary* story from the promotional materials. Instead, it is another part of the flux of ideas and beliefs that contribute to the ideology of the language.

The study of language attitudes toward English involved the interviewing of a small sample of Japanese nationals who had studied the language at higher education level, and had an extended history of interest in the subject. Its purpose was to interrogate their views on their motivation for learning English, and the role that their experience of learning and their current language abilities play in their life. This data could then be used as a cross-referent for the themes that have been identified in the first half of the chapter.

Again, it is worth placing this approach within the context of similar research paradigms in order to draw out the specific character of the present strategy. The work on motivation alluded to at the beginning of the chapter gauges the opinions of individuals about their attitude to language or language learning. While much of this is psychometric in design, and attempts to quantify the correlation between attitude and learning success, the nature of the attitudes and the classifications that can be posited based on a survey of these attitudes constitute an important data source for how language is perceived. For our purposes therefore, the substance and articulation of such perceptions can reveal much about the dominant language ideologies within a group. For some, however, there is a distinction to be drawn between *ideology* and *attitude* in this context. Baker (1992: 14–15) suggests that:

> The difference ... is ... partly about different traditions of research, theory and expression, particularly between sociology and social psychology.... Ideology tends to refer to codifications of group norms and values. At an individual level, ideology tends to refer to broad perspectives on society – a philosophy of life.... A psychological approach to attitude will tend to acknowledge both the group and individual representations of attitude (perhaps with more accent on the individual).

Drawing upon this distinction, we can suggest that if attitudes are taken to be more individualized dispositions, recurrent patterns within the expression of attitudes in a community can be taken as evidence of the more structured belief systems that constitute ideologies. It is this that the present research study aims to examine. Of interest is not the correlation between individual attitudes and learning success or language proficiency, but trends of belief within the cohort which constitute an ideology of the language.

Writing on the method employed by folk linguistics, Preston (1999: xxv) recommends that '[o]nce it has been decided that the folk facts...are worth knowing, it remains only to visit the folk and find them out'. The folk in this instance were selected according to the following criteria. They were all Japanese nationals currently living and working in Japan. Each had studied an English course at tertiary level, and had spent some time on a study abroad programme in an English-speaking country, and thus had a background which bore witness to a particular investment in learning the language. The table in Figure 7.5 gives an indicative breakdown of these aspects of their biography. The sample pool for participants was specifically kept small so that individualized qualitative data could be gathered, which could then be analyzed in some detail (Kvale, 1996: 102).

The method of interview was via email, with an initial questionnaire inviting open responses to a selection of questions, and with a succession of follow-up interviews then pursuing particular topics of interest. This method allowed for considered rather than ad hoc replies, giving the participants the opportunity to reflect upon relevant issues. As the object of research was the rationalizations made by participants over their attitude to English and the role it plays within their life, the scope for considered responses is seen as a requirement for the process. From a practical point of view, this method also facilitated an ongoing conversation with participants which could be continued over several weeks, regardless of impediments related to schedule or physical location. The participants

Name	Age	Occupation	English Education	Residence Abroad
Chie	30–35	Office worker	Undergraduate study	3 years in UK
Naoto	25–30	IT professional	Undergraduate study	1 month in Canada
Asako	25–30	Office worker	Undergraduate study	6 months in UK
Eiko	35–40	University lecturer	Postgraduate study	10 years in UK & US
Miho	25–30	Music industry	Undergraduate study	4 years in UK

Figure 7.5 Table of interview participants

were offered the chance to respond either in English or Japanese, but the majority replied in English.[4]

Analysis of the data looked to identify within the content of the replies recurrent patterns of rationalization, the justification for behavior and the association of ideas related to the language. To an extent, the surface form of expression was considered, as assumptions and associations can be expressed in the choice of metaphors and conceptual schemata (Lakoff, 1993). As Deignan (2006) explains, '[i]n many cases, linguistic metaphors represent subconscious choices on the part of the speaker or writer, whose choice of language is partly constrained by the conceptual structures shared by members of his or her community'. Micro sociolinguistic features of the responses, on the other hand, were not evaluated as the focus was not on individual linguistic form and variety, but rather on conceptual attitude (and particular recurrent patterns of shared attitude) toward the idea of the language. In addition to allowing us to trace certain of the entrenched beliefs which constitute the symbolic meaning of English, the interview data also offers insights into the personalized rationalizations of individuals, which can provide salutary contrast to the deterministic picture of attitudes to English which is liable to emerge from much of the promotional literature.

The role of English as an important skill for work was a key theme in responses about motivations for learning the language, though English appeared to have lost some of the symbolic value it once had in this regard. Chie, for example, who spent three years living in London in her early thirties before returning to Japan where she now works in a large computer company in Tokyo, spoke of her desire to learn other languages:

> I was interested in Spanish and Italian. So I learned both of them. Now I want to learn French again. When I was in junior college I had to learn it but I wasn't interested at that moment so I spent horrible hours.... If I could manage to use another language, I could get a good job and salary as well. There are a lot of English speakers in Japan, so we need a second foreign language now.

For Chie it appears that the cultural capital that English once represented has been diminished because so many people in Japan now speak the language. It no longer constitutes the sort of 'specialized' knowledge that gives access to better job prospects, and thus it is necessary to have alternative linguistic skills. Here, then, it is not the instrumental value of the language in itself that is important, but it is how these skills are distributed amongst the population that appears to constitute the rationalization for a desire for English. Paradoxically, for Chie the perception is that the more people that speak the language (i.e. the more that it does indeed move toward becoming a global language), the less helpful it is for giving access to enhanced job prospects.

Naoto, who is in his late 20s, works in the same company as Chie. He too studied English at university, but only spent one month studying abroad, in Canada. He works in the international trading section of the company, and does have to use English in the course of his job, and as such considers that he has fulfilled the initial ambition that motivated him to learn the language: 'I thought being fluent in English would help me get a job that I wanted and it did help, at least a little.' Despite this, his views on the general necessity of English fluency for everyday Japanese life are significantly different from those expressed in the government rhetoric of the *Frontier Within* document (CJGTC, 2000a). In his opinion

> The Japanese, in general, are not very good at learning foreign languages because very few people have much necessity to speak English well. We might need to be good at exams and might need good TOEIC score, [but] very few really find them in need to communicate in business level English.... When we go sightseeing, we don't need to be fluent, and don't need to use precisely appropriate words.

The pattern of associations here is between proficiency in language learning and the sociolinguistic context of contemporary Japanese society. There is, in this account, still an instrumental motivation for learning the language however, and one specifically linked to the pragmatic needs of Japanese life. The language is seen to play a role within the existing social system, and thus pursuing the type of English needed to excel in entrance exams or the TOEIC is of importance for advancing within the current social structure. Naoto is clear, though, in his opinion that English for communicative purposes is not a priority for many people in Japan. Furthermore, despite the fact that he does equate English skills with success in a globalized business world, he does not do so entirely without qualification, concluding his remarks by saying that now 'I want to be able to speak Chinese. The reason is simply because the Chinese population would be more dominant in business in future'. The Chinese language (in some abstract, monolithic form) has replaced English as a symbol of global business opportunity as part of the wider narrative of the rise of China as an economic power.

Asako, a woman in her mid-20s who studied for a degree in English Communication at a four-year college before going to work for a local manufacturing company in a small town in central Japan, is of the opinion that her English skills are of integral importance to the position she now holds, 'I use English to communicate with customers, so it must be an essential skill for me to speak English. If I cannot speak English,

I would not be in the current section. English is very very important for my current job!' However, she notes that such a direct relationship between the skills learnt at university and those sought by an employer is not necessarily the norm. She relates the story of one of her classmates who studied in the United States for a year after graduation and then went to England for three months and to Hong Kong for nine months, but who has failed to find a position in which she can utilize her knowledge of English, despite working for a firm which trades internationally:

> I think [my friend] wanted a job [which] needed English ability. Now she works for a manufacturing company and she has been placed in the personnel section even though there are many jobs [in the company] using English. She does not use English at work, she said. We do not know where we will be positioned in the company.

This last comment refers to the way that companies in Japan mostly hire employees not on the basis of job-specific skills, but according to their general academic and social background. Thus, for example, graduates of the top universities will be employed by the leading companies, and it is only once they have joined the organization that they will be assigned a role, for which they will then be given in-house training. In such a system, it is aptitude for education rather than the results of education that are valued, and specific skills and knowledge are of secondary importance to the social status which is defined by university of graduation, as well as other variables such as gender and age (Kobayashi, 2007). The cautionary tale of Asako's friend, therefore, gives the lie to the simplistic equation of English ability and career prosperity. This would appear to be a good example of the limits of the decontextualized instrumental orientation toward English, based upon a naïve reading of the discourse which sees English as a key attribute for upward mobility in the globalized labor market.

A further intriguing comment from Asako relates to her belief that learning a new language can lead to self-knowledge and an increased awareness of one's own cultural identity which, she suggests, is to be gained by means of an anthropological distance facilitated by English ability:

> I would like to work in the world, not only in Japan. I want to have a wide view. [With English] I have one of the tools to communicate with foreigners, and I think I would use that tool.... I would like to see Japan from far from Japan. I cannot notice that Japan is a strong country as long as I live in Japan, but if I live in a foreign country I would see that clearer than I do in Japan. I think it is a

good thing to live in foreign countries and to learn about my own country.

Here again, the motivation for learning English is focused back upon Japanese society itself, and exhibits a mixture of nationalistic pride and cultural inquisitiveness. This appears to be the very opposite of a traditional, simplistic conception of integrative motivation as Asako does not desire to become part of a foreign culture, but rather to use her exposure to a foreign culture as a way of drawing attention to the distinctiveness of her native culture. At the same time, she subscribes to an instrumentalist ideology of language in her use of the metaphor of English as an important tool for use within the globalized labor market.

In accord with the examples from the promotional literature, it is in the realm of gender politics that the social values of non-Japanese cultures are assigned most importance. In the responses from the informants the most noticeable expression of this concerned what Block (2006: 93) has termed a 'discourse of difference between [the] Japanese and English [languages]'. Such a view contrasts the strict hierarchical organization of honorific speech in Japanese, which imposes exacting rules of usage according to one's social position, against the more 'democratic' structuring of interpersonal forms in English (in rationalizing the difference, the ideology of iconicity (Gal & Irvine, 1995) transfers attributes associated with national culture onto the grammatical system of the language). Within this context, English is often said to be a liberating language for Japanese women, as it imposes less constraints on them expressing their thoughts and emotions. A number of the participants in the current study appeared to voice attitudes in keeping with this discourse. For example, when asked to comment on why she thought English classes were particularly popular among women in Japan, Eiko, a woman in her late thirties who spent much of her twenties in the United States and England and now lectures at a two-year college in a rural area of Japan, had the following to say:

> More women express their own opinions in English than men. As you know, in Japan many women are still oppressed by men and communities. If women speak English, they might feel more open and express their true feeling.

Another participant, Miho, who works for a music company in Tokyo, was of a similar opinion:

> In Japanese, I need to select a proper way from many choices for the expression... [and] need to read the atmosphere in the conversation,

somebody's feeling.... For example, I can say 'No' quite easily in English, but I can't say 'No' in Japanese.

These views do, of course, see English specifically in terms of its difference from Japanese, and thus the valorization of English is once again a rejection of the system they are living in as much as anything else. Comments from Asako seem to highlight the underlying social factors involved. She suggests that it is actually a lack of fluency and familiarity with the pragmatic conventions of English-speaking cultures that results in a more 'direct' form of expression, before going on to imply that it is being in a different environment that allows for a different manner of communication, rather than anything essential in the languages themselves:

> I think we do not know many ways to express ourselves in English. We have a lot of ways to express feelings, and sometimes we use ambiguity words in Japanese. But we do not know so many ways to express ourselves in English, and we only know how to express our real feelings. So, it is sometimes easier to express ourselves in English. I think that it is important to say what you think in foreign countries, but it is not always a good thing to express our real feelings in Japan.

Conclusion

Although the responses of the informants do not give quite as vivid or uncluttered a picture of the aspirational associations for English as the promotional examples, they are nevertheless illustrative of a similar pattern of desires which are made meaningful against the backdrop of contemporary Japanese social structures. An important point that we can make in summation is that the 'English' referred to throughout this discourse is far from unitary, and instead this one signifier embraces a range of linguistic varieties and language-related concepts. As was discussed at the beginning of this chapter, the *why* will determine the *what*, and the type of English that is desired will depend on the details of that desire. For example, an instrumental orientation such as that expressed by Naoto, who learnt English in the hope of getting a job in an international trading company, is going to require a very different variety of the language from that required by those wishing to pass the exams that regulate the hierarchically structured academic and corporate spheres of Japanese society (Sasaki, 2008). Despite the substantial differences that these two purposes will demand of the learning process and the language product, both are valid reasons for engaging with English education, and they both represent different aspects of the presence that English occupies in contemporary Japanese society.

Another role played by 'English' in Japan that is revealed in the data above is the way that the *pursuit* of the language becomes a means of expressing one's identity and of negotiating aspects of one's native culture. In this case, linguistic competence need not be the desired outcome at all, but instead it is an engagement with the processes represented by English language learning – and by the status and meaning that the language has in contemporary Japan – that appears to be the true object of the motivation. The implications of this, and of the various different Englishes that the aspiration motif invokes and creates, must need alter our conception of the meaning of a 'global' language, and prompt us to broaden the scope of our enquiry when formulating programmes of research and language regulation in applied linguistics. I shall return to this issue in the final chapter of the book, but before moving to that I will conclude the examination of the Japanese context with a look at how the discourse of English in Japan works not only to assign conceptual meanings to the language, but also to shape what does and does not count as 'English' in Japan.

Chapter 8
The Unknown Language

An Imaginary Japan

> The Japanese people are the deliberate self conscious creation of certain individual artists.... In fact, the whole of Japan is a pure invention. There is no such country, there are no such people ... [T]he Japanese people are, as I have said, simply a mode of style, an exquisite fancy of art. (Wilde, 1908: 47–48)

There is a lengthy tradition of using Japan as a touchstone for debates about Western thought: In European literature, an imaginary conception of the nation has been a locus for cultural speculation since the late 19th century, when Japan was first 'opened up' to the rest of the world. In the immediate aftermath of this, Western interest in the aesthetics and artistic culture of the country was rife, and yet, as the character of Vivian in Oscar Wilde's *The Decay of Lying* notes, the culture being celebrated was in many ways pure idealization. Western tracts on the subject were exercising an Orientalism (Said, 1979) by means of which they imagined the place as a counterpoint to occidental society and civilization. As Nunokawa writes, 'part of a long line of fashions [in the 1880s] given over to the celebration of the artificial, the rage for things Japanese was as much as anything else a longing for an exoticism removed from the realm of the real' (2003: 48). By offering a substitute vision of social cohesion and expression, one in which meaning is secondary to harmony and style, critics were able to deconstruct the belief system upon which Western society is predicated, and offer instead an alternate vision of civilization. And indeed, much this same process continues today, and can be seen in writings ranging from those of cultural critics such as Jean Baudrillard (1988) to science fiction authors like William Gibson (2001).

In the latter half of the 20th century, when once again Japan's relationship with the West was being reconfigured, Roland Barthes developed a similar fascination with the country.[1] For Barthes (1982), writing in the aftermath of a few brief visits, Japanese culture offered an alternate paradigm against which he could analyze his own perception of culture, and it was the closed meaning and impenetrability he saw in the society that acted as the greatest catalyst for his theorizing. Of the Japanese language, he writes

> The dream: to know a foreign language and yet not to understand it: to perceive the difference in it without that difference ever being recuperated by the superficial sociality of discourse, communication or vulgarity. (p. 6)

Here he ascribes to the language – a language he neither spoke nor understood; nor indeed had any interest in speaking or understanding – properties which enable him to challenge directly his understanding of occidental culture. As Thody (1977: 123) explains

> Barthes makes it clear from the very beginning [of *Empire of Signs*] that it is quite pointless to try to call Western society seriously into question unless one actually begins by attacking its view of language as essentially instrumental.... Just as Western story-telling is wrong because it has traditionally set out to help the reader see meaning in his own experience by explaining the behaviour of certain other people in rational and comprehensible terms, so Western language is wrong because it tries to express ideas. It should, instead, delight in diagrams which explain nothing because there is nothing to be explained and which consequently exist as art forms in their own right.

For Barthes, it is the 'emptiness' of the sign that he finds in Japanese culture that is to be celebrated (Ikegami, 1991), and which can lead us away from the reliance on the fixed meanings to which the West condemns itself.

If we adapt this formula we can, perhaps, gain an insight into the way in which, in extreme (though numerous) examples, a similar process is at work with the English language in Japan. Within Japanese society the English language, held up in policy and public discourse as a tool for accessing the greater world beyond the shores of Japan, works as much as a shade obscuring the international community and reflecting back ideas of Japanese insularity. It has a complex, highly contested, and much appropriated meaning – existing both as the pre-eminent vehicle for global communication, but at the same time an 'unknown language' (Barthes, 1982: 6) which seemingly does not conform to the precepts of occidental logic and instrumental use. And it is in this way that a study of the functions and various existences of the language within Japanese society can be used to interrogate preconceptions about the nature of

English, especially within the context of its developing role as a global language.

In this final chapter of the case study, therefore, I wish to consider the relationship between mainstream ideas of English language use within Japan – those focusing primarily upon its use as a communicative code for the relay of ideational meaning – and the many other ways in which it is dispersed across the wider cultural landscape. What I have been discussing over the length of this book can, perhaps, be summarized by saying that the English language in Japan has a dual existence: On the one hand, it *is* a communicative code of the sort that mainstream linguistics and its various subdisciplines are wont to study; it is also, though, a cultural symbol – an idea, whose meaning is discursively constructed and then utilized as part of wider social and cultural debate. The two are, of course, linked at every moment – the idea of the language will influence its use; and use of the language will contribute to the idea – but it is often the case that in debate and regulation of the language one aspect is privileged almost exclusively over the other, and the actuality of the language's existence within society is ignored in favor of an idealized conception of what a global language should be. It has been my contention that in looking at the example of Japan we can begin to effectively problematize this equation. For whereas Barthes championed in Japan the profusion of 'empty' signs which could be appreciated as all process and no product, I would suggest that the use and display of English within Japan, while not conforming solely to the totalizing strictures of formalized denotational meaning, is nevertheless still semiotically active both in the ludic terms to which Barthes refers, but also as a vehicle for ideological meaning. An investigation into the signifying power of 'language which is not interpreted as language' therefore can allow us to reformulate the multifunctional role that linguistic behavior plays within the social environment.

English Encounters

In her survey of the social significance of loanwords in a rural community in Japan, Hogan (2003: 48) records the view of one of her informants that people in urban areas do not even notice instances of English-derived vocabulary and consider them a natural part of the everyday social environment, while in the countryside the population is very aware (and antithetically disposed to) the use of what they consider to be 'English' (which for them includes the variety of loanwords – both *gairaigo* and *wasei-eigo* – that punctuates the vernacular). There is, in this single observation, the importance of what is understood as English for the interpretation of language practices. In Chapter 3, I discussed, with reference to assumptions about the ontology of language, the importance of the question of what does and does not count as language for an understanding of the role that language is accorded within society. Decisions over the boundary between language and nonlanguage or between what is perceived as being part of the English language and what is not are ideologically informed ones, and thus are liable to be another productive focus of investigation. To explore this further therefore, I will present in the first half of this chapter the results of a small empirical study into people's perspectives on the extent to which the English language features as an everyday part of life in Japan. The results of this survey, as we shall see, can provide exemplary insights into the positioning and subsequent consequences of this interpretation of a borderline between sanctioned and unsanctioned language behavior.

As was mentioned in the introduction, one of the motivating factors in the choice of Japan as the case study for this book was the way in which the Japanese lived environment, especially in urban areas, has a great density of visual information, much of it in the form of linguistic signage. The urban physical landscape of the country is engraved with information, and a high proportion of this takes the form of signs in the Roman alphabet, many of them spelling out ostensibly English slogans (Backhaus, 2005). In addition to this, broadcast media, both television and radio, will be regularly punctuated by the marked use of English-derived vocabulary (Moody, 2006), as well as the use of longer lexical sequences in English and some overt cases of bilingualism. To gauge the amount of English that people come across in their daily lives, therefore – and to provide some contextual background for the arguments developed in the book – another small-scale research project was designed in which a number of people were asked to keep a structured diary on selected days in order to record the amount and type of English they encountered during that day.

The rationale for this study was comparatively straightforward: It was intended to provide empirical data about the intensity of the visual and oral display of English in contemporary Japanese society, and to offer a snapshot of the diversity in form and dispersal of the language. Rather than rely on statistical accounts of the number of citizens enrolled in English classes at the various educational levels, or on other such officially published records of the penetration of English within society,[2] my interest instead was on receiving a detailed, informant-centered account of the full range of English-related language behavior as encountered in the course of everyday activities. This approach is again based on the model of surveys favored in folk linguistics. Perceptual dialectology, for example, will canvas people's beliefs about language variety by investigating how they categorize and evaluate different dialects and accents (Preston, 1999). The object of analysis in such cases will be the overtly stated opinions of the nonspecialist on specific linguistic variables. My study adapted this approach, and instead of exploring the categorization of dialect, it aimed to examine perceptions about the quantity, dispersal and nature of English that was encountered in everyday activity. The original plan was to carry out a pilot study which would provide data about the areas of distribution and types of written and oral English which were encountered so that these could then be used to create a more targeted questionnaire for use in a subsequent, larger study. As it transpired, the follow-up study was rendered unnecessary due to the results generated by the initial survey.

The participants for the study were chosen to be a rough cross-section of society in terms both of English ability and other demographic factors. The specific intention was to examine a contrast of daily routines as well as established relationships with the language, and thus participants were picked from both rural and urban environments, and included those in full-time employment or education, as well as those whose routine was more oriented to the household. As the study at this initial stage of the process was intended to provide basic contextual information rather than extensive ethnographic detail, a sample of only eight participants was chosen. The questionnaire was offered in both English and Japanese, and consisted of a brief section about biographical background (including any history of English language study), followed by structured prompts for the recording of the amount and type of English-related language that was encountered during the day. This daily journal section was divided into three categories: the first relating to the media (television, radio, advertising or signage); the second asking about the use of English to communicate with friends, acquaintances or work colleagues; and the final category enquiring about participation in any language study activities. Guidelines were given for each section, with leading questions intended to highlight the type of entry that might be applicable (e.g. advertising slogans, brand names or songs on the radio). What was to count as 'English', however, was not specified in any explicit way, and no limitations were set as to whether it should include katakana English or solely Romaji English for the written language, or the extent to which various levels of linguistic borrowing might be included. (The lack of explicit directives about this issue proved, ultimately, to be a productive flaw in the research design.) Each participant was then asked to complete one such structured journal entry for four randomly selected days.[3]

The results of the project initially appeared confusing and counterintuitive. Rather than providing the types of data that were anticipated, and that would have answered the original research question, the responses instead recorded a very low frequency of encounters with English. Of the eight participants, none recorded sightings of English-language slogans on T-shirts or other fashion items; none noted the prevalence of English-language names for shop signs or on advertising hoardings. The only areas in which encounters with English were recorded were when listening to music and watching movies, or in correspondence with 'native speaker' acquaintances. One participant, for example, a woman in her 20s named Kazumi, who works as a hospital nurse in a mid-sized city in the west of Japan and who had studied English in the UK for a year, recorded in each diary that the only encounter with the English language she had was when she listened to Western pop music, or, on one occasion, when she wrote an email to a British friend. Despite commuting to work in the center of town, during the course of which she would almost certainly have come across English-language display in advertisements and on an assortment of civic signs, she always answered in the negative for that section of the questionnaire. An even more emphatic pattern emerged from the responses of Aiko, a woman in her mid-30s who had spent a large part of her adult life studying in English-speaking countries, but had recently returned to Japan to search for work and was living in one of Japan's largest cities in the central region of the country. Again, the only affirmative answers came when she related that she had watched an international news bulletin on the television, and had emailed an English-speaking friend. There was no mention of encountering any of the English that is ubiquitously embedded within the context of the everyday Japanese landscape.

From an analysis of the responses of Kazumi and Aiko, the only English that was acknowledged as being English as such was that directly related to a British or American source (for example, British pop music, an American film or a conversation with a friend from Britain). All the other English language display that they would likely have encountered appears not to have qualified, and thus did not merit a place in the journal. Seiko, a housewife in her late 50s, whose daily routine is centred mostly around the home and the local shops, also recorded only instances of English that were related in some form to the culture of the dominant English-speaking nations. She recorded watching an American drama on the television in which one of the actors had spoken English, and hearing of the theme song from an American movie on the radio. On two out of the four days on which she completed the journal, she recorded no contact with English at all.

Perceptual Disjuncture and Ideological 'Erasure'

Though by no means definitive, these results do suggest an interesting phenomenon about the existence of English within Japan, or rather, about the *perception* of this existence. What they appear to indicate is a form of perceptual disjuncture between entrenched ideas about language use, and the actuality of everyday language practices. What in effect is happening is that a prevailing ideology that informs the way people speak or consciously think of the language is at odds with the way people actually use it, resulting in an evident disparity between perception and practice. Despite the ubiquitous presence of signs, adverts, brand names and loanwords in Japan, all exhibiting an English origin, these various types of language use appear not to be sanctioned as real or authentic English according to the interpretive standards of these participants and are thus rendered invisible in the survey. The prevailing language ideology in this case, therefore, not only conceptualizes the language in a particular way (it produces preconceived ideas of what the language is and what its functions are), but in doing so it invalidates other forms or interpretations of the language's existence.

The apparent gap between language behavior and the rationalization of that behavior or between conflicting rationalizations of the same behavior has long been a focus of interest for linguistic anthropology. Although Boas (1911: 71) may have dismissed 'the faulty reasoning [of] ... secondary explanations' expressed by the nonexperts he studied, the opinions that people hold about their language use have become a dedicated field of enquiry in folk linguistics. Preston (1999: xxiii) provides a useful model of what he sees as the three approaches to language data, in which language attitudes and opinions are the third node on the triangle (Figure 8.1).

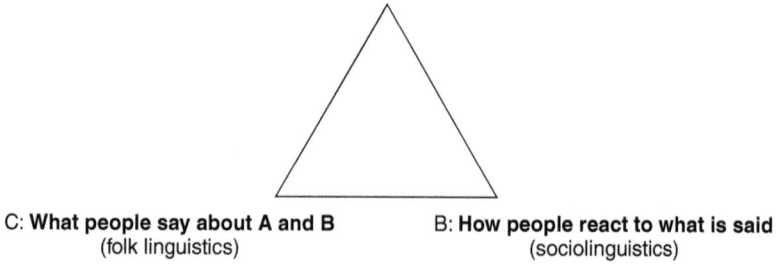

Figure 8.1 Preston's triangle of approaches to language data (adapted)

Perceptual dialectology (the branch of folk linguistics with which Preston is most concerned) begins with the assumption that folk beliefs (C) and scientifically recorded data (A) will be divergent, and that there will not be an exact match between the perception and the production of dialect. Language ideologies theory suggests that there are degrees of consciousness about one's linguistic actions, which range from the discursive to the practical (Kroskrity, 2006: 505). A discursive consciousness of one's actions is one in which they are raised to an explicit level in terms of conscious understanding and articulated within discourse; a practical consciousness is where they remain embodied in procedural knowledge. Based on the results of explorations in this area, the identity of perception and product does not appear in any sense to be the norm.

The disjunct between a dominant ideology and actual practice can take a number of forms. For example, Bamgbose (1982: 100) records how 'In our teaching and examinations [in Nigeria] we concentrate on drilling and testing out of existence forms of speech that even the teachers will use freely when they do not have their textbooks open before them'. In commenting on this statement, Kachru and Nelson (2001: 18) suggest, 'people do not always speak the way they think they do, and linguistic insecurity is perhaps one of the chief motivations for linguistic prescriptivism'. In Bamgbose's case, it would perhaps be wrong to suggest that there is a disjuncture in perception between the rationalization of linguistic behavior and actual practice. Instead, we can say that the dominant ideology within the Nigerian education system that produces the prescriptive discourse embodied in teaching practices is in conflict with the habitual and unregulated practices of those same teachers.[4]

Gal and Irvine (1995: 974) use the term 'erasure' to designate a process whereby a dominant ideology renders certain aspects of sociolinguistic usage invisible in order to constrain the interpretation of linguistic behavior to a particular stereotype. They write '[b]ecause a linguistic ideology is a totalising vision, elements that do not fit its interpretive structure – that cannot be seen to fit – must either be ignored or transformed'. In other words, a dominant ideology will produce a selective interpretation of sociolinguistic behavior, and privilege or suppress any aspects of actual practice which do not accord with the language-based rationalizations which provide a meaning-frame for that action. The designation and interpretation of the cultural significance of loanwords in Japan can be seen to operate according to a similar process. In certain contexts, an ideology of cultural difference will classify some lexical items as *foreign* imports, while in other contexts they will be used as semiotic resources with no overtly specific political inflexion. In both cases, the linguistic phenomena are the same, but there is a difference of perception according to social context. In the case referred to in Chapter 5, where the former prime minister railed against foreign imports, we could perhaps categorize his behavior as a form of *strategic* perceptual disjuncture as the motivation for ignoring the nature of actual practice (his government's own use of foreign imports) was a deliberate statement of beliefs about ethnolinguistic nationalism.

In all these cases, however, the way in which a particular aspect of linguistic behavior is perceived and interpreted appears either to contract the observable phenomena (as recorded by the researcher) or to conflict with other interpretations of the same aspect of behavior. In other words, there is a significant difference of expressed opinion (between subject and researcher, or between different subjects) where agreement would have been expected. And it is in the nature and details of this discrepancy that we can read the ideologies which are influencing the interpretation of this linguistic behavior. So, for example, the case cited by Hogan shows a disjuncture between the perceptions of loanwords in two communities separated in terms of geographical environment. From this, we can speculate that the different community beliefs are producing different interpretations of the same linguistic behavior, and that an analysis of this differential will provide insights into the language ideologies of the two communities.

In the case of data from this current survey, the perception of what counted as English (when the concept was not defined explicitly in advance) proved to be built on a number of ideological assumptions. The disconnect between societal practices (the prevalence of what I had expected would be interpreted as English language forms within the social landscape) and the actual interpretation of that practice within the context of the discourse of English as a global language was the product of a complex of beliefs concerning the language. Such attitudes were not revealed in the initial survey data however, but in later interviews with the participants. In place of the original intention to execute a wider survey exploring language perception by means of a structured questionnaire, I instead followed up the pilot study with dedicated interviews with the original participants. As with the interviews discussed in Chapter 7, the intention was to elicit opinions and rationalizations about both the informants' encounters with English in the course of the everyday, and their attitude toward these encounters. Of interest were the overt judgments and categorizations of the participants. During the interviews, I also asked the participants to reflect on these judgments and categorizations in the light of what could be perceived as discrepancies between their behavior (or my interpretation of it) and the rationalization of that behavior. Of interest was not only why there should be a disjuncture between the two interpretations, but the nature of the participants' qualifications for their own interpretations.

Kazumi's response appears to accord with the interpretation that it is when the language is used as the predominant or sole mode of communication – and particularly when it is used as the medium of conversation – that it counts as 'English'. Other uses have been subsumed into Japanese language practice:

> I think that *gairaigo* and *romaji* [words written in the Roman alphabet] are not 'English'. I think we use English in our daily life, but we use them as if they were real Japanese. I mean, those words are English but when we use those words, we don't realise they are English. It is when I hear the conversation which some people speak in English, I think I encounter 'English'.

In these comments and a further clarifying statement she made that '*gairaigo* is Japanese, because when people use them, they are not going to think they are English', she is explicit that it is the perception about what does and does not count as 'real English' that forms the basis of beliefs about the language.

Aiko explained that words that were simply written in the Roman alphabet did not come under the category of any particular language, 'if I see English words in an advertisement, I count [them] as mark[s], not English. For instance, Coke, Prius, IMB and Sony.' To this, she added that while she would consider longer phrases used in advertisements or on television as being in English, she would, nevertheless, ignore them, 'I don't read the sentences in English on advertisements of magazines and TV, because... I think they are not meaningful. I look at the advertisement as image. In other words, I mainly look at the picture... I think the company prints English sentences on the advertisement to look better and cool.' Here it is not form alone that constitutes the English language, but the specific context in which it is used. If the language is displayed or utilized for a predominantly symbolic rather than semantic function, the usage is overlooked entirely. Here a process of erasure very self-consciously takes place according to presuppositions about the purpose of English.

Semiotic Hierarchies

One of the consequences of the perceptual disjuncture between different types of language use is the creation of semiotic hierarchies, whereby precedence is given (at least in conscious interpretation) to certain modes or functions of language behavior over others. Jakobson (1990: 72), in his 1958 lecture on 'Linguistics and Poetics', writes '[o]bviously we must agree with Sapir... that, on the whole, "ideation reigns supreme in language", but this supremacy does not authorize linguistics to disregard the "secondary factors"'. For Jakobson these 'secondary factors' include the other communicative functions of the linguistic utterance, and his six-part model of the orientations and functions of language has been a foundational statement in the development of semiotics. In light of the work done on multimodality in recent years, we can maybe expand upon this statement and suggest that it should also include the functions of all modes of semiotic behavior which contribute to the communicative act.

The concept of multimodality within communication theory has sought to codify the manner by which most human communication, from the printed text to face-to-face conversation, utilizes multiple semiotic modes which combine to produce a holistically realized message (Kress & van Leeuwen, 2001). The complexity and significance of what to a linguist would be referred to as 'paralinguistic' features (e.g. tone of voice and gesture in spoken interaction; typography and layout in written communication (Goodman, 2006: 250)) is theorized as being an integral aspect of the communicative act in multimodal theory. Perceptual disjuncture produced by a dominant language ideology – which, as was discussed earlier, is most often the referential ideology (Silverstein, 1979) – results, however, in the privileging of the 'linguistic' message in a multimodal text, and the establishment of a semiotic hierarchy which gives more weight to the denotational meaning encoded in the lexico–grammatical structure of the text, even when the structural motivation for that text may lie predominantly with one of the other functions. In other words, the referential ideology – which, by privileging the denotational function, assumes for language an ontology which has it as a bounded, transparent system – excludes from conscious interpretation the signification being performed by other semiotic modes. There is, then, a perceptual disjuncture between the way the text is being overtly interpreted (as a linguistic phrase encoding a verbal meaning) and the other semiotic work occurring.

What is of key significance for the present discussion is that it is this perceptual disjuncture that allows for the symbolic meaning of the language. It is the way that what counts as language (or a language) is closed down, the way that the boundary itself is constructed, which in effect creates the idea of the language. What is of interest, then, is not so much what actually does or does not count as language in a society, but the assumptions and debates that are mobilized in the process of creating this boundary.

In Chapter 2, I wrote of how the various approaches to a global English, in order to regulate language practice, first have to regulate the *concept* of the language. For English to qualify as a candidate for a universal code of communication according to Quirk's principles, for example, the language has to be limited to a particular standard, both decontextualized and static. The concept of this language can then be made real through institutionally sanctioned ideologies which produce curricula, textbooks and classroom practice to enforce it, but such regulation first involves closing down the meaning of what counts as English. Pennycook (2007: 108–109), in his discussion of the 'myth' of English as an international language, makes a similar point when arguing that we need to question whether in fact, 'something called English' really exists. He goes on to say

> It is assumed a priori that there is such a thing as English. This view is reinforced by excluding those types of English and...those types of speakers, that don't fit what is deemed to be English, and then employing the circular argument that, if it doesn't fit, it isn't English. A core system of English is assumed, with deviations from this core that destabilise the notion of system discounted.

When the concept of English is regulated in this way, practice is necessarily influenced by the consequences. Practice itself, though – how the language is actually used – can never be regulated in such a precise or effective way, and it is this that leads to the perceptual disjuncture discussed above.

A further point of note is that regulating the concept of the language produces two distinct categories of linguistic behavior. There is 'language' itself – which is the traditional focus of interest for linguistics and its associated disciplines[5] – and there is nonlanguage. As Harpham (2002: 42–43) writes 'Any theoretically coherent account of language must exclude some observable or inferable features, dimensions, or aspects of language; and these denied elements will necessarily exert a certain pressure on the object that is produced by their exclusion'. We have then a model comprising the privileged class of 'real' or correct language, and a hinterland of unlicensed or disregarded language behavior, which has been 'erased' (Gal & Irvine, 1995) from the official or dominant discourse of the language. And the *idea* of English is forged in the friction between the two; that is, in the creation of the boundary itself (see Figure 8.2).

The book so far has been concerned primarily with ways in which this symbolism boundary is set, and the discourses and debates that are involved in the process of creating a shape for what is to qualify as 'English', both in Japan and in more general applied linguistic theory. Yet it is important to note that the disregarded linguistic residue plays a significant semiotic role in society as well, both as the differential against which 'language' is defined, but also as a complex of semiotic behaviors in its own right. In the last part of the situated case study, therefore, I wish

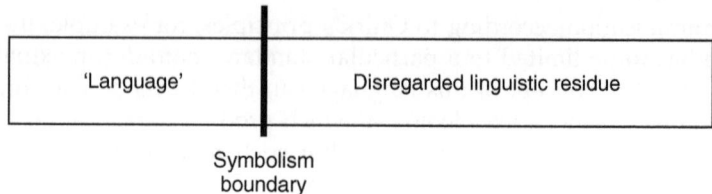

Figure 8.2 The hierarchy of semiosis and the symbolism boundary

to consider the ways in which this operates, both in contributing to the ideologies of English, as well as in offering an alternative perspective on the way that English exists in a globalized context. I will explore this with the aid of two examples.

The Disregarded Linguistic Residue

In Chapter 5, I discussed the presence of ornamental English in Japan, where primarily aesthetic factors rather than denotational linguistic meaning motivate language display. For a fluent speaker of Standard English guided by an ideology structured around denotation, linguistic practices such as the example below of a slogan on a T-shirt (Figure 8.3) are often interpreted as laughably meaningless or incompetent misuses of proper English. I also suggested that the critical reception of such cases is further aggravated by hegemonic attitudes about the validity of all

Figure 8.3 T-shirt design

nonstandard usage, and by a form of proprietorialism that not only views other cultural uses of English as incorrect (wrong rather than different), but sees them as an abuse of native speaker orthodoxies. There is, then, a strong perspectivist aspect to the interpretation of a text such as the one below, and for the case of the native or expert speaker, this is likely to be guided by the semiotic hierarchy that promotes the denotational content of the linguistic sign over other semiotic functions.

If one considers the functional purpose of this particular text though, denotational meaning is likely to be of insignificant importance. The semiotic work being done by the slogan on a T-shirt such as this is unlikely to be primarily referential, either in design or practice (it is not attempting to communicate a conceptual message), and thus to fault it for some flaw in the orthographic or lexico–grammatical composition of such a message (in this case a spelling mistake motivated by phonological transference) is to stubbornly uphold the normative precepts of these dominant ideologies (referential + proprietorial) and ignore the input of other functions. Of course, within an entirely non-Anglophone context, these dominant ideologies do not hold, and thus the semiotic hierarchy will most likely be reversed. Borrowing Jakobson's idea of the poetic function, and, for the written word, expanding it to include the visual impact as well (we might want to talk instead of an 'aesthetic' function), we can suggest that it is this that is central to the structure of the text. As Jakobson writes, '[t]he poetic function is not the sole function of verbal art but only its dominant, determining function, whereas in all other verbal activities it acts as a subsidiary, accessory constituent' (1990: 76). In this particular example, there is abundant evidence of aesthetic considerations structuring the combination of elements: there is visual symmetry in the proliferation of Os, Q and D in the main phrase, as well as their embedding in the concentric ovals of the image, and then there is the assonance that accompanies them ('D*o*n't qu*o*te'). As a text, its coherence is manifest in the aesthetic arrangement of resources, rather than the denotational; and as soon as denotational meaning is removed from the equation, this becomes apparent.

Globalization is still a context of significance for this design, because the choice of English does likely have a trace of symbolic meaning to it (along the lines of 'English = internationalism'). The language is still signifying therefore, both in an aesthetic *and* broadly symbolic way, but it does not do so as a communicative code for the expression of denotational meaning in the manner privileged by formal linguistics. Having said that, within the context of what is traditionally understood as 'English as a global language', this text will probably be viewed, by those who speak English as a global language, as referential code; and thus as an incompetent attempt at accurate or meaningful English, and it is likely to be ridiculed for such failings (is likely, for example, to feature as part of a gallery of similar humorous mistakes on the internet). Again, we can draw on Hymes's concept of second language relativity (1966) here, and consider the way in which the form may remain unchanged as the text passes across linguistic and cultural boundaries, but the function will necessarily be different. In this case, when the text enters into an English-speaking context and relies for its meaning on the interpretation by English speakers socialized outside the Japanese context, it indexes a complex of globalization-linked language ideologies, including some of the following: (1) the referential ideology which privileges the denotational meaning of the words; (2) the 'global language' ideology which suggests that the function of such a language is neutral code for communication; (3) the proprietorial ideology which views solecisms of form as violations of the conventions of English-speaking cultural decorum; and (4) a discourse of Japanese foreign language incompetence, promoted by internet sites such as *www.engrish.com*. When the text exists within the culture in which it was produced, however, the salience of these ideologies in the overall semiotic act is likely to be far less pronounced, if not nonexistent.

Dual-process Interpretation of English

While the example of the T-shirt slogan may rely on a context mostly external to the culture in which it was produced for the indexing of many of these wider ideologies of globalization and language, there are examples from within mainstream Japanese culture itself where language-linked social practice gains its substantive meaning from similar ideologies, while at the same time displaying a use of the language well beyond that licensed in such dominant ideologies. In such cases, there is, on the one hand, a hegemonic portrayal of English as something which *is* foreign and exotic to Japanese culture, yet on the other there is a ludic quality which results in such practices becoming a distinct form of cultural production in their own right and an integral part of the local cultural landscape.

One such example is the popular slot 'Karakuri Funniest English' in the television variety show, *Sanma no Karakuri Terebi* from TBS. The format of this programme has an American born Caucasian host, Thane Camus (TC in the transcript below), asking a member of the public to relate a short anecdote in Japanese and then to try to explain it in English. The host is bilingual, but the participants are not, and thus they inevitably make mistakes in their translations, which provides rich comedy for the studio audience. While the segment is part of an entertainment show, it borrows the clothing of a language education scenario: the anecdotes are always themed around an idiom or set phrase, and the whole situation is framed as a 'lesson' in English usage. In the excerpt transcribed below (originally broadcast on 29 October 2000), the lesson is based around the apparently well-known phrase 'my tragedy' [*watashi no higeki*], and the man (M in the transcript below) is thus being prompted to recount an incident full of personal disappointment.

As is often the case with Japanese television, subtitles are superimposed on the screen, spelling out what the participants have said. These can be used for particular effects, with the color, size and style of the font emphasizing aspects of the utterance (i.e. being of semiotic significance in the multimodal construction of the message) or prompting the audience to interpret it in a particular way. For an interaction of this sort, which is bilingual in nature, these subtitles also provide translations of the utterances, but again the purpose is to create a particular effect. The result is a complicated multimodal presentation, and, as we can see from an analysis of the excerpt, this complexity indicates sophisticated and innovative exploitation of English language resources, which belie many of the assumptions inherent in the prevailing ideologies.

(*Note about transcription:* Both the spoken exchanges between the participants, as well as the accompanying on-screen subtitles are included in the transcript; the former in the left-hand column, the latter in the right. Often the subtitles repeat exactly the spoken utterances, but they also modify or emphasize aspects of it and a color scheme is employed to enable this. Japanese has been transliterated into the Roman alphabet with a direct translation by me included in square brackets afterward. The onscreen subtitles mostly provide both the English and Japanese version of each utterance, and thus for this, my own translation of the Japanese is included only if there is an omission or notable difference of interpretation in the translations provided. Where aspects of either the speech or the on-screen transcription is of marked significance, a note to this effect is included in the relevant *Comments* column.)

	Spoken dialogue	Comments	On screen subtitles	Comments
TC:	What is your (.) job? *Shokugyô* [job]?		What is your job? (*Anata no shokugyô ha nan desu ka?*)	In blue text
M:	*Kajitetsudai* [housekeeper]		*Kajitetsudai*	In red text

(Continued)

Spoken dialogue	Comments	On screen subtitles	Comments
TC: *Kajitetsudai* [housekeeper]? English please		*Kajitetsudai.* English please. (*Kajitetsudai wo eigo de onegai shimasu*)	In blue text
M: (2) **Health** keeper	Marked Japanese-English pronunciation	*Herusu kîpâ* [written in katakana]. (*Kenkô ijisha*) [written in kanji: health keeper]	Katakana in purple text; kanji in red
TC: (laughing) Please tell me your *watashi no higeki* [my tragedy] story		Please tell me your *watashi no higeki* story. (*Anata no 'watashi no higeki' hanashi wo oshiete kudasai*)	In blue text
M: *Kanojo no tame ni daietto wo shitan desu yo. Soshitara 140 kiro made yaseta noni furarechaimashita.* [I went on a diet for my girlfriend. Although I managed to slim down to 140 kg, she ditched me]		*Kanojo no tame ni daietto wo shitan desu yo. Soshitara 140 kiro made yaseta noni furachaimashita*	In green text
TC: Okay. English please	Hand gesture summoning the man to reply	English please. (*Eigo de onegai shimasu*)	In blue text
M: I am (2) one hundred forty (3) kilogram (2) and (3) my girlfriend (5) shaking me	Spoken with katakana pronunciation, and very slowly	I am 140kg and my girlfriend shaking me (*140 kiro aru watashi wo kanojo ga furimawashita*) [My girlfriend shook me, who weighs 140 kg]	In purple text. Each word being spelt out as he speaks it After a pause and in red text

TC:	(laughing) Do do you have me...message to er...before girlfriend?	TC's speech accommodating to M's pronunciation and grammar	Do you have massage [sic] before girlfriend? (*Mae no kanojo ni nani ka messêji ga arimasu ka?*)	In blue text
M:	*Hai* [yes] *Koibito yo modotte oide.* [Please come back to me, my sweetheart.]	Turns to camera Bows	*Koibito yo modotte oide*	In red text
TC:	Na (.) English please		English please. (*Eigo de onegai shimasu*)	In blue text
M:	'*Koibito*' *tte eigo de nan to iun desu ka ne?* [How do you say *koibito* in English?]		'*Koibito*' *tte eigo de nan to iun desu ka ne?*	In green text
TC:	*Koibito*? Erm, 'lover'		Lover. (*Koibito*)	In blue text
M:	Please come back (1) my (1) **lebâ** [liver]		Please come back my **Lebâ** [written in katakana] (*Modotte oide watashi no kanzô*) [Please come back my liver]	In purple text. In red text. After a pause, also in red text
TC:	(laughs)	Holds his head in his hand		

Transcription conventions

- (.) = brief pause
- (2) = timed pause – two seconds
- (laugh) = transcription of a sound etc. that forms part of the utterance
- words in *italics* are in Japanese
- words in square brackets are translations of the Japanese
- words in bold = specific mispronunciations.

The general set up of this example, then, mocks the supposed inability of the average Japanese to speak English, by laughing at the uneven utterances that ensue when a random passerby tries to construct an English sentence. This particular television programme is often viewed by commentators as a type of self-reflexive criticism on the part of Japanese society: a contributor to the open-source *Everything2* website, for example, in an article about the English conversation school sector in Japan, sees it as illustrative of the way that 'Japanese media of all types strongly support the image that Japanese, no matter how much they study, simply cannot speak English'.[6] And yet a close look at the actual language practices involved shows it to be a great deal more complicated than this.

We can begin a detailed analysis by observing that the framing of the interaction does indeed index discourses related to this trend for a self-critical attitude to foreign language learning ability. This is represented in the following way: (1) the format mimics an educational setting, and is structured around a 'lesson'; and (2) it comprises a stereotypical encounter between a prototypical 'native speaker' (blond Caucasian) and a non-English speaking Japanese person. The humor is then based on the preconception that the Japanese participants will obviously make mistakes in their spoken English, and that the native speaker will look on incredulously. The humor actually works, however, by dint of the fact that the audience of the show *understand* at the level of the linguistic utterances themselves that mistakes have been made, and also that they can appreciate the resulting word play. When the man says 'health' instead of 'house' the audience must realize this is a mistake, and furthermore have some conception of the nonsense term that this results in. When the man is tripped up by the polysemy of the verb *furu* (in the passive form *furareru* and the compound *furimawasu* in the conversation) and picks the literal meaning 'to shake' over the figurative meaning 'to ditch one's girlfriend', the audience must be aware that this same polysemy is not found in an English equivalent, and that the resulting image is an absurd one. The format thus relies on a sophisticated level of linguistic interpretation, while being predicated on the prejudice that such sophistication in language use is beyond the capabilities of the average Japanese. This, then, is a further case of perceptual disjuncture, in which actual observable practice and the perception of the participants of that practice are at odds. In this way, the programme assists in the reproduction of the dominant 'Japanese people are ineffective users of English' ideology despite bearing witness to a far more nuanced and extensive form of the influence of globalization on native language practices.

These twin effects of comprehension and apparent miscomprehension are achieved here by the orchestration of multiple semiotic modes, and though I wish to argue that the English use here is not as inexpert as it is presented, it is *in combination* with other semiotic resources that it generates its richness of meaning. In part, comprehension of the 'mistakes' is aided by the on-screen subtitles, which allow for pronunciation difficulties to be exaggerated and interpreted as inappropriate puns. The jokes are thus assisted, with the on-screen translation making the most of any possible deviation from American Standard English in pronunciation, vocabulary choice or syntax, and, through a system of color-coding, prompting the audience toward a particular response (the pattern goes from blue, through purple, to red, with the latter indicating a punch line or moment of optimum incompetence). Often it is the *form* that is thus being privileged in these exchanges – which relates maybe to the importance placed upon formal aspects of language in the institutional education system and the prevailing exam culture. Privileging the form, of course, allows for word play, and yet, as I have suggested, it is 'assisted' word play, which depends not merely on the participant making mistakes (meaningless or abstract phonological articulations), but on him making mistakes that are funny if you understand English.

Let us take as an example the final solecism perpetrated by the unfortunate participant. When asked to give a message to his former girlfriend he fails to clearly pronounce the word 'lover', and ends up saying something which approximates as 'Please come back my liver'. That we are meant to interpret the mispronunciation in this way is made very clear by the subtitles, which firstly transcribe the offending word in katakana (the syllabary used for foreign imports), and then further force the point home by translating this into the native Japanese word for 'liver'. Yet there is a certain liberty being taken with the Japanese language in order to maximize the humorous potential of the mistake. When written in katakana the loanword *lebâ* [liver] refers to food, whereas the Japanese original [*kanzô*] is used exclusively as a medical or biological term (the distinction in meaning between the two terms is of the same quality as that between the French loans *mutton* and *pork* and the Anglo–Saxon *sheep* and *pig*). The two Japanese words, therefore, are not synonyms within the language, and thus by using them in this way in the on-screen translation the programme makers are going out of their way to construct a plausibly cautionary narrative that upholds the prejudice about poor English ability in Japanese society.

Also of note is that all the English words that are mispronounced or lead to the mistakes in this excerpt are ones that do actually exist in the Japanese lexicon as loanwords. The words *health*, *keeper*, *love* and *liver* are all established parts of the contemporary Japanese word-stock, and thus their pronunciation is likely to be familiar to the audience. Again, the actual nature of English influence on Japanese linguistic practices is mobilized for the very purpose of obscuring that nature, and promoting an idea of the language which conforms to mainstream discourses about cultural difference and language as an index of distinct cultural identity.

One might also point out that the transcript itself exhibits spelling mistakes (*massage* for *message*), and uses elliptical grammar ['Do you have massage before girlfriend?' (Do you have a message for your ex-girlfriend)], while the interviewer accommodates his speech to that of the participant in this same exchange. Yet none of this is *meaningful* for the substantive function of the language within the context of an entertainment show. What is meaningful here is the possibilities for linguistic play that are created by the processes of globalization, and that exist as a consequence of constructing specific ideologies about the place that English has within Japanese society. For while the dominant conceptualizations of the language may, in one respect, be reinforced by this type of language-related social practice; it also allows other ways for English language practices to be incorporated within the cultural landscape, and for English, in some unlicensed and inadmissible form, to become a part of the fabric of Japanese society.

Conclusion

Barthes continues his meditations on the significance of the 'Unknown Language' by suggesting the following:

> One chapter by Sapir or Whorf on the Chinook, Nootka, Hopi languages, by Granet on Chinese, a friend's remark on Japanese opens up the whole fictive realm... permitting us to perceive a landscape which our speech (the speech we own) could under no circumstances either discover or divine. (1982: 6–7)

In the early 21st century, when ownership of English is disputed, when the unitary meaning of the concept of the language is challenged and, with increasing frequency, rejected altogether, the insights of the ethnographer's gaze that Barthes invokes here can and maybe should be directed back at what we already know. As linguistic practices around the world evolve under the influence of rapid social change, consideration of the shape that the English language takes, the functions to which it is put and the convictions and ideologies that grow up around it – all these can enable us to look at this language that is apparently so familiar, about which we seemingly have such firm beliefs, and consider the multiplicities that it contains.

In his discussion of globalized standards of English at the turn of the millennium and of the future of English as an international language, Yano expresses the opinion that

> Japan is a typical country where English is and will certainly stay a foreign language in that it will function only as a means of communication with non-Japanese in international settings. It will probably never be used within the Japanese community and form part of the speaker's identity repertoire. There will not be a distinctly local model of English, established and recognisable as Japanese English, reflecting the Japanese culture and language. (2001: 127)

A view such as this is predicated on a cluster of assumptions about language which close down the meaning of the word until it refers to only a part of the totality of linguistic behavior. As far as the likely emergence of a 'Japanese English' along the lines of the Kachruvian world Englishes model is concerned, Yano's prediction will likely prove to be correct, and it is within debate about such a variety that he expresses this opinion. However, there is also ample evidence to suggest that English – as both concept and practice – already exists as a site and as a vehicle for cultural expression and for the brokering of identity in Japan, and that there are distinctive and expansive uses of the language which can claim an 'authentic' Japanese character. In other words, the existence of English within Japan – which is both extensive and deep-rooted – is not merely superficial and faddish, but plays a significant cultural role within the country.

Chapter 9
Rival Ideologies in Applied Linguistics

An Ontology of English in Japan

The focus of this book has been on the way in which the English language is positioned in Japanese society. The basic methodological approach has been to explore how the language actually exists as both concept and resource in various and diverse settings, rather than to work from preconceptions about what a global language should be. In essence, the book has attempted to provide an ontology of the English language in Japan, using the opinions and behaviors of people and institutions to trace the shape of this. The intention has been to show that the way in which the language is positioned in society and the symbolic meanings with which it is invested are bound up with a complex of values and contestations which relate to political, cultural and social issues that constitute the variegated and dynamic identity of modern Japan. The question we then come to, though, is how does this ontology of English in Japan relate to the broader concept of English as a global language. Where does *this* picture of English fit into the dialogue about monocentric or polycentric approaches to the language, for example, and how might it inform current debates about English in the world that are being pursued within the discipline of applied linguistics?

To consider these questions, I will take a step back and look once again at how the language is conceptualized in research paradigms in contemporary applied linguistics thought. And I will do this not in terms of the abstract question of what English is understood to mean within debates about its global nature or role, but by considering the specific question of what form of English should best be used as a teaching model around the world. The rationale for framing the discussion around this question is the pivotal and formative role that education plays in the life of the language. In the current ecology of world languages, English is very often an additional tongue, and its acquisition is most usually the product of formal education. As such, the domain of education becomes a key mediating factor in the existence of the language, and it is here that debates about what English is are reified, and that ideas about the language become disseminated into the social environment.

Education is also one of the pre-eminent sites for the regulation of language and linguistic behavior. As Foucault (1972: 227) explains

> Education may well be, as of right, the instrument whereby every individual, in a society like our own, can gain access to any kind of discourse. But we well know that in its distribution, in what it permits and in what it prevents, it follows the well-trodden battle-lines of social conflict.... What is an education system, after all, if not a ritualisation of the word; if not a qualification of some fixing of roles for speakers [?]

Education is the site for the superintendence not only of what can and cannot be said, and of what passes for and is passed on as knowledge, but also of the form that articulation takes. And though such regulation, in the guise most notably of 'evaluation', is integral to all linguistic interaction to a certain extent (an issue to which I shall return later in the chapter), it is at its most explicit, its most co-ordinated, and its most institutionally sanctioned, in the processes of education. The question 'what form of English should be taught around the world?' does not, therefore, provide an arbitrary context for the more fundamental query about what English is, but instead foregrounds the key mechanisms by which the concept and the shape of the language is regulated.

To this, we should add that research and scholarship that explores English-related language practices within the context of the language's status as a universal tongue will themselves, whether by conscious intent or not, be a prelude to some form of regulation. Although a sociolinguistics of English use around the world, or a linguistic–anthropological study of the English language practices of diverse worldwide communities, will be predominantly descriptive exercises, they take place within the shadow of the unstable concept of the universal language, and as such their descriptive data will be interpreted within this conceptual framework. Rather than remaining simply descriptive, they themselves become instruments of regulation, adding to the debate about how the language exists within the world, and how knowledge of this existence should influence educational practices.

Even in the recent past, the question of what English is, and what form of the language should be taught, was not considered unduly problematic. The answer often began and finished with the expert native speaker. Chomsky's (1965: 3) famous prefatory assertion, 'Linguistic theory is concerned primarily with an ideal speaker–listener, in a completely homogenous speech-community, who knows its language perfectly' points unequivocally to what it considers the source of linguistic expertise; and this same source, in the shape of an educated and representative member of the dominant social class of a particular nation or culture, easily assumed the mantel of teaching model for a foreign language. As Davies (2003: 103) notes, 'in spite of his own genuine wish for linguistic competence not to be applied to areas such as language learning and teaching, Chomsky's theory was widely made use of in applied fields'. This teaching model has proved to be flawed on two accounts, however. Firstly, the concept of 'native speaker' is theoretically vague and far from being a secure scientific category; and secondly, given the multifarious roles that English plays around the world, the insistence on a normative model tied to one social group within one particular culture is more divisive than is commonly considered necessary or acceptable.

The purpose of this final chapter, therefore, is to revisit contemporary approaches to the question of what variety or standard should be used as a teaching model around the world, and consider how the specific symbolic meanings for the language that have been explicated in the previous chapters – those meanings that are written into the fabric of Japanese society – equate with the way the general debate over English as a world language is presently evolving. The intention is to try to incorporate significant structural factors from the language ideologies that constitute the symbolic meaning of English in Japan into the debates about the function and cultural implications of a global language that are currently a major preoccupation for applied linguistics research and theorizing.

Rival Authenticities

One persuasive approach to the question of what variety or standard should be used as a teaching model is that it should reflect the actual circumstances in which the language is most commonly used now. Given the rapid sociological changes produced by globalization, the traditional typological model of global English is often considered to be anachronistic now. Where the map of world English usage was conventionally divided up into the EFL, the ESL and the EMT countries – each grouping highlighting a particular function for the language within the community so designated (Carter & Nunan, 2001) – shifts in the demographics of worldwide English users have complicated this pattern. Japan, for example, was traditionally considered a part of what Kachru has described as the Expanding Circle, and was thus seen as an English as a *Foreign* Language country. Yet, the contention in many quarters is that the use of this terminology masks the way in which the language is actually used in contemporary globalized contexts, and that it is no longer the case that the inhabitants of Japan wish to use the language primarily for conversing with speakers from the main English-language countries (i.e. 'native speakers'), as the EFL tag would suggest. Scholars such as Jenkins (2005: 144) maintain that instead

> It is now widely accepted that the world's largest number of English speakers come from the countries of the *expanding circle* and that the majority of communication involving the use of English by its non-native speakers does not involve its native speakers. In other words, the changing function of English around the world [means that it is]... a vehicle primarily for lingua franca (NNS–NNS) interaction.

The argument here is that, given this new global context in which demographic distribution of English-users means that those who have it as an additional language statistically outnumber those who have it as a mother tongue, previous beliefs about teaching models need to be revised. Yet despite the shift in patterns of usage, 'control over the norms of how it "should be used" is still assumed to rest with the *minority* of its speakers, namely English native speakers' (Seidlhofer, 2005: 170). In other words, in what used to be referred to as EFL countries, the 'realities' of English usage have changed (Jenkins, 2006: 158), and this, it is argued, should be a determining factor in decisions about the variety used as a teaching model.

At issue here is what constitutes the *authentic* circumstances in which the language is used. As was discussed in Chapter 6, authenticity, be it concerned with the nature of the language itself or of the type of interaction in which the language is used, is not an unproblematic concept. Although often co-opted as an authoritative reference point against which phenomena can be judged, and which can be used as a foundation stone for the construction of argument, the concept is, in fact, a site for ideological struggle, and its invocation often has both an epistemic and rhetorical purpose behind it. In the field of sociolinguistics, Coupland (2003: 419) has identified a pattern amongst claims to authenticity which, he contends, is a determining factor in the structure and ambition of the discipline as a whole:

> a large part of the dominant sociolinguistic agenda over many decades has been to defend one cluster of traditionally authentic phenomena and processes, in opposition to a different cluster.... Sociolinguistics has defended *vernacular authenticities* in the domain of language, and has set itself ideologically against *establishment authenticities*.

Sociolinguistics, he suggests, has promoted the usage of speakers who are on the margins of traditional sites of social power as being more 'real' than those who conform to conventions that are valued in establishment or institutional environments. According to this formula, the latter are liable to constrain their language use to ensure it accords with artificial norms, and this enforced practice is the site for the reproduction of linguistic (and other political) inequalities.

We can discern an emergent trend in the field of world English which parallels this pattern. The Quirk–Kachru debate, for example, is structured around much of this distinction – the monocentric standard versus sociolinguistic diversity. The argument from demographics outlined above also follows a similar pattern: 'vernacular authenticities' in this formula would correspond to lingua franca communication scenarios, with 'establishment authenticities' being the institutional models codified within mainstream textbooks and curriculum resources. The result is that scholars such as Jenkins and Seidlhofer privilege the 'vernacular' use of English, and suggest that this is the more authentic framework for language in the world today.

One of the consequences of this type of approach is to essentialize particular groups of speakers. As Bucholtz (2003: 400) notes

> The idea of authenticity gains its force from essentialism, for the possibility of a 'real' or 'genuine' group member relies on the belief that what differentiates 'real' members from those who only pretend to authentic membership is that the former, by virtue of biology or culture or both, possess inherent and perhaps even inalienable characteristics criterial of membership.

In other words, to describe something as authentic is to relate it to a stable and coherent set of characteristics which constitute the understanding of the reality of that object. In the case of a group of speakers, it is to promote certain elements of their linguistic behavior and to suggest that these elements considered together are an essential quality for qualification as part of that group. The danger of such an approach is that it results in a form of reductionism.

There are two issues of particular interest here. One is that, as Coupland points out, the claim for authenticity invariably works for a specific agenda, and thus has a political purpose behind it (though often this need not register as a conscious concern of the theorizing or research). One of the motivating factors behind the approach that claims lingua franca usage among non-native speakers as the 'reality' for the majority of English-users in the world is to return power to those disenfranchised by the hegemony of the (Western) English speaking countries. To a degree, essentializing such a speaker is a necessary part of the process of prosecuting such an agenda – it focuses attention on one specific aspect of usage, and attempts to valorize this above other factors which have previously been used as determinants in the argument. The process thus works as what Spivak has called 'strategic essentialism' (Bucholtz, 2003; Spivak, 1988) in that it accepts some of the reductionist ramifications inherent in the act of essentialism in order to create a strong, cohesive identity for a group who would otherwise be marginalized or ignored. A 'strategic essentialism' of this sort is therefore often considered a preliminary process, offering the otherwise disenfranchised group an initial voice in the debate which, once secured, can then be refined to produce a more nuanced and heterogeneous position.

As noted, this approach necessarily foregrounds only certain aspects of linguistic behavior, and simplifies (for strategic reasons) the language use involved. In a dialogic argument attempting to redress historical inequality, it can therefore be a useful tool; as a framework for prolonged and context-sensitive analysis of linguistic behavior however it has its limitations. If we take as an example the argument from demographics for English as a lingua franca, we can see both the advantages and limitations. It may well be the case that statistically the majority of speakers around the world use English for NNS–NNS lingua franca purposes, and thus the pursuit of a research agenda which highlights this will have the effect of providing such users with an autonomous linguistic identity and a degree of sociolinguistic recognition. This statistical fact in itself, however, need not be a determining factor for people's orientation to and adoption of a particular variety. While it may be true that there are more non-native speakers than native speakers in the world these days, the proportion of global power and influence that belongs to those native speakers (not simply by virtue of them being native speakers, of course, but because they are natives in economically rich and politically powerful countries) is greater than what it is for the non-native speakers. If one of the purposes of lingua franca communication is to enable international trade and the participation in world markets, then the distribution of economic power is likely to present an alternative picture of the statistical 'realities' of contemporary global society, and the standard recognized by those who currently *hold* this economic power will, by default, become the model to which those wishing to gain access to this power are likely to aspire.[1]

There is then a false syllogism in the original argument: It is not necessarily the case that people orient toward 'native speaker' varieties simply because they are varieties spoken as a mother tongue; it is equally as likely that they orient toward these varieties because they are the ones spoken by people with economic (and political) power. It may very well be the case that the two factors coincide – and indeed the causal dynamic that has resulted in the current elevated position of English in the hierarchy of world languages is a *result* of the economic and political power of the countries that speak it (Crystal, 1997: 7). But there are actually two separate issues here: One is to do with ideas of fluency and expertise based on psycholinguistic assumptions about native speaker intuition and the extent to which this should act as an arbiter for the 'authenticity' of a model of the language; and another is to do with ideologies of the language based on observations and beliefs about its associations with particular social and cultural values. The English as a Lingua Franca position is to dispute the argument from psycholinguistic assumptions, but ignore the argument from ideology. It would undermine the argument that suggests that 'native speaker' norms are inherently more correct because linguistics has traditionally based its observations on the expert native speaker (Howatt & Widdowson, 2004: 358), and instead it would offer an alternative interpretation of legitimacy centered around actual use. But in prosecuting this position (for strategic ends), these scholars do not acknowledge that the attraction of such norms might be due to other sociopolitical factors which are obscured by the vagueness of the term 'native speaker'. The argument from demographics produces one sort of 'reality', but the argument from economic power produces a quite different one.

Of course, speculation about the 'realities' of worldwide usage based on this argument from economic power falls into the same trap as the original argument from demographics. It too is in danger of claiming legitimacy for one particular standard based on an *a priori* understanding of the role that the language occupies in people's lives. And it is here that research into the complex of local ideologies which create the meaningful context in which the language actually operates becomes important. As has been shown for the Japanese case, the orientations that both institutions and individuals have toward the language are related to issues of policy, and cultural and social identity and thus there is a deep-rooted integrity to them which needs to be acknowledged by the research community. In the case of Japan, the context is one in which it is neither simply international lingua franca purposes nor the appeal of economic power which produces the meaning that is associated with the language, but rather one that involves also the negotiation of cultural identity within a society that is being recast by globalizing forces.

Evaluation as Interpretation

The lingua franca approach, in common with many conceptualizations of English as a global language, puts great stress on 'intelligibility', and this is one key area where an approach that combines linguistic precepts with context-specific ideologies is essential for successful language regulation. As Bamgbose (1998: 11) has noted, '[p]reoccupation with intelligibility has often taken an abstract form characterised by decontextualised comparisons of varieties', where form is discussed without consideration of the interpersonal strategies that convert this form into embodied linguistic behavior. Even corpus approaches which look to record 'real' examples of usage are likely to be found wanting when it comes to the effects and interpretation of actual communicative acts. As Ferguson (2006: 176) notes, 'while corpora are certainly useful in determining, for example, the frequency of particular constructions over a wide range of texts, they tend to be less informative about the contextual conditions under which a particular feature was produced'. To downplay the influence of this context as mostly irrelevant for a tolerable degree of 'intelligibility' is, then, to ignore all but the ideational function of language, and run the risk of misinterpreting the way that communication is effected.

We can illustrate the importance of the subtle but crucial influence that elements of context can play by examining one current debate in world English which relates directly to the different agendas articulated through rival claims to authenticity. This is the controversy over the use of the term 'error' to refer to aspects of non-native speech. The debate here is concerned with the politics of characterization: the battle between 'errors' versus 'innovations'; between 'deficient forms' versus 'emergent features'. One side of the argument runs that if a particular feature of language used by a non-native speaker diverges from that of the native speaker standard but does so habitually and systematically, then it should not be considered an error, even if it violates the orthodox form of language modeled by mainstream textbooks or other codified authorities on language (see Jenkins, 2000: 160, for the expression of such a view, and Seidlhofer, 2004: 228, for further commentary). The contention is that a feature that occurs with regularity within a particular speech community should be considered a legitimate part of the grammar of the variety used by that speech community. The counterposition is the one that advocates a single and authoritative standard as the base against which all usage is best judged (e.g. Görlach, 2002), and thus, implicitly, regards the use of terms such as 'innovation' and 'emergent feature' as a type of prevarication, which is liable to have the effect of degenerating the language (Görlach talks of 'broken, deficient forms' and 'a decline, decay or mangling of English' (p. 12)).

Unfortunately, a decontextualized summary of the two approaches does not allow for clear-cut adjudication between them. Abstract theoretical assertions of this sort can offer no definitive answer to which side is right and which is wrong in practice. We can, however, provide a theoretical precept which will settle the argument as it occurs in real-life scenarios. And this is the aforementioned issue of evaluation. As Blommaert (2006b: 520) says: 'Language use ... is intrinsically normative, not in the sense that it always follows established rules, but in the sense that every act of communication will be subject to assessment on grounds of (often implicit) shared complexes of indexicalities – the complexes of indexicalities that provide the basis for speech communities'. In other words, marked features such as unorthodox usage will be interpreted according to the ideologies of language which constitute the context of interaction between interlocutors. The interpretation will depend on the participants involved, their social and geographical background, the purpose of the interaction as well as various other psychological variables and prejudices. Indeed, the only certainty that we can ascribe to the encounter is that the form of what is said *will* be evaluated, and will thus become part of the overall communicative message that is expressed/interpreted. It is not within the executive power of applied linguistics scholarship to prescribe the rules by which this encounter proceeds and thus determine *a priori* whether an instance of unorthodox usage is interpreted as an 'error', an 'emergent feature', a creative usage or anything else. The call for a change in conceptualization within the teaching community could, of course, filter through to influence in some form the ideologies that determine interpretation, and doubtless this is the ultimate intention of those who advocate such a position. It is unlikely, however, that there will be a direct relationship between such a call and the actual act of interpretation, as the interpretation will be determined by a myriad of social and cultural factors, of which the well-meaning intentions of the professional applied linguist will likely only constitute a rather minor part.

As a side note, it is worth adding that non-native speaker 'errors' of this sort are not necessarily interpreted negatively, and can in fact assist in creating an exchange that works toward mutual intelligibility. Blommaert (2003: 610) points out, 'In practical terms [these metapragmatic aspects of language usage] may ... offer us an understanding of why non native English of [this] kind ... often meets considerable interpersonal tolerance for deviation from "standard" English in pronunciation, lexis and style'. In other words, interlocutors will interpret certain features of usage as errors if they wish to interpret them as errors (that is to say, if the ideological matrix that constitutes the context – composed of issues related to status, location, shared or divergent background, etc – prompts such interpretation), but that paradoxically, by seeing these features as errors (as the output of someone from outside the speech community), the interlocutors may well orientate themselves toward the interaction by seeing it as a lingua franca exchange and adapting their own usage accordingly, thus facilitating a productive act of communication.

The Limitations of a Lingua Franca Usage Model

Language regulation (be it in the context of policy, education or research) which is not sensitive to the ideologies 'on the ground', therefore, is not simply offering an opposing view of the role that language should play within society, but failing to perceive *how* language functions within society. As has been shown with the Japanese case, the ideologies on the ground will invariably exist for a particular reason, and contribute to a wider ecology of social behavior, of which linguistic behavior is but a part. The political desire to alter language regulation practices so that they are less complicit in the production and reproduction of social inequalities can remain an important rationale for applied linguistics research and TESOL theorizing, yet it needs to be understood as operating within a context in which local beliefs about the language can play a positive role in the negotiation of national, cultural and personal identity, and can be a significant political factor in their own right. As such, decontextualized debates about apparently divisive issues such as native speaker norms and language as a vehicle for Western values may well take on a quite different complexion when they are embedded within a specific culture.

How, though, does this observation help us with our discussion of what variety of English should be taught? A legitimate question at this stage would be whether it is fair to critique approaches to worldwide English from the point of view of total linguistic behavior, and by discussing not simply language as practice but language as concept as well. Are we really contrasting like with like here? After all, advocates of the lingua franca communication position are very clear that they are talking of a specific use of the language. Seidlhofer (2001: 146), for example, defines the function as follows:

> The term 'lingua franca' is understood in the strict sense of the word, i.e. an additionally acquired language system that serves as a means of communication between speakers of different first languages, or a language by means of which the members of different speech communities can communicate with each other but which is not the native of either.

The concept of global English here is one that is tied specifically to communication. As such, it seeks to present the most pragmatic and politically acceptable way in which a shared linguistic code can operate as part of the communicative repertoire for world citizens in order to facilitate the expression of ideas across speech community boundaries.

It is no accident that advocates of this position look to the history of reduced Englishes for inspiration in this task. Writing of Ogden's *Basic English*, Palmer and Hornby's *Thousand-Word English* and West's *Service List*, Seidlhofer and Jenkins (2003: 145) state that '[t]hese anticipate, and offer many profound insights into, many of the EWL [English as a World Language] issues that we are confronted with today'. Building on the insights of their predecessors, the ELF approach is explicit about the need to draw up a framework which will provide empirically based insights into the way in which the central purpose of lingua franca communication can be achieved. Such a strict narrowing of the parameters of what a language *should* do does not have a particularly successful pedigree however (Graddol, 1996: 186). A major fault in any such project appears to be that while theorists can ignore the many peculiarities of natural languages in favor of their own choice of functional use, speakers do not have the same luxury when the language is loosed into the oxygen of actual use. All the variables that appeared so neatly contained on the page of the research article are suddenly producing real-life effects and combining in unpredictable ways when embodied by living interlocutors.

Widdowson (2003: 55) offers a modified approach to the issue of lingua franca communication which highlights certain necessary constraints that need to apply for the success of the project. He suggests that the English language exists around the world as a result of two different kinds of development: 'One of them is primary and local and takes the form of varieties which are dialect-like in that they serve the immediate everyday social needs of a community. The other is secondary and global and takes the form of registers associated with particular domains of institutional and professional use'. He is drawing here on Halliday's distinction between dialects and registers (Halliday *et al.*, 1964): the former being a variety with reference to the user, the latter with reference to its use. In other words, one variety is associated primarily with a particular community, and the other with a type of communication. In this way, Widdowson sees the variety that is used for international communication purposes (English as an International rather than a Second Language) as one practiced by discourse communities which are founded on a shared need to communicate across traditional linguistic barriers, and thus develop specific linguistic strategies for this purpose.

Such a conceptualization refines the formula of lingua franca use, pointing to the role played by the professional or social domain in which encounters take place. And indeed, instances in which reduced Englishes do operate in an effective functional manner appear to be those tied specifically to the needs of the domain in which they operate, so much so that as registers many of them warrant their own name: for example, Seaspeak, Airspeak and so on. Yet by this stage in the process we have moved rather far from the wider topic of English as a global language, and cannot practicably offer the specialized register approach as an answer to the question of what variety of English should be used as a general teaching model.[2]

What seems to be the problem is that the communicative code rationale appears, at first glance, to be the main and proper purpose for a global language – after all, what is the point of a global language if not to facilitate international communication. As such, approaches predicated on this belief appear logically sound. The data from the Japanese case study show, however, that the language is never limited to this role – that a global language (or at least the use of *English* as a global language) – involves a far more complex set of factors, many of which compromise the rationale for a purely lingua franca approach. Of course, one could suggest that the uses described in the previous chapters are in fact all *intranational* uses, and are related to the positioning of English *within* Japan. Yet they also all draw upon the concept of English being an international language and on the value and attraction of its 'global' status. And it is this conceptual understanding of the language that provides the context in which the language is used, and thus becomes a determining factor in the character and nature of that use. Divorcing the use of the language from the complex set of beliefs which constitute its existence within society is neither practicable nor, one could argue, possible.

Conclusion

In conclusion, if our question is what variety or standard of the language should be taught, the answer – one of seemingly pure equivocation – will be: this depends. This answer is not quite as facetious as it sounds however. The mechanism *by which* it depends is the key issue here, and should feature as part of the answer to the question. The form and meaning of a language will always be specific to the circumstances in which it is used, and thus choosing one particular variety as a teaching model will never be sufficient to satisfy the many issues that have been raised during the course of the lengthy and ongoing debates about English education in the world today. To suppose that it is simply a matter of choosing the correct variety of the language – that this act alone can resolve the political and ethical issues about inequality, as well as the ideational and interpersonal issues about productive communication – is a mistake. What is needed is an awareness of what forms have what functions and what meanings in specific contexts, and *how* it is that these are determined. Choosing an appropriate variety will depend on the ends to which learners wish to use the language and the reasons they have for learning it. It will depend on the beliefs about the language current in the society in which these users live and the beliefs of the speech community with which they wish to converse. As such, the choice of any standard or variety needs to be accompanied by an integrated programme of anthropological awareness that incorporates an understanding of the various ideologies which produce meanings for the language, be they at a macro symbolic level, or at a micro metapragmatic level.

Arguments about world benchmarks (about prestige varieties and standards) versus demographic and sociolinguistic realities are, in themselves, never going to be accurate enough in their appraisal of the *in situ* practice which determines attitudes toward the language. Indeed, we can go further and say that a definitive statement on the standard to be used as a teaching model can never be made as every articulation about the language and every slight and simple act of language regulation alters in some form and some place the complex of ideologies about the language which influences its use and interpretation. If, as scholars such as Calvet (2006) argue, English (or any named language) is simply an abstraction from the practices of those who use and represent it, then each act of use and representation is likely to alter its shape and existence, and each act of codification will alter the entity it attempts to codify.

The idea of the language – which transforms into ideologies as it is expressed through material practices – is a key part of what constitutes the way the language actually exists in any one context or society. These ideologies can be read from the relations between English and the national language; from the relations between English and the individual's identity in the local society and his or her projected identity in the wider (imaginary) context of global society; and in the relations between the language and local culture. These relationships – which, in the Japanese case, give rise to the motifs of globalization, of authenticity and of aspiration – produce the idea of the language as it exists and is understood in a given society, and their examination will reveal the assumptions about the language that contribute to its ontological reality, affect the attitudes toward it and the ways in which it is used.

If intelligibility were the primary concern for the success of a global language, then decisions about a model for teaching could be resolved on the basis of rudimentary linguistic knowledge. Concord over the choice of a particular standard (selected according to pragmatic concerns such as the distribution of expert speakers and the availability of the resources of codification, maybe) could happily be buttressed by the inherent flexibility of natural languages to accommodate diversity of form and delivery and remain comprehensible (thanks to redundancy in much grammatical construction, the abundance of synonyms in the lexis, a phonemic system which locates significance in differential rather than determined forms, pragmatic strategies for the negotiation of meaning etc.). The combination of these factors, plus natural patterns of social organization in groups committed to communication that create the conditions for a discourse community (Swales, 1990) and see language adapt accordingly, would suggest that mutual intelligibility is achievable without great trouble (with some coordinated planning and the ready availability of suitable resources).

But a global language is not simply a matter of mutual intelligibility. The role that ideology plays in language conceptualization and language use results in a far more complex picture of what a global language is. As an inherent part of linguistic behavior, implicated in both procedural knowledge (metapragmatics) and propositional knowledge (symbolic meaning), ideology links language to a range of other social concepts and practices: with cultural and political beliefs being indexed in every act of speech, while the very concept of 'a language' is a political construction or invention (Pennycook & Makoni, 2007).

The struggles produced by the ideological nature of languages are magnified, of course, with a *global* language, which does not share the relative stability of discrete community- or society-based cultural beliefs. A global language juxtaposes worldview with worldview, and implicit norms with divergent implicit norms to a far greater extent than a national or community language. The consequences of this are that, as has been shown in the Japanese case, the language (both as practice and idea) can be co-opted for a range of political and cultural purposes and can become the site for the expression and negotiation of an understanding of one's place within the world.

This does not void the practical utility of the language as a lingua franca – ideational communication still occurs, and English (in its multiple forms) is doubtless the pre-eminent language for international communication in this current phase of world history. But it means that crucially the language operates in other ways as well: many of which can affect the actual nature of communication (through the role ideology plays in evaluation and interpretation); and others which allow it a different dynamic role within the lived experience.

Ultimately, we need to consider English as a Global Language as a composite of function and concept which gains its meaning and value from the mediating role it plays in the social lives of people who understand their lives to be lived in a global context. And while this is not to deny the key instrumental role the language has as an effective means of communication, it can point us in the direction of a broader understanding of the consequences of the way in which English is increasingly being positioned as the pre-eminent international language.

Notes

2 The Concept of English as a Global Language

1. McArthur (2003: 56) proposes the term 'English Language Complex' as an umbrella term for the many different incarnations of the language that can be called English. Mesthrie (2006: 382–383), in adopting this terminology in place of his own use of the 'language family' metaphor, gives a useful list of subtypes. His proposal for what should or should not be included in such a list utilizes a 'prototype' definition of the term 'English'.
2. Such a contention involves something of a polarization of trends within the field, and I follow Jenkins (2006) here, both in adopting such a framework for analytic purposes, and also in the use of the specific terminology. I shall look, in Chapter 3, at a broader mapping of contemporary approaches to the issue.
3. Quirk (1985: 6), for example, in a famous pronouncement, suggests '[t]he relatively narrow range of purposes for which the non-native needs to use English (even in ESL (English as a second language) countries) is arguably well catered for by a single monochrome standard that looks as good on paper as it sounds in speech'. Here, he is prescribing a very specific functional use of the language, yet still according it the name of 'English'.
4. Modifiers which create the many three letter acronyms (ELF (English as a lingua franca), EIL (English as an international language), EFL (English as a foreign language), etc) do, of course, endeavour to effect a certain refinement of reference, yet the compatibility between term and concept is always an issue of contention, with different parties promoting different definitions. See Jenkins (2007: 3–4) for an example of discussion around this issue.
5. Harpham's use of the word 'arbitrary' is an intertextual echo of the fundamental tenet of Saussurean linguistics, and is to be read as a polemical refutation of positivist approaches to the language sciences in which the object of research is considered as self-evident and secure. It is not meant absolutely – rather there is a certain arbitrary quality to all conceptualizations of language which disqualifies them from claiming ahistorical universality.
6. Ibuki was Minister of Education, Culture, Sports, Science and Technology from 26 September 2006 to 25 September 2007.
7. All quotes about McPal are taken from the company's promotional literature, and translated from the Japanese (http://www.mcpal.jp – accessed 15 December 2006).

3 Language Ideology and Global English

1. Kachru's (1985) influential model of English in the world draws distinctions between an Inner Circle comprised of countries where English is used as a native language (e.g. the UK and the US); an Outer Circle, where the language has institutional status and is acquired mostly as an additional language (e.g. India or Singapore); and an Expanding Circle, where it is traditionally used as a foreign languages (e.g. most European countries).

2. Peirce's tripartite typology of signs distinguishes between those which resemble their object (icons), those which have a relationship of contiguity with their object (indexes) and those which have a conventional but otherwise arbitrary relationship with the object (symbols).
3. Peircean scholars such as Kockelman (2005) employ portmanteau terms such as indexical-symbols or iconic-indices to indicate the combinatory nature of relations between sign and object.

4 English in Japan: The Current Shape of the Debate

1. For an incisive discussion of ideologies of the English language within the mainstream Japanese media, see Kubota (1998).
2. The history of JALT dates back to much the same time as the publication of *The Teaching of English in Japan*, as it was in 1975 that the organization, originally called the Kansai Association of Language Teachers, began. In 1977, it changed its name to JALT and became a TESOL affiliate.
3. We can find a similar historical framework being utilized as background context for many other studies. Honna and Takeshita (2002) and Torikai (2005), for example, both gloss some general historical background as context for their detailed analyses of recent educational policy reforms.
4. The Ministry of Education (*Monbusho*) was renamed as part of a reorganization of government agencies in January 2001, and is now known as the Ministry of Education, Culture, Sports, Science and Technology (*Monbu Kagakusho* in Japanese, though most often referred to by the acronym MEXT). Subsequent references in the book will refer to *Monbusho* for the pre-2001 ministry, and MEXT for the post-January 2001 ministry, as this is the most common pattern of usage in the literature.
5. The Test of English for International Communication (TOEIC) and Test of English as a Foreign Language (TOEFL) are administered by ETS (Educational Testing Service) in the USA. The former is intended to measure competency in English for everyday use in a business environment, while the latter for 'academic' English. The TOEIC was developed following a request from Japan's Ministry of International Trade and Industry and is a very popular qualification in Japan.
6. *Nihonjinron* is the genre of pamphlets and books dealing with the 'uniqueness of the Japanese'. The topic is discussed in further detail in Chapters 5 and 6.
7. Torikai (2005) has a rather different interpretation of this trend based on a reading of the *Action Plan*. She notes that while the word 'communication' is used 41 times in the 15 page document, the word 'culture' appears only 7 times. She takes this as evidence of a shift away from the 'language = culture' ideology, and writes 'It is fair to conclude in summary that the government's rationale for their decisions on the purpose and objectives of English language education is to accommodate globalisation' (p. 251). Kawai (2007), meanwhile, sees a clash between governmental discourse (in the *Frontier Within* document) and public reaction: according to her, the former de-culturises the language and presents it as a functional tool of communication, while the latter is more ready to associate language with 'foreign culture' and worry about its influence on Japanese culture and identity.
8. Two qualifications need to be noted here. High school education in Japan is not compulsory, despite the fact that the majority of those graduating from junior high school do continue to the next stage of secondary education. In addition, the *Course of Study* refers to 'foreign language' education, not English alone. In practice, however, English is very much the predominant language.

Notes

5 Globalization: 'Enriching Japanese Culture Through Contact with Other Cultures'

1. A simple act of subtraction of the figures given in surveys such as Crystal (2008: 5), which estimates that approximately 2 billion people in the world have 'a basic level of conversational competence in English', from the total global population (approximately 6.6 billion) indicates the number of speakers who neither speak nor are learning English.
2. 'Panel tells real estate agents to treat foreigners better', *Japan Times*, 20 March 2003; 'Govt unveils plan to boost English skills of Japanese', *Yomiuri Shimbun*, 20 March 2003.
3. A recent survey suggested that little more than 50% of the population thought foreign residents should be afforded the same human rights as Japanese nationals. 'Japanese play down foreigners' rights: survey,' *Japan Times*, 13 April 2003. See also the United Nation's 'Diène Report on Discrimination and Racism in Japan' for a full discussion of the state of multiculturalism in the country (Diène, 2006).
4. From 1868 to 1870 and 1875 to 1885 the Meiji government ran an overseas scholarship programme which produced 'the nucleus of the intellectual elite of late Meiji Japan' (Marshall, 1998: 298).
5. The concept of the 'sakoku mentality', predicated upon the idea of absolute isolationism, is one that is frequently recorded in the 'historical frame' of the discourse of ELT in Japan, as outlined in Chapter 4.
6. Unfortunately, in the case of Mary Arden's house, they are being authentic to Stratford-upon-Avon's idea of authenticity, which was dealt a blow in 2000 when it was discovered that this was not actually the house that Shakespeare's mother had lived in, despite having been promoted as such as a tourist attraction for 70 years.
7. The park's Web site is keen to draw attention to the fact that this is 'the first reconstruction of this building in the world, and that even in Stratford it is only the foundations that still remain', http://www.rosemary-hill.jp/scp/new.html – accessed 20 January 2005.
8. Chiba Prefecture promotional material, http://www.pref.chiba.jp – accessed 14 April 2007.
9. The concept of the 'loanword' is itself predicated on the metaphor of LANGUAGE IS A POSSESSION, and thus operates as part of this wider conceptual frame. The term 'English-derived vocabulary' has been used in some recent scholarship (Hogan, 2003; Miller, 1997; Stanlaw, 2004) to counter the way that 'loanword', as Hogan (2003: 44) expresses it, 'reduce[s] dynamic linguistic innovation to a one-way flow of signs'.
10. 'Koizumi puts a lid on kana bafflegab', *Asahi Shimbun*, 18 May 2002.
11. *Sutoppu za ondanka taisô*, http://www.team-6.jp/tis/index.html – accessed 15 April 2007.
12. Another striking aspect of this example is that one would expect the matrix language (which in this case is Japanese) to determine syntactic structure (Myers-Scotton, 1993), but in this case the word order conforms to Standard English syntax. In Japanese, the imperative of the verb would follow the noun phrase: 温暖化を止めようたいそう (*ondanka wo tomeyou taisô*). The result is that the clause operates as if the noun phrase is a nonce borrowing from Japanese into English, although the wider discourse context is Japanese.
13. There are also poetic motivations for the structure. *On-dan-ka* consists of three syllables, the first two repeating the final 'n' sound, while the last two have a common 'a' vowel. In addition, *sutoppu-za* and *on-dan-ka* both end with the same 'a' vowel, and consist

of an identical number of morae, thus providing internal scansion and rhyme for the phrase:

す-と-っ-ぶ-ざ (5 morae)
お-ん-だ-ん-か (5 morae)

14. I will return to this perception–practice gap with the discussion of 'perceptual disjuncture' in Chapter 9.
15. The English language version of this document translates this as '... introducing it in an appropriate fashion in *their* languages' (my emphasis). In the Japanese, the reference to the 'international language' (*kokusai gengo*) is explicit however (Kawai, 2007: 44).
16. The example of the Gaba language school promotional material is analyzed in greater detail in Chapter 7.
17. The National Institute for Japanese Language has a committee which publishes recommendations about native alternatives for foreign imports, http://www.kokken.go.jp/public/gairaigo/ – accessed 17 April 2007.
18. *Académie française* at http://www.academie-francaise.fr/ –accessed 18 April 2007. *Kokuritsu Kokugo Kenkyûjo* at http://www.kokken.go.jp – accessed 4 November 2006. In recent months, the *Kokken* Web site has been redesigned and this title page has been dispensed with. The result is a far more text-heavy homepage, although the English version of the name is still featured prominently.
19. From the exhibition 'Japan Series' at Mizuma Art Gallery, Tokyo, 10 July–10 August 2002.
20. From the exhibition 'Girl! Girl! Girl!' at Tokyo Opera City Art Gallery, 5 August–15 October 2003.
21. Chinese 'loans', as well as the use of the Chinese writing system, had been absorbed into the Japanese language by the eighth century (Hoffer, 2002).

6 Authenticity: 'More English than England Itself'

1. All quotes about British Hills are taken from the company's promotional literature, http://www.british-hills.co.jp – accessed 4 July 2005.
2. Information for sales figures for 2002, compiled by the Yano Research Group. *Japan Times*, 4 June 2004. See also Gottlieb (2001).
3. Until October 2007, Nova was Japan's largest private language school chain, with more than 900 branches and close to half a million students. In the second half of 2007, the company collapsed after the Ministry of Economy, Trade and Industry ordered it to suspend part of its operations over irregularities in its business practices. The Nagoya-based company G.Communication took over the running of a proportion of the schools in November 2007, and retains the brand name in some of its marketing strategies.
4. Information taken from the Nova Group publicity material, and translated from the Japanese, http:// www.nova.ne.jp – accessed 4 July 2005.

7 Aspiration: 'Enhancing Lifestyles and Living Out Dreams'

1. Information taken from the Gaba company publicity material.
2. We should not suppose, of course, that this is an authentic survey of the public's attitudes toward English. It is the product of an advertising agency, and has thus been composed for a particular commercial function. Although the inclusion of the employment status of the participants offers a certain layer of situated authenticity, the identities of the

Notes 173

purported informants remain hidden, and thus a high modality is withheld. The impression given, therefore, is that these people are types rather than individuals, however idiosyncratic the ambitions attributed to them may be.
3. All quotes taken from *Ryûgaku Access*, Vol. 4, 2006, p. 21. Translated from the Japanese with assistance from Noriko Inagaki, who also provided much valuable background information about ALC.
4. The research was carried out over several months in the second half of 2005. The purpose and output procedures were discussed with all participants, and informed consent was received orally. Names have been changed to ensure anonymity.

8 The Unknown Language

1. Barthes is explicit about the fact that the Japan he is writing about is an imaginary construct. He continually places the name of the country in quotation marks, and insists that he is not talking about Japan as a political country, but as a cultural space.
2. Statistical information of this sort is regularly published by MEXT and other nongovernmental organisations. For example, in 2002 the ministry reported that 318 universities in Japan offered coursework in English, which was up from 256 the previous year. In 2003, they reported that approximately 90% of the 22,526 public elementary schools had introduced English-language activities into the curriculum, http://www.mext.go.jp – accessed 15 May 2007.
3. The research was carried out in November and December 2005. The purpose and output procedures were discussed with all participants, and informed consent was received orally. Names have been changed to ensure anonymity.
4. Gal and Irvine (1995: 993) note, however, 'the linguistic ideologies that rationalise and create order in historically contingent sociolinguistic situations are not limited to ordinary speakers. Professional observers of language have been equally adept at regularising linguistic descriptions and the boundaries between languages they demarcate in grammars, maps, and monographs'.
5. Blommaert's (2008) study of the role played by the *esquisse grammaticale* in the 'birth' of African languages in the mid-20th century provides an example of the way in which the codification of certain specific aspects of linguistic behavior involved a process of demarcating what was understood, by the linguistics community, as a particular language. He writes that '[t]he record ... included certain things at the same time as it obscured other things; it made certain things visible while it made other things invisible; it demarcated a particular – pocket-size – collection of phenomena as being "language"' (p. 306).
6. http://www.everything2.com/index.pl?node_id=1494527 – accessed 14 June 2007.

9 Rival Ideologies in Applied Linguistics

1. Figures cited in Graddol (2006: 62) suggest that English accounts for 28.2% of the global economy, and is the language with the greatest individual share of this economy.
2. Bruthiaux (2003: 168) makes a similar point when arguing that 'restricted profession-based codes' cannot be considered to constitute the basis for a variety of English.

References

Adjoe, C. (2006) Language policy and planning in Ghana: A monolingual ideology, ethos and discourses in a multilingual society? Unpublished PhD, Institute of Education, University of London.

Aspinall, R. (2006) Using the paradigm of 'small cultures' to explain policy failure in the case of foreign language education in Japan. *Japan Forum* 18 (2), 255–274.

Backhaus, P. (2005) Signs of multilingualism in Tokyo – a diachronic look at the linguistic landscape. *International Journal of the Sociology of Language* 175/176, 103–121.

Bailey, K. (2006) Marketing the eikaiwa wonderland: Ideology, akogare, and gender alterity in English conversation school advertising in Japan. *Environment and Planning D: Society and Space* 24 (1), 105–130.

Baker, C. (1992) *Attitude and Language*. Clevedon: Multilingual Matters.

Bambrough, P. (1994) *Simulations in English Teaching*. Buckingham: Open University Press.

Bamgbose, A. (1982) Standard Nigerian English: Issues of identification. In B. Kachru (ed.) *The Other Tongue: English Across Cultures* (pp. 99–111). Urbana, IL: University of Illinois Press.

Bamgbose, A. (1998) Torn between the norms: Innovations in world Englishes. *World Englishes* 17 (1), 1–14.

Barthes, R. (1982) *Empire of Signs* (R. Howard, trans.). London: Cape.

Baudrillard, J. (1983) *Simulations* (P. Foss, P. Patton and P. Beitchman, trans.). New York: Semiotext(e).

Baudrillard, J. (1988) *America* (C. Turner, trans.). London: Verso.

Baudrillard, J. (1994) *Simulacra and Simulation* (S.F. Glaser, trans.). Ann Arbor: University of Michigan Press.

Bauman, Z. (1999) *Culture as Praxis*. London: Sage.

Befu, H. (1983) Internationalization of Japan and Nihon Bunkaron. In H. Mannari and H. Befu (eds) *The Challenge of Japan's Internationalization: Organisation and Culture* (pp. 232–266). New York: Kodansha International.

Berns, M. (2005) Expanding on the expanding circle: Where do WE go from here? *World Englishes* 24 (1), 85–93.

Block, D. (1996) Not so fast: Some thoughts on theory culling, relativism, accepted findings and the heart and soul of SLA. *Applied Linguistics* 17 (1), 63–83.

Block, D. (2006) *Multilingual Identities in a Global City: London Stories*. Basingstoke: Palgrave Macmillan.

Block, D. (2008) On the appropriateness of the Metaphor of LOSS. In R. Rubdy and P. Tan (eds) *Trading Language: Of Global Structures and Local Market Places* (pp. 187–203). London: Continuum.

Blommaert, J. (2003) Commentary: A sociolinguistics of globalization. *Journal of Sociolinguistics* 7 (4), 607–623.
Blommaert, J. (2005) *Discourse: A Critical Introduction*. Cambridge: Cambridge University Press.
Blommaert, J. (2006a) Ethnopoetics as functional reconstruction: Dell Hymes' narrative view of the world. *Functions of Language* 13 (2), 255–275.
Blommaert, J. (2006b) Language ideology. In K. Brown (ed.) *Encyclopaedia of Language and Linguistics* (2nd edn, Vol. 6, pp. 510–522). Oxford: Elsevier.
Blommaert, J. (2008) Artefactual ideologies and the textual production of African languages. *Language & Communication* 28 (4), 291–307.
Boas, F. (1911) *Handbook of American Indian Languages*. Washington, DC: Smithsonian Institution and Bureau of American Ethnology.
Bolton, K. (2005) Where WE stands: Approaches, issues, and debate in world Englishes. *World Englishes* 24 (1), 69–83.
Bourdieu, P. (1990) *The Logic of Practice* (R. Nice, trans.) Cambridge: Polity.
Bourdieu, P. (1991) *Language and Symbolic Power* (G. Raymond, trans.). Cambridge: Polity.
Boyle, D. (2003) *Authenticity: Brands, Fakes, Spin and the Lust for Real Life*. London: Flamingo.
Breen, M. (1985) Authenticity in the language classroom. *Applied Linguistics* 6 (1), 60–70.
Breen, M. and Candlin, C. (1980) The essentials of a communicative curriculum in language teaching. *Applied Linguistics* 1 (2), 89–112.
Browne, C.M. and Wada, M. (1998) Current issues in high school English teaching in Japan: An exploratory survey. *Language, Culture and Curriculum* 11 (1), 97–112.
Brumfit, C. and Johnson, K. (1979) *The Communicative Approach to Language Teaching*. Oxford: Oxford University Press.
Bruthiaux, P. (2003) Squaring the circles: Issues in modeling English worldwide. *International Journal of Applied Linguistics* 13 (2), 159–178.
Brutt-Griffler, J. (2002) *World English: A Study of its Development*. Clevedon: Multilingual Matters.
Bucholtz, M. (2003) Sociolinguistic nostalgia and the authentication of identity. *Journal of Sociolinguistics* 7 (3), 398–416.
Butler, Y.G. and Iino, M. (2005) Current Japanese reforms in English language education: The 2003 'Action Plan'. *Language Policy* 4 (1), 25–45.
Calvet, L.J. (2006) *Towards an Ecology of World Languages* (A. Brown, trans.). Cambridge: Polity.
Carroll, T. (2001) *Language Planning and Language Change in Japan*. Richmond: Curzon.
Carter, R. and Nunan, D. (2001) Introduction. In R. Carter and D. Nunan (eds). *The Cambridge Guide to Teaching English to Speakers of Other Languages* (pp. 1–6). Cambridge: Cambridge University Press.
Chandler, D. (2002) *Semiotics: The Basics*. London: Routledge.
Chomsky, N. (1965) *Aspects of the Theory of Syntax*. Cambridge, MA: M.I.T. Press.
CJGTC (Prime Minister's Commission on Japan's Goals in the Twenty-First Century) (2000a) *The Frontier Within: Individual Empowerment and Better Governance in the New Millennium – Chapter 1 Overview*.

CJGTC (Prime Minister's Commission on Japan's Goals in the Twenty-First Century) (2000b) *The Frontier Within: Individual Empowerment and Better Governance in the New Millennium – Chapter 6 Japan's Place in the World*.
Clammer, J. (1997) *Contemporary Urban Japan: A Sociology of Consumption*. Oxford: Blackwell.
Clammer, J. (2000) In but not of the world? Japan, globalization and the 'End of History'. In C. Hay and D. Marsh (eds) *Demystifying Globalization* (pp. 147–167). Basingstoke: Palgrave Macmillan.
Coleman, H. (ed.) (1996) *Society and the Language Classroom*. Cambridge: Cambridge University Press.
Connor, U. (1996) *Contrastive Rhetoric: Cross-Cultural Aspects of Second-Language Writing*. Cambridge: Cambridge University Press.
Cook, V. (1999) Going beyond the native speaker in language teaching. *TESOL Quarterly* 33 (2), 185–209.
Coupland, N. (2003) Sociolinguistic authenticities. *Journal of Sociolinguistics* 7 (3), 417–431.
Creighton, M. (1995) Imagining the Other in Japanese advertising campaigns. In J. Carrier (ed.) *Occidentalism: Images of the West* (pp. 135–160). Oxford: Clarendon Press.
Crystal, D. (1997) *English as a Global Language*. Cambridge: Cambridge University Press.
Crystal, D. (2008) Two thousand million? *English Today* 93 (24) (1), 3–6.
Culler, J. (1975) *Structuralist Poetics: Structuralism, Linguistics and the Study of Literature*. London: Routledge.
Dale, P. (1986) *The Myth of Japanese Uniqueness*. London: Croom Helm.
Davies, A. (2003) *The Native Speaker: Myth and Reality* (2nd edn). Clevedon: Multilingual Matters.
Deignan, A. (2006) Conceptual Metaphor Theory. Available online: http://creet.open.ac.uk/projects/metaphor-analysis/index.cfm.
Diène, D. (2006) *Report of the Special Rapporteur on Contemporary Forms of Racism, Racial Discrimination, Xenophobia and Related Intolerance: Mission to Japan*. New York: Office of the United Nations Commissioner for Human Rights.
Dörnyei, Z. (2005) *The Psychology of the Language Learner: Individual Differences in Second Language Acquisition*. Mahwah, NJ: Lawrence Erlbaum Associates.
Dougill, J. (1995) Internationalisation – as if it mattered. In K. Kitao (ed.) *Culture and Communication* (pp. 61–73). Kyoto: Yamaguchi Shoten.
Duranti, A. (1997) *Linguistic Anthropology*. Cambridge: Cambridge University Press.
Eagleton, T. (1991) *Ideology: An Introduction*. London: Verso.
Eco, U. (1994) *The Search for the Perfect Language* (J. Fentress, trans.). Oxford: Blackwell.
Ferguson, G. (2006) *Language Planning and Education*. Edinburgh: Edinburgh University Press.
Fishman, J.A., Cooper, R.L. and Conrad, A.W. (1977) *The Spread of English: The Sociology of English as an Additional Language*. Rowley, MA: Newbury House Publishers.

Foucault, M. (1972) *The Archaeology of Knowledge and the Discourse on Language* (A.M. Sheridan Smith, trans.). New York: Pantheon.
Foucault, M. (1983) The culture of the self. *UC Berkeley Lectures and Events*. Berkeley Language Center: The Regents of the University of California.
Foucault, M. (1991) *The Foucault Reader*. P. Rabinow (ed.) London: Penguin.
Gal, S. and Irvine, J. (1995) The boundaries of languages and disciplines: How ideologies construct difference. *Social Research* 62 (4), 967–1001.
Gardner, R.C. and Lambert, W.E. (1972) *Attitudes and Motivation in Second-Language Learning*. Rowley, MA: Newbury House.
Gee, J.P. (1999) *An Introduction to Discourse Analysis: Theory and Method*. London: Routledge.
Gibson, W. (2001) Modern boys and mobile girls. *The Observer*, 1 April. Available online: http://www.guardian.co.uk/books/2001/apr/01/sciencefiction fantasyandhorror.features.
Giddens, A. (1991) *Modernity and Self-Identity: Self and Society in the Late Modern Age*. Cambridge: Polity.
Giddens, A. (1999) *Runaway World: How Globalization is Reshaping our Lives*. London: Profile.
Gillham, B. (2000) *Case Study Research Methods*. London: Continuum.
Goodman, S. (2006) Word and image. In S. Goodman and K. O'Halloran (eds) *The Art of English: Literary Creativity*. Basingstoke: Palgrave Macmillan in association with The Open University.
Görlach, M. (2002) *Still more Englishes*. Amsterdam: John Benjamins.
Gorsuch, G. (2001) Japanese EFL teachers' perceptions of communicative, audiolingual and Yakudoku activities: The plan versus the reality. [Online]. *Education Policy Analysis Archives* 9 (10). Available online: http://epaa.asu.edu/epaa/v9n10.html.
Gottlieb, N. (2001) Language planning and policy in Japan. In N. Gottlieb and P. Chen (eds) *Language Planning and Language Policy: East Asian Perspectives* (pp. 21–48). Richmond: Curzon Press.
Graddol, D. (1996) Global English, global culture? In S. Goodman and D. Graddol (eds). *Redesigning English: New Texts, New Identities* (pp. 181–237). London: Routledge.
Graddol, D. (2006) *English Next: Why Global English may Mean the End of 'English as a Foreign Language'*. London: British Council.
Graddol, D., Leith, D. and Swann, J. (eds) (1996) *English: History, Diversity, and Change*. London: Routledge.
Hall, I. (1998) *Cartels of the Mind: Japan's Intellectual Closed Shop*. New York: W. W. Norton.
Halliday, M.A.K. (1978) *Language as Social Semiotic*. London: Edward Arnold.
Halliday, M.A.K., McIntosh, A. and Strevens, P. (1964) *The Linguistic Sciences and Language Teaching*. London: Longman.
Halpin, D. (2003) *Hope and Education: The Role of the Utopian Imagination*. London: Routledge.
Harpham, G. (2002) *Language Alone: The Critical Fetish of Modernity*. New York: Routledge.

Hashimoto, K. (2000) 'Internationalisation' Is 'Japanisation': Japan's foreign language education and national identity. *Journal of Intercultural Studies* 21 (1), 39–51.

Hashimoto, K. (2002) Implications of the recommendation that English become the second official language in Japan. In A. Kirkpatrick (ed.) *Englishes in Asia: Communication, Identities, Power and Education* (pp. 63–74). Sydney: Language Australia Ltd.

Hawkes, D. (2003) *Ideology*. London: Routledge.

Hayes, C. (1979) Language contact in Japan. In W. Mackey and J. Ornstein (eds) *Sociolinguistic Studies in Language Contact: Methods and Cases* (pp. 363–376). The Hague: Mouton.

Heath, S.B. (1989) Language ideology. In E. Barnouw (ed.) *International Encyclopedia of Communications* (Vol. 2, pp. 393–395). New York: Oxford University Press.

Heidegger, M. (1962 [1927]) *Being and Time* (J. Macquarrie and E. Robinson, trans.). Oxford: Blackwell.

Heller, M. (1982) Negotiation of language choice in Montreal. In J. Gumperz (ed.) *Language and Social Identity* (pp. 108–118). Cambridge: Cambridge University Press.

Hendry, J. (2000a) Foreign country theme parks: A new theme or an old Japanese pattern? *Social Science Japan Journal* 3 (2), 207–220.

Hendry, J. (2000b) *The Orient Strikes Back: A Global View of Cultural Display*. Oxford: Berg.

Hoffer, B. (2002) The impact of English on the Japanese language. In R. Donahue (ed.) *Exploring Japaneseness: Japanese Enactments of Culture and Consciousness* (pp. 263–273). Westport, CT: Ablex.

Hogan, J. (2003) The social significance of English usage in Japan. *Japanese Studies* 23 (1), 43–58.

Holborow, M. (1999) *The Politics of English*. London: Sage.

Holliday, A. (2005) *The Struggle to Teach English as an International Language*. Oxford: Oxford University Press.

Honna, N. (1995) English in Japanese society: Language within language. *Journal of Multilingual and Multicultural Development* 16 (1–2), 45–62.

Honna, N. and Takeshita, Y. (2002) English education in Japan today: The impact of changing policies. In W.K. Ho and R.Y.L. Wong (eds) *English Language Teaching in East Asia Today: Changing Policies and Practices* (pp. 183–211). Singapore: Eastern Universities Press.

Hood, C. (2001) *Japanese Education Reform: Nakasone's Legacy*. London: Routledge.

Hoshiyama, S. (1978) A general survey of TEFL in postwar Japan. In I. Koike (ed.) *The Teaching of English in Japan* (pp. 104–114). Tokyo: Eichosha.

Howatt, A.P.R. and Widdowson, H.G. (2004) *A History of English Language Teaching*. (2nd edn). Oxford: Oxford University Press.

Hyde, B. (2002) Japan's emblematic English. *English Today* 18 (3), 12–16.

Hymes, D. (1966) Two types of linguistic relativity (with examples from Amerindian ethnography). In W. Bright (ed.) *Sociolinguistics: Proceedings of the UCLA sociolinguistics conference, 1964* (pp. 114–167). The Hague: Mouton.

Ike, M. (1995) A historical review of English in Japan (1600–1880). *World Englishes* 14 (1), 3–11.

References

Ikegami, Y. (1991) Introduction: Semiotics and culture. In Y. Ikegami (ed.) *The Empire of signs: Semiotic Essays on Japanese Culture* (pp. 1–24). Amsterdam: John Benjamins.
Itoh, M. (1998) *Globalization of Japan: Japanese Sakoku mentality and U.S. Efforts to Open Japan*. New York: St. Martin's Press.
Jakobovits, L. (1981) Authentic language teaching through culture-simulation in the classroom. *Bulletin of the Canadian Journal of Applied Linguistics* 4 (1), 9–30.
Jakobson, R. (1990) *On Language*. Cambridge, MA: Harvard University Press.
Jameson, F. (1984) Postmodernism, or the cultural logic of late capitalism. *New Left Review* 146, 53–93.
Jenkins, J. (2000) *The Phonology of English as an International Language*. Oxford: Oxford University Press.
Jenkins, J. (2003) *World Englishes: A Resource Book for Students*. London: Routledge.
Jenkins, J. (2005) Teaching pronunciation for English as a lingua franca: A sociopolitical perspective. In C. Gnutzmann and F. Intemann (eds) *The Globalisation of English and the English Language Classroom* (pp. 145–158). Tübingen: Gunter Narr Verlag.
Jenkins, J. (2006) Current perspectives on teaching World Englishes and English as a Lingua Franca. *TESOL Quarterly* 40 (1), 157–181.
Jenkins, J. (2007) *English as a Lingua Franca: Attitude and Identity*. Oxford: Oxford University Press.
Johnson, K. and Johnson, H. (eds) (1998) *Encyclopedic Dictionary of Applied Linguistics*. Oxford: Blackwell.
Jones, K. (1982) *Simulations in Language Teaching*. Cambridge: Cambridge University Press.
Kachru, B. (1985) Standards codification and sociolinguistic realism: The English language in the outer circle. In R. Quirk and H.G. Widdowson (eds) *English in the World* (pp. 11–30). Cambridge: Cambridge University Press.
Kachru, B. (1986a) *The Alchemy of English: The Spread, Functions, and Models of Non-Native Englishes*. Oxford: Pergamon Press.
Kachru, B. (1986b) The power and politics of English. *World Englishes* 5 (2–3), 121–140.
Kachru, B. (1991) Liberation linguistics and the Quirk concern. *English Today* 7 (1), 3–13.
Kachru, B. (2005) *Asian Englishes: Beyond the Canon*. Hong Kong: Hong Kong University Press.
Kachru, B. and Nelson, C. (2001) World Englishes. In A. Burns and C. Coffin (eds) *Analysing English in a Global Context* (pp. 9–25). Oxford: Routledge.
Kachru, B. and Smith, L. (1985) Editorial. *World Englishes* 4 (2), 209–212.
Kachru, B. and Smith, L. (1995) Introduction. *World Englishes* 14 (1), 1–2.
Kasper, G. (1997) The role of pragmatics in language teacher education. In K. Bardovi-Harlig and B. Hartford (eds) *Beyond Methods* (pp. 113–141). New York: McGraw-Hill.
Kawai, Y. (2007) Japanese nationalism and the global spread of English: An analysis of Japanese governmental and public discourses on English. *Language and Intercultural Communication* 7 (1), 37–55.
Kay, G. (1995) English loanwords in Japanese. *World Englishes* 14 (1), 67–76.

Keane, W. (2003) Semiotics and the social analysis of material things. *Language & Communication* 23 (3–4), 409–425.
Kelsky, K. (1999) Gender, modernity, and eroticized internationalism in Japan. *Cultural Anthropology* 14 (2), 229–255.
Kelsky, K. (2001) *Women on the Verge: Japanese Women, Western Dreams*. Durham, NC: Duke University Press.
Kerr, A. (2001) *Dogs and Demons*. New York: Hill and Wang.
Kitao, K. and Kitao, S.K. (1995) *English Teaching: Theory, Research and Practice*. Tokyo: Eichosha.
Klein, N. (2000) *No Logo*. London: Flamingo.
Kobayashi, Y. (2007) Japanese working women and English study abroad. *World Englishes* 26 (1), 62–71.
Kockelman, P. (2005) The semiotic stance. *Semiotica* 157 (1–4), 233–304.
Koike, I. (ed.) (1978) *The Teaching of English in Japan*. Tokyo: Eichosha.
Koike, I. and Tanaka, H. (1995) English in foreign language education policy in Japan: Toward the twenty-first century. *World Englishes* 14 (1), 13–25.
Kramsch, C. (1993) *Context and Culture in Language Teaching*. Oxford: Oxford University Press.
Kramsch, C. (1998a) The privilege of the intercultural speaker. In M. Byram and M. Fleming (eds) *Language Learning in Intercultural Perspectives: Approaches Through Drama and Ethnography* (pp. 16–31). Cambridge: Cambridge University Press.
Kramsch, C.J. (1998b) *Language and Culture*. Oxford: Oxford University Press.
Kress, G. and van Leeuwen, T. (2001) *Multimodal Discourse: The Modes and Media of Contemporary Communication*. London: Arnold.
Kress, G. and van Leeuwen, T. (2006) *Reading Images: The Grammar of Visual Design*. (2nd edn). London: Routledge.
Kristeva, J. (1989) *Language, the Unknown: An Initiation into Linguistics* (A.M. Menke, trans.). London: Harvester Wheatsheaf.
Kroskrity, P. (2006) Language ideologies. In A. Duranti (ed.) *A Companion to Linguistic Anthropology* (pp. 496–517). Malden, MA: Blackwell.
Kubota, R. (1998) Ideologies of English in Japan. *World Englishes* 17 (3), 295–306.
Kubota, R. (1999) Japanese culture constructed by discourses: Implications for applied linguistics research and ELT. *TESOL Quarterly* 33 (1), 9–35.
Kvale, S. (1996) *InterViews: An Introduction to Qualitative Research Interviewing*. Thousand Oaks, CA: Sage.
Lakoff, G. (1993) The contemporary theory of metaphor. In A. Ortony (ed.) *Metaphor and Thought* (2nd edn, pp. 202–251). Cambridge: Cambridge University Press.
Lakoff, G. and Johnson, M. (1980) *Metaphors We Live by*. Chicago: University of Chicago Press.
Lessard-Clouston, M. (1998) Perspectives on language learning and teaching in Japan: An introduction. *Language, Culture and Curriculum* 11 (1), 1–8.
Littlewood, W. (1981) *Communicative Language Teaching: An Introduction*. Cambridge: Cambridge University Press.
LoCastro, V. (1996) English language education in Japan. In H. Coleman (ed.) *Society and the Language Classroom* (pp. 40–63). Cambridge: Cambridge University Press.

Lucy, J. (1993) Reflexive language and human disciplines. In J. Lucy (ed.) *Reflexive Language: Reported Speech and Metapragmatics*. Cambridge: Cambridge University Press.
Lummis, D. (1976) *Ideorogi to shiteno eikaiwa [English Conversation as Ideology]*. Tokyo: Shobunsha.
Maher, J.C. and Yashiro, K. (eds) (1995) *Multilingual Japan: An Introduction*. Clevedon: Multilingual Matters.
Makoni, S. and Meinhof, U.H. (eds) (2003) *Africa and Applied Linguistics*. Amsterdam: John Benjamins.
Mannheim, K. (1936) *Ideology and Utopia: An Introduction to the Sociology of Knowledge*. London: Routledge & Kegan Paul.
Marshall, B.K. (1998) Professors and politics: The Meiji academic elite. In P. Kornicki (ed.) *Meiji Japan: Political, Economic and Social History, 1868–1912* (Vol. 4, The end of Meiji and early Taisho, pp. 296–318). London: Routledge.
Matsuda, A. (2003) The ownership of English in Japanese secondary schools. *World Englishes* 22 (4), 483–496.
McArthur, T. (2003) World English, Euro-English, Nordic English? *English Today* 19 (1 (73)), 54–58.
McKay, S. (2002) *Teaching English as an International Language: Rethinking Goals and Approaches*. Oxford: Oxford University Press.
McVeigh, B. (2002) *Japanese Higher Education as Myth*. New York: M.E. Sharpe.
Mencken, H.L. (1947) *The American Language: An Inquiry into the Development of English in the United States*. London: Routledge.
Mesthrie, R. (2006) World Englishes and the multilingual history of English. *World Englishes* 25 (3/4), 381–390.
MEXT [Ministry of Education, Culture, Sports, Science and Technology] (2002) *The Course of Study*. Tokyo: Ministry of Education.
MEXT [Ministry of Education, Culture, Sports, Science and Technology] (2003) Regarding the Establishment of an Action Plan to Cultivate 'Japanese with English Abilities'.
MEXT [Ministry of Education, Culture, Sports, Science and Technology] (2006) Press Release, 29 September 2006.
Miller, L. (1997) Wasei-eigo: English 'loanwords' coined in Japan. In J. Hill, P.J. Mistry and L. Campbell (eds) *The Life of Language: Papers in Linguistics in Honor of William Bright* (pp. 123–139). Berlin: Mouton de Gruyter.
Miller, R.A. (1967) *The Japanese Language*. Chicago: University of Chicago Press.
Molnar, A. (1996) *Giving Kids the Business: The Commercialization of America's Schools*. Boulder, CL: Westview.
Monbusho [Ministry of Education] (1989) *The Course of Study*. Tokyo: Ministry of Education.
Moody, A. (2006) English in Japanese popular culture and J-Pop music. *World Englishes* 25 (2), 209–222.
Morrow, P. (1987) The users and uses of English in Japan. *World Englishes* 6 (1), 49–62.
Myers-Scotton, C. (1993) *Duelling Languages: Grammatical Structure in Codeswitching*. Oxford: Clarendon.
Nakane, C. (1998) *Japanese Society*. Berkeley, CA: University of California Press.

Niño-Murcia, M. (2003) 'English is like the dollar': Hard currency ideology and the status of English in Peru. *World Englishes* 22 (2), 121–142.
Nunokawa, J. (2003) *Tame Passions of Wilde: The Styles of Manageable Desire*. Princeton, NJ: Princeton University Press.
Okano, K. and Tsuchiya, M. (1999) *Education in Contemporary Japan: Inequality and Diversity*. Cambridge: Cambridge University Press.
Omura, K. (1978) From the Phaeton Incident up to the Pacific War. In I. Koike (ed.) *The Teaching of English in Japan* (pp. 91–103). Tokyo: Eichosha.
Ono, R. (1992) Englishized style repertoire in modern Japanese literature. *World Englishes* 11 (1), 29–50.
Paikeday, T. (1985) *The Native Speaker is Dead!* Toronto and New York: Paikeday.
Pennycook, A. (1994) *The Cultural Politics of English as an International Language*. London: Longman.
Pennycook, A. (1998) *English and the Discourses of Colonialism*. London: Routledge.
Pennycook, A. (2000) The social politics and the cultural politics of language classrooms. In J.K. Hall and W. Eggington (eds) *The Sociopolitics of English Language Teaching* (pp. 89–103). Clevedon: Multilingual Matters.
Pennycook, A. (2001) *Critical Applied Linguistics: A Critical Introduction*. Mahwah, NJ: Lawrence Erlbaum.
Pennycook, A. (2003) Global Englishes, Rip Slyme, and performativity. *Journal of Sociolinguistics* 7 (4), 513–533.
Pennycook, A. (2007) The myth of English as an international language. In S. Makoni and A. Pennycook (eds) *Disinventing and Reconstituting Languages* (pp. 90–115). Clevedon: Multilingual Matters.
Pennycook, A. and Makoni, S. (2007) Disinventing and reconstituting languages. In A. Pennycook and S. Makoni (eds) *Disinventing and Reconstituting Languages* (pp. 1–41). Clevedon: Multilingual Matters.
Phillipson, R. (1992) *Linguistic Imperialism*. Oxford: Oxford University Press.
Piller, I. and Takahashi, K. (2006) A passion for English: desire and the language market. In A. Pavlenko (ed.) *Bilingual Minds: Emotional Experience, Expression, and Representation* (pp. 59–83). Clevedon: Multilingual Matters.
Preston, D. (1998) Folk metalanguage. In A. Jaworski, N. Coupland and D. Galasinski (eds) *Metalanguage: Social and Ideological Perspectives* (pp. 75–101). Berlin: Mouton de Gruyter.
Preston, D. (1999) Introduction. In D. Preston (ed.) *Handbook of Perceptual Dialectology, Volume 1* (pp. xxiii–xl). Amsterdam: John Benjamins.
Prime Minister's Office (2008) Prime Minister's speech 17 January 2008.
Quirk, R. (1968) *The Use of English* (2nd edn). London: Longman.
Quirk, R. (1985) The English language in a global context. In R. Quirk and H. Widdowson (eds) *English in the World: Teaching and Learning of Language and Literature* (pp. 1–6). Cambridge: Cambridge University Press.
Quirk, R. (1990) Language varieties and standard language. *English Today* 6 (1), 3–10.
Rampton, M.B.H. (1990) Displacing the 'native speaker': Expertise, affiliation, and inheritance. *ELT Journal* 44 (2), 97–101.
Rampton, B. (1995) *Crossing: Language and Ethnicity Among Adolescents*. London: Longman.

Rampton, B. (1999) Styling the other: Introduction. *Journal of Sociolinguistics* 3 (4), 421–427.
Reischauer, E.O. (1977) *The Japanese*. Cambridge, MA: Harvard University Press.
Reischauer, E.O. and Jansen, M.B. (1988) *The Japanese Today: Change and Continuity*. Cambridge, MA: Belknap Press.
Ritzer, G. (1996a) McUniversity in the postmodern consumer culture. *Quality in Higher Education* 2, 185–199.
Ritzer, G. (1996b) *The McDonaldization of Society: An Investigation into the Changing Character of Contemporary Social Life*. Thousand Oaks, CA: Pine Forge Press.
Ritzer, G. (1999) *Enchanting a Disenchanted World: Revolutionizing the Means of Consumption*. Thousand Oaks, CA: Pine Forge Press.
Robertson, R. (1992) *Globalization: Social Theory and Global Culture*. London: Sage.
Robertson, R. (1995) Glocalization: Time-space and homogeneity-heterogeneity. In M. Featherstone, S. Lash and R. Robertson (eds) *Global Modernities* (pp. 25–44). London: Sage.
Said, E.W. (1979) *Orientalism*. New York: Vintage Books.
Sakai, S. (2005) Introduction. *World Englishes* 24 (3), 321–322.
Sakui, K. (2004) Wearing two pairs of shoes: Language teaching in Japan. *ELT Journal* 58 (2), 155–163.
Sasaki, M. (2008) The 150-year history of English language assessment in Japanese education. *Language Testing* 25 (1), 63–83.
Savignon, S.J. (1972) *Toward Communicative Competence: An Experiment in Foreign Language Teaching*. Philadelphia: Center for Curriculum Development.
Seargeant, P. (2008) Language, ideology and 'English within a globalized context'. *World Englishes* 27 (2), 217–232.
Seargeant, P. (2009) Language ideology, language theory, and the regulation of linguistic behaviour. *Language Sciences* 31 (4), 345–359.
Seidlhofer, B. (2001) Closing a conceptual gap: The case for a description of English as a Lingua Franca. *International Journal of Applied Linguistics* 11 (2), 133–158.
Seidlhofer, B. (ed.) (2003) *Controversies in Applied Linguistics*. Oxford: Oxford University Press.
Seidlhofer, B. (2004) Research perspectives on teaching English as a lingua franca. *Annual Review of Applied Linguistics* 24 (1), 209–239.
Seidlhofer, B. (2005) Standard future or half-baked quackery? Descriptive and pedagogic bearings on the globalisation of English. In C. Gnutzmann and F. Intemann (eds) *The Globalisation of English and the English Language Classroom* (pp. 159–173). Tübingen: Gunter Narr Verlag.
Seidlhofer, B. and Jenkins, J. (2003) English as a lingua franca and the politics of property. In C. Mair (ed.) *The Politics of English as a World Language* (pp. 139–154). Amsterdam: Rodopi.
Selinker, L. (1972) Interlanguage. *International Review of Applied Linguistics* 10, 209–31.
Shelton, B. and Okayama, E. (2006) Between script and pictures in Japan. *Visible Language* 40 (2).
Shimizu, K. (1995) Japanese college student attitudes towards English teachers: A survey. *The Language Teacher* 19 (10), 5–8.
Shimizu, Y. (1993) *Kotoba no kuni [Land of words]*. Tokyo: Shueisha.

Silverstein, M. (1979) Language structure and linguistic ideology. In P. Clyne, W. Hanks and C. Hofbauer (eds) *The Elements of a Parasession on Linguistic Units and Levels* (pp. 193–247). Chicago: Chicago University Press.
Skehan, P. (1989) *Individual Differences in Second-Language Learning*. London: Edward Arnold.
Spivak, G.C. (1988) Subaltern studies: Deconstructing historiography. In R. Guha and G.C. Spivak (eds) *Selected Subaltern Studies* (pp. 3–32). Oxford: Oxford University Press.
Stanlaw, J. (1992) English in Japanese communicative strategies. In B. Kachru (ed.) *The Other Tongue: English across Cultures* (pp. 178–208). Urbana, IL: University of Illinois Press.
Stanlaw, J. (2004) *Japanese English: Language and Culture Contact*. Hong Kong: Hong Kong University Press.
Stapleton, P. (2000) Culture's role in TEFL: An attitude survey in Japan. *Language, Culture and Curriculum* 13 (3), 291–305.
Storry, R. (1990) *A History of Modern Japan*. Harmondsworth: Penguin.
Strevens, P. (1992) English as an International Language: Directions in the 1990s. In B. Kachru (ed.) *The Other Tongue: English Across Cultures* (pp. 27–47). Urbana, IL: University of Illinois Press.
Sturtridge, G. (1981) Role-play and simulations. In K. Johnson and K. Morrow (eds) *Communication in the Classroom* (pp. 126–130). Harlow: Longman.
Swales, J. (1990) *Genre Analysis: English in Academic and Research Settings*. Cambridge: Cambridge University Press.
Takahashi, S. (2001) The global meaning of Japan: The state's persistently precarious position in the world order. In G.D. Hook and H. Hasegawa (eds) *The Political Economy of Japanese Globalization* (pp. 19–39). London: Routledge.
Takashi, K. (1992) Language and desired identity in contemporary Japan. *Journal of Asian Pacific Communication* 3 (1), 133–144.
Thody, P. (1977) *Roland Barthes: A Conservative Estimate*. London: Macmillan.
Toolan, M. (2003) English as the supranational language of human rights? In C. Mair (ed.) *The Politics of English as a World Language: New Horizons in Postcolonial Cultural Studies* (pp. 53–65). Amsterdam: Rodopi.
Torikai, K. (2005). The challenge of language and communication in twenty-first century Japan. *Japanese Studies* 25 (3), 249–256.
van Lier, L. (1996) *Interaction in the Language Curriculum: Awareness, Autonomy, and Authenticity*. London: Longman.
Verschueren, J. (1995) The pragmatic return to meaning: Notes on the dynamics of communication, conceptual accessibility and communicative transparency. *Journal of Linguistic Anthropology* 5 (2), 127–156.
Whorf, B.L. (1956) *Language, Thought and Reality*. Cambridge, MA: MIT Press.
Widdowson, H. (1979) *Explorations in Applied Linguistics*. Oxford: Oxford University Press.
Widdowson, H. (1994) The ownership of English. *TESOL Quarterly* 28 (2), 377–389.
Widdowson, H. (1996) Comment: Authenticity and autonomy in ELT. *ELT Journal* 50 (1), 67–68.
Widdowson, H. (2003) *Defining Issues in English Language Teaching*. Oxford: Oxford University Press.
Wilde, O. (1908) *Intentions, and The Soul of Man*. London: Methuen.

Williams, R. (1976) *Keywords: A Vocabulary of Culture and Society*. London: Fontana.
Wittgenstein, L. (1953) *Philosophical Investigations* (G.E.M. Anscombe, trans.). Oxford: Blackwell.
Woolard, K. (1989) *Double Talk: Bilingualism and the Politics of Ethnicity in Catalonia*. Palo Alto, CA: Stanford University Press.
Woolard, K. (1998) Introduction: Language ideology as a field of inquiry. In B. Schieffelin, K. Woolard and P. Kroskrity (eds) *Language Ideologies* (pp. 3–47). Oxford: Oxford University Press.
Yano, Y. (2001) World Englishes in 2000 and beyond. *World Englishes* 20 (2), 119–131.
Yano, Y. (2008) Comment 5. *World Englishes* 27 (1), 139–140.
Yoshimoto, M. (1994) Images of empire: Tokyo Disneyland and Japanese cultural imperialism. In E. Smoodin (ed.) *Disney Discourse: Producing the Magic Kingdom* (pp. 181–199). New York: Routledge.
Yoshino, K. (1992) *Cultural Nationalism in Contemporary Japan*. London: Routledge.

Index

Abe, Shinzo 15, 16
academic apartheid 56
Académie française 80-81
Adjoe, Casimir 120
aesthetic function 145
Aida, Makoto 84
akogare 122
ALC 116, 124
appropriation 78-79
artefactual view of language 31, 33, 43
aspiration 100, 106-111, 114, 117, 119-121
authenticity 67, 70, 89-94

Bamgbose, Ayo 139, 161
Barthes, Roland 132-134, 152
Baudrillard, Jean 67, 72, 100, 103, 132
Bauman, Zygmunt 37, 74
Berns, Margie 24
Block, David 45, 122, 129
Blommaert, Jan 31, 33, 162
Bolton, Kingsley 22, 24
Bourdieu, Pierre 28
Breen, Michael 58
British Hills 87-88, 100-104
Brown, Gordon 6
Browne, Charles 51-52
Brutt-Griffler, Janina 24
Bucholtz, Mary 158-159

Candlin, Christopher 58
Chomsky, Noam 155-156
Clammer, John 85
communicative language teaching (CLT) 50, 52, 59
conceptual case studies 64-65
conceptual metaphor theory 34
Coupland, Nikolas 157-158
Course of Study 50-51, 53-54, 56-59, 61
creole 7, 13
Crystal, David 11-12, 63
culture 36-38

Dejima 69, 72
discourse 4, 65

disregarded linguistic residue 143-144
dochakuka 73
Dougill, John 54-55

eikaiwa 25, 94-95, 99, 110
Empire of Signs 133
English as a foreign language (EFL) 51, 60, 97, 109-110, 113, 156-157
English as a lingua franca (ELF) 12, 23, 91, 92, 106, 110, 159-160, 164
English as an international language (EIL) 6, 9, 13, 64, 76, 91, 93-94, 97, 110, 153
English Today 8
erasure 139, 141
ethnographic epistemology 33
ethnography 5
evaluation 155, 162
exam system 52

family resemblances 7, 13
Ferguson, Gibson 161
Foucault, Michel 33, 155
Fundamental Law of Education 15, 54

Gaba language school 80, 110-111, 119, 122
gaikoku mura 70-73, 87, 102
gairaigo 75, 134, 141
Gal, Susan 139, 143
Gardner, Robert 109, 113
Geos language school 95, 104, 110
Gibson, William 67, 132
Giddens, Anthony 89, 120
globalization 63-64, 66
glocalization 73-74
Gorsuch, Greta 51

habitus 28
Halpin, David 107
Harpham, Geoffrey 14, 143
Heath, Shirley Brice 26
Heidegger, Martin 32
Heller, Monica 31
Hendry, Joy 71, 102
Hogan, Jackie 134, 140

Index

Honna, Nobuyuki 46-47, 59
Hymes, Dell 82, 146

Ibuki, Bunmei 15-16, 54
Ichihara, Hiroko 84
iconicity 30, 129
ideology 27-29
Ike, Minoru 48-49
indexicality 29-32, 77, 79, 82, 162
interlanguage 10
Irvine, Judith 139, 143
Itoh, Mayumi 54

Jakobson, Roman 141-142, 145
JALT 46, 87
Jenkins, Jennifer 12, 13, 96, 106, 157, 158, 164
JET program 51, 56

Kachru, Braj 8-11, 23, 24, 82, 139, 153, 156, 158
Kant, Immanuel 33
Karakuri Funniest English 146
Kawai, Yuko 55
Kerr, Alex 58, 72
Kobayashi, Yoko 121
Koike, Ikuo 46-48, 53
Koizumi, Junichiro 15, 76-77
kokusaika 54, 56-57, 72-73, 80
Kramsch, Claire 92-93, 104
Kress, Gunther 114-116
Kristeva, Julia 13
Kroskrity, Paul 26, 64
Kubota, Ryuko 33, 79

Lambert, Wallace 109, 113
language ideology 25-27, 28-29
language regulation 9
linguistic anthropology 4, 24, 27, 34, 138
loanwords 75-77, 82, 134, 139, 140, 151
LoCastro, Virginia 52, 58
Lummis, Douglas 25

Mannheim, Karl 27
Maruyama Shakespeare Country Park 70-71, 72
Matsuda, Aya 93-94
McDonald's 17, 19, 99
McDonaldization 99
McPal 17-20, 32, 34, 38
McVeigh, Brian 55, 96
Meiji Restoration 48, 49, 50, 54, 55, 69
Mencken, H.L. 7
metapragmatics 28-29, 31-32, 162, 166-167

MEXT – *see* Ministry of Education
Ministry of Education 6, 50, 57, 61, 68, 80
Monbusho – *see* Ministry of Education
monocentrism 10, 12, 16, 35, 154, 158
motivation 107, 109-110, 113, 120, 123, 124, 129, 131
multimodality 41, 142, 147

Nakasone, Yasuhiro 50, 54, 56
National Institute for Japanese Language 80-81
native speaker 10-11, 13, 56, 88, 92-93, 95-98, 101, 104, 145, 150, 155-162
nihonjinron 55, 73-75, 84, 97
Nova language school 95-99, 104

Oishi, Yuka 117-119, 122, 124
Orientalism 67, 132
ornamental English 77-78, 83, 85, 144
ownership of English 34, 152

Peirce, C.S. 29-30
Pennycook, Alastair 24, 82, 93, 143
perceptual disjuncture 138-143, 150
Phillipson, Robert 23, 24
pidgin 7, 13
pluricentrism 10, 12, 16, 35, 154
Preston, Dennis 125, 138, 139
promulgation function 78-80, 113

Quirk, Randolph 8-11, 13, 22, 23, 106, 143, 158

referential ideology 29, 34, 142, 146
Reischauer, Edwin 46, 47, 53
Ritzer, George 99-100, 102
Robertson, Roland 73-74
ryûgaku 114, 116-117, 119, 122-123
Ryûgaku Access magazine 116-117, 122

sakoku 48, 54, 69
Sanma no Karakuri Terebi 146
second language relativity 82, 146
Seidlhofer, Barbara 158, 163, 164
semiotic hierarchies 141-142
Shimizu, Yoshinori 84
Shogakukan 17, 99
Silverstein, Michael 25-26, 29-30
simulation 100-104
Stanlaw, James 76, 82
strategic essentialism 159
study abroad programmes – *see ryûgaku*
Survey of English Usage 22-23
symbolic meaning 3-5, 29-31, 64-65, 142, 167

TESOL 6, 23, 50, 59, 92, 93, 94, 104, 163
theme parks 70-72, 87, 100, 102, 104
totalizing fallacy 35, 53, 75, 102

Ujino, Muneteru 82-84, 86

van Leeuwen, Theo 114-116
Verschueren, Jeff 41

Wada, Minoru 51-52
wasei-eigo 75-76, 82, 134

Wilde, Oscar 132
Williams, Raymond 36
Wish magazine 114-116, 117, 120
Wittgenstein, Ludwig 7
Woolard, Kathryn 26, 28, 29, 31, 32
World Englishes 9, 46, 49
World Standard Spoken English (WSSE) 11-12

yakudoku 48
Yano, Yasukata 153

For Product Safety Concerns and Information please contact our EU Authorised Representative:

Easy Access System Europe

Mustamäe tee 50

10621 Tallinn

Estonia

gpsr.requests@easproject.com

www.ingramcontent.com/pod-product-compliance
Ingram Content Group UK Ltd.
Pitfield, Milton Keynes, MK11 3LW, UK
UKHW022217250326
4937IPUK00005B/33